YANKEE CORRESPONDENCE

Civil War Letters between
New England Soldiers and the Home Front

A NATION DIVIDED:
NEW STUDIES IN CIVIL WAR HISTORY

James I. Robertson,
GENERAL SERIES EDITOR

This project was developed by the New England Foundation for the Humanities, supported by the New England state humanities councils, and funded by the National Endowment for the Humanities.

YANKEE CORRESPONDENCE

Civil War Letters
between New England Soldiers
and the Home Front

Edited by NINA SILBER AND
MARY BETH SIEVENS

UNIVERSITY PRESS OF VIRGINIA
Charlottesville and London

The University Press of Virginia
Copyright © 1996 by the New England Foundation for the Humanities

First published 1996

(∞) The paper used in this publication meets the minimum requirements of the
American National Standard for Information Sciences—
Permanence of Paper for Printed Library Materials, ANSI Z39.48-1984.

Library of Congress Cataloging-in-Publication Data
Yankee correspondence : Civil War letters between New England soldiers
and the home front / edited by Nina Silber and Mary Beth Sievens.
    p.   cm. — (A Nation divided)
Includes index.
ISBN 0-8139-1668-2 (cloth : alk. paper)
    1. United States—History—Civil War, 1861–1865—Personal
narratives. 2. Soldiers—New England—Correspondence. I. Silber,
Nina. II. Sievens, Mary Beth. III. Series.
E464.Y36   1996
973.7'81—dc20   95-46983
                                                                     CIP

Printed in the United States of America

CONTENTS

Foreword, *by Sarah Getty*
ix

Introduction: "Any Letter from Father, Girls?"
I

ONE
The Military Experience
25

TWO
The Meaning of the War
55

THREE
Views of the South
83

FOUR
Politics on the Home Front
109

FIVE
The Personal Sacrifices of War
129

SIX
The Morse Family Correspondence
155

Index
167

ILLUSTRATIONS

"Off for the War" envelope 2

Group of the Connecticut Sixth 3

Group of rural African Americans at Drayton's plantation 4

Surgeon Moulton and family 5

Camp of the Ninth Maine on Morris Island 6

Third Rhode Island cemetery 7

Sleeping with no covering but our blankets 8

Field music unit of the Third New Hampshire 9

"The Innocent Cause of all the trouble" envelope 10

Abraham Lincoln envelope 11

Daily Calls 12

James Hopkinson's place on Edisto Island 13

Women teaching African-American soldiers 14

Planting sweet potatoes 15

Ladies Anti-Slavery Society preamble 16

Ballots 17

Abraham Lincoln: "We Cherish His Memory" envelope 18

Henry Carruth receipt 19

"My only support" envelope 20

Rebs and Yanks burying their dead 21

B. F. Morse 22

Wabash Minstrels 23

FOREWORD

THIS VOLUME OF letters was created as part of a larger project " 'The Civil War': A Second Look," funded by the National Endowment for the Humanities. The project presented a public reading, viewing, and discussion series that brought adult New Englanders together with humanities scholars to explore the interpretation of the Civil War in novels, biographies, and the PBS television series "The Civil War." The project also presented "Telling the Story: The Media, the Public, and American History" a national conference held in April 1993.

Perhaps the most satisfying element of these activities was the overwhelming personal interest in the Civil War evinced by people in every part of New England. Family history and the sharing of family memorabilia, including letters, turned out to be an important part of almost every public program. It is in the spirit of sharing those intimate stories that this collection of letters has been created. While many famous New Englanders played a leading role in public events before and during the Civil War, we wanted to tell the little-known story of individual soldiers and those they left behind. In the absence of any other collection with focuses on New England and on the home front, we hope to fill a gap and reach a wide audience both within the region and beyond.

The New England Foundation for the Humanities was created by the six New England humanities councils and relies on their continued collaboration and support as we build bridges between the general public and the many professions and organizations involved, in the broadest sense, in the education of our citizens. This collection, drawn from the holdings of New England archives ranging from local historical societies to major university collections, is an example of the kind of cooperative effort we exist to promote.

We are grateful to Nina Silber for her enthusiastic work as editor of the volume and to Mary Beth Sievens for her painstaking research and annotation. Thanks are also due Holly Holdman for her preparation of the manuscript and her imaginative pursuit of illustrations, in which she was aided by Sherry

Wilding-White of the New Hampshire Historical Society. Finally, we are indebted to our editor at the University Press of Virginia, Dick Holway, for his astute and good-natured assistance.

Sarah Getty
Executive Director
New England Foundation for the Humanities

YANKEE CORRESPONDENCE

Civil War Letters between
New England Soldiers and the Home Front

INTRODUCTION

"Any Letter from Father, Girls?"

"VERY FEW LETTERS were written in those hard times that were not touching, especially those which fathers sent home. In this one little was said of the hardships endured, the dangers faced, or the homesickness conquered. It was a cheerful, hopeful letter, full of lively descriptions of camp life, marches, and military news, and only at the end did the writer's heart overflow with fatherly love and longing for the little girls at home." In describing this fictional missive, sent by the absent Mr. March to his family of "little women" in rural New England, Louisa May Alcott perhaps did not depict the typical correspondence written and read by New Englanders during the Civil War years. Certainly some letters (including those Alcott wrote herself while working as a nurse in Washington, D.C.) did assume a cheerful and optimistic tone, seeking to allay the fears of friends and family. But a considerable number, as this collection bears out, spoke more explicitly about dangers and hardships, and especially about frustrations with the army, home-front suffering, and government policies. Nonetheless, the author of *Little Women* underscored one significant feature of the Civil War years: the crucial role of letters in allowing correspondents to maintain the bonds that war had temporarily severed. As Alcott observed, when Mrs. March returned home after her day's activities, she always posed her "usual question": "Any letter from Father, girls?" Tens of thousands of New Englanders in the war years no doubt had the same query frequently on their lips.[1]

This present collection of letters, documenting some of the correspondence between New England soldiers (and other participants in wartime activities) and friends and family, is, in part, a testament to the power of letter writing in the Civil War years. As numerous scholars have suggested, Civil War letters provided a link to the domestic and community values that were so important to Victorian Americans. Describing correspondence in the Union army, Sanitary Commission worker Mary Livermore remarked that "there never was an army so intent on corresponding with the kindred and friends left behind." Some believed that letters could even soften the tough and tenacious world of military masculinity. According to one Union soldier, the arrival of mail in camp made the men "subdued and gentle in manner." Another suggested that a letter from his mother made one depraved soldier renounce his sinful ways. "You have no idea what a blessing

---

1. Louisa May Alcott, *Little Women* (New York, 1993), 12, 185; for Alcott's wartime correspondence, see Louisa May Alcott, *Hospital Sketches* (Cambridge, Mass., 1960).

letters from home are to the men in camp," he explained. "They make us better men, better soldiers."[2]

New Englanders were not, of course, the nation's only letter writers. As historian James McPherson has observed, when the Confederate and Union armies squared off, they represented "the most literate armies in history to that time"; both Northern and Southern soldiers were avid writers and readers of all forms of written communication. Indeed, the Civil War unleashed a veritable onslaught on the U.S. postal system. About 90,000 letters passed through Washington, D.C., on a daily basis, heading to or from Union soldiers in the eastern armies. An equal number passed through Louisville en route to or from federal troops in the West. The Confederacy, too, was besieged not only with wartime correspondence but also with the immense challenge of routing the mail through a ravaged and war-torn society.[3]

2. Mary Livermore, *My Story of the War* (Hartford, 1887), 140; soldiers quoted in Gerald Linderman, *Embattled Courage* (New York, 1987), 94. Like Linderman, Reid Mitchell also underscores the importance of letters in reaffirming domestic values for Civil War soldiers. See Mitchell, "The Northern Soldier and His Community," in Maris Vinovskis, *Toward a Social History of the Civil War* (Cambridge, Mass., 1990), 84.

3. James McPherson, *What They Fought For, 1861–1865* (Baton Rouge, La., 1994), 4; Linderman, *Embattled Courage,* 94. Mary Livermore cites the same figures as Linderman regarding Union correspondence (Livermore, *My Story of the War,* 140–41).

Off for the War

Envelopes with decorations printed to the left on the front were common during the Civil War. This decoration is one of many expressing political views, patriotic fervor, and family sentiment. (New Hampshire Historical Society, no. 4292)

Soldiers of the Sixth Connecticut on Hilton Head Island, S.C. (New Hampshire Historical Society, no. F2438)

New Englanders were, in this regard, not different; they did, however, represent the vanguard of Americans' commitment to literacy and education. Certainly it was no accident that the Romantic literary renaissance, nurtured by writers like Hawthorne, Emerson, and Thoreau, grew and flowered in the heart of Yankeedom. New Englanders took their reading and writing very seriously. The literacy rate among adult Southern whites stood at 80 percent in 1860, while in New England over 95 percent of the adult population were able to read and write. Public schooling figures reveal a sharper contrast: three-quarters of New England children attended school whereas only one-third of the South's white children received any kind of regular education. In the antebellum period the state of Massachusetts had more public high schools than did all the Southern states combined.[4]

Indeed, the questions of education, literacy, and letter writing point to a larger debate concerning New England's distinctiveness in the nineteenth century. Many Americans living at the time of the Civil War, especially those outside the region, would no doubt have affirmed the existence of a unique New England sensibility. Confederate soldiers frequently revealed a bias against New England, identifying it as the hotbed of abolitionism and thus the region most responsible for bringing on

4. James McPherson, *Battle Cry of Freedom* (New York, 1988), 19–20.

Rural African Americans at Drayton's plantation on Hilton Head Island. The women in the fore-ground are sitting on drying cotton retrieved from ships sunk by the Union navy. (New Hampshire Historical Society, no. F3809)

the war. Yet much of the evidence also runs counter to the stereotypes that were prevalent during the war and persist to the present day. The region did contain pockets of intense abolitionist feeling, but there was by no means a widespread en-dorsement of emancipation. In fact, as many of the letters in this collection reveal, New Englanders could be just as scornful of abolitionism as any other white American in the 1860s.[5]

Rather than view New England as a distinctive geographic entity, it is perhaps more useful to view this region as the embodiment of Northern distinctiveness in the Civil War period. That is, as a region New England best reflected those social and economic trends that had begun, increasingly, to set the Northern states apart from the region south of the Mason-Dixon Line. Antebellum Americans affirmed New England's pacesetting status when they used the word *Yankee* to denote not only Northern characteristics but New England features more specifically. The re-gion epitomized Northern economic progress and "Yankee" ingenuity. Between 1790 and 1860, for example, New Englanders churned out new innovations and in-

5. On Confederates' anti–New England feelings, see Reid Mitchell, *Civil War Soldiers* (New York, 1988), 26–27.

The wife and child of Surgeon Moulton of the Third New Hampshire accompanied him to the field. (New Hampshire Historical Society, no. F2428)

ventions at an astonishing rate. When the war began New England was the most urban and industrialized region of the United States, with 37 percent of its population residing in towns of 2,500 or more. Most of the region, of course, remained rural, especially New Hampshire and Vermont, which had minimal urban development by the time of the war. But as railroads and canals began to open up new and more productive agricultural regions to the west, New England farming experienced a noticeable decline. And, as agriculture declined, New Englanders increasingly sought their fortunes in a number of important commercial and manufacturing centers—like Lynn, Lowell, Fall River, and Pawtucket—places with some of the most advanced manufacturing methods then available and places that made crucial contributions to the war effort. Indeed, Springfield rifles and Lynn shoes, not to mention the uniforms made by Hartford correspondent John Norton, were most certainly factors in the final success of the Union army.[6]

In addition to its economic profile, antebellum New England also possessed social and cultural characteristics that revealed the growing chasm between North and South. Literacy and school attendance reflected this gulf, with the Northern

6. McPherson, *Battle Cry,* 19; Philip Paludan, *"A People's Contest": The Union and Civil War, 1861–1865* *(New York, 1988),* 151.

Camp of the Ninth Maine on Morris Island, S.C. (New Hampshire Historical Society, no. F4283)

literacy rate nearly equaling that of New England. But regional distinctiveness embraced a broader cultural differentiation that went far beyond reading and writing. James McPherson, along with other historians, has suggested that the difference between North and South reflected a break between a gemeinschaft and gesellschaft society. In other words, while Southern life emphasized such values as tradition, hierarchy, status, and deference, Northern life had begun to move in the direction of a mobile, impersonal, and bureaucratic way of life. New Englanders, to a great extent, epitomized the gesellschaft qualities of the antebellum North. The extension of trade and transportation networks into even the more rural parts of New England brought profound change in the form of reliance on market exchange and manufactured goods. Household production for home use declined more quickly in New England than in other Northern regions. Likewise, as New England farm earnings declined, the Yankee population became especially mobile. By 1860 one-third of Connecticut and New Hampshire residents had left their homes; four out of ten in Vermont also had picked up stakes and moved in search of better opportunities. In general, New England by 1860 was a region beset by change, mobility, and modernization.[7]

Finally, in political terms the movement to end slavery did assume a unique hold on New England's political culture. In part, this stemmed from the unique inter-

7. On gemeinschaft and gesellschaft distinctions, see James McPherson, "Antebellum Southern Exceptionalism: A New Look at an Old Question," *Civil War History* 29 (Sept. 1983): 220–44; figures on New England change and mobility appear in American Social History Project, *Who Built America: Working People and the Nation's Economy, Politics, Culture, and Society* (New York, 1989), 1:235–38.

The Third Rhode Island cemetery on Hilton Head Island. (New Hampshire Historical Society, no. F4281)

mingling of Protestant revivalism and reform. Beginning around 1810, New England churches had been singularly affected by a wave of evangelical revivals known as the Second Great Awakening. New England was not the only region in the country to experience this awakening, but the revival movement here possessed a type of influence and political component which it did not have elsewhere. In New England religious enthusiasm often led to reform, including a movement to end what many saw as the most heinous sin of all, Southern slavery. Hence, abolitionism gained a powerful base in New England, especially around Boston. Likewise, those political groupings that tended to sympathize with abolitionist views—the so-called Conscience wing of the Whig party and the radical faction of the Republican party—all had strong support in the New England region. In terms of Republican politics in the 1850s, the state of Vermont was considered to be the most radical of all.[8]

Of course, significant sectors of New England society were not abolitionists or radicals; in the towns and cities, one could even find strong support for the Democratic party. Moreover, industrial workers in New England and elsewhere often displayed a strong antiwar sentiment in the period right before the outbreak of hostilities. Yet despite the political diversity there was strong support through-

8. McPherson, *Battle Cry*, 20–21, 8; Eric Foner, *Free Soil, Free Labor, Free Men* (New York, 1970), 107.

"We were out from the first of June untill the tenth with nothing but our ruber blankets it rained steadily," reported Henry C. Glines on June 13, 1862.

out New England (and throughout the North) when it came to responding to the Confederate attack on Fort Sumter in April 1861 and Lincoln's call for 75,000 troops to "maintain the honor, integrity, and existence of our National Union." The Northern states, including New England, enthusiastically met and exceeded Lincoln's demands. Within three days of Sumter, Massachusetts had sent its first two regiments to war. On April 19 one of those units—the sixth Massachusetts—experienced the Civil War's first official combat casualties when it was attacked by an angry secessionist mob in Baltimore, Maryland.[9]

For all the alacrity with which the Massachusetts men responded, the New England contribution to the Union army did not, even in proportional terms, exceed that of other Northern regions. Nonetheless, the New England states did furnish a considerable number of troops in light of their relatively small population base. A total of 363,000 New England soldiers participated in the war effort, with nearly 150,000 troops coming from Massachusetts alone. Drawn from a population of 3,135,283, these Yankee combatants represented more than 10 percent of the inhabitants of New England. In Vermont 55 percent of the men between eighteen and forty-five took up arms. With such a significant proportion of the population at war, New England and its residents could not help but be dramatically affected by the four years of conflict. The letters that follow provide a glimpse of some of the changes and dramas that unfolded.[10]

9. Paludan, *People's Contest*, 15.

10. Troop numbers derived from Frederick H. Dyer, *A Compendium of the War of the Rebellion* (New York, 1959), 1:11; population numbers from U.S. Civil War Centennial Commission, *The United States on the Eve of the Civil War as Described in the 1860 Census* (Washington, D.C., 1963), 6; figures for Vermont from Paludan, *People's Contest*, 157.

Field music unit of the Third New Hampshire mess. (New Hampshire Historical Society, no. F4282)

In various, and oftentimes subtle ways, the letter writers in this volume revealed the imprint of their regional experience. New England soldiers, throughout the war, carried aspects of their New England identity with them. They enlisted, as did the men of all other parts of the country, as local boys, as soldiers with the home-town company. Because states and local communities, not the federal government, bore the main responsibility for raising the army, regiments were named according to state affiliation: the Second Rhode Island, the Twenty-seventh Connecticut Volunteers, or the more famous Twentieth Maine and Massachusetts Fifty-fourth. Such state and local affiliations undoubtedly gave soldiers a certain pride, the type of pride that led one soldier in this collection, Justus Gale, to write enthusiastically about the "spunkey boys of Vermont." Yet in other ways a terrible price could be paid for this localized system of organization, especially if one of these regiments experienced an unusually high casualty rate. Rhode Islander Thomas Nickerson explained the way local affiliation shaped the enlistment process and the potentially devastating consequences of this practice: "i came home and took my Father and two of my Brothers and came out in the Co which i am now in at present. i have also got a Brother in law and a cousin in the same Co. with me. so you see if we have a battle that we stand a narrow chance to all get of[f] without some of us being hirt." For many New England companies, Nickerson's prophecy proved to be a costly reality.

While state and local affiliations guided the enlistment process, regional sensibilities were often nurtured once the soldiers found themselves far from home. Soldiers displayed their New England origins most forcefully in their assessments of the South and the Southern landscape. To some extent they echoed a more generalized Northern defense of "Yankee energy" and "Yankee industry," but often with a New England slant. Many, for example, were struck by the absence of neat and orderly houses and New England–style villages. "You miss entirely," wrote Rhode Island soldier Henry Spooner, "that taste and neatness in the building and surroundings which is apparent about nearly every New England dwelling." Robert Hubbard of Connecticut echoed Spooner's words. "You miss the taste and neatness of New England homes," Hubbard explained. Clearly Hubbard's and Spooner's nearly identical complaints had to do with more than just inanimate surroundings. Behind their words was a critique of Southern work habits. And in this sense many New England soldiers reiterated certain principles of the Republican party's "free labor" philosophy—its celebration of Northern energy and ingenuity,

The sentiments in this envelope decoration suggest an economic reason for the Civil War. (New Hampshire Historical Society, no. F4293)

which stood in stark contrast to Southern idleness. In keeping with this view, many New England soldiers found much to criticize in the Southern way of life. They spoke of Southern indolence, alluded to Southern ignorance, and recoiled against Southern drinking habits. According to Justus Gale, liquor was as common in the South "as watter is in Vermont."[11]

New England religious sensibilities likewise appeared in many of these assessments of Southern society. Not only did several writers view the cataclysm of war

11. Foner, *Free Soil*, 11–72.

This envelope decoration includes a portrait of Abraham Lincoln. (New Hampshire Historical Society, no. F4294)

through an intensely religious framework, but many also attempted to shield themselves from the improprieties of army life or the alleged evils of Southern living by maintaining a firm wall of Christian propriety. To William Walker, for example, nothing so clearly revealed Southerners' immorality as their boisterous celebration of Christmas. This experience offered Walker "additional proof . . . that

1861

Head Quarters Fifth Regiment New-Hampshire Volunteers,

CAMP JACKSON, October 8, 1861.

DAILY CALLS.

Revielle (Roll Call)	6 o'clock A. M.	
Breakfast	6½ " "	
Surgeon's Call	7 " "	
Sergeant's Call	7½ " "	
Guard Mounting	8 " "	
Company Drill	9 " "	
Cease Drill	11 " "	
Officers' Drill	11.10 " "	
Cease Drill	12 o'clock M.	
Dinner	12½ " P. M.	
Fatigue to be beaten by the drums	1 " "	
Company Drill	2 " "	
Cease Drill	4 " "	
Officers' Drill	4.10 " "	
Dress Parade (Roll Call)	5 " "	
Retreat and Supper immediately after Dress Parade.		
Tattoo (Roll Call)	8½ o'clock P. M.	
Taps	9 " "	

The Fatigue Call will be sounded by the Drums, and all Calls will be sounded in front of the Guard Tent.

At Revielle, Retreat and Tattoo, all the Field Music will assemble in front of the Guard Tent.

The Light Infantry Revielle, Retreat and Tattoo will be sounded by the Buglers, and afterward played by the Drummers and Fifers.

Five minutes before Revielle, Retreat or Tattoo, the call for the assembly of the Field Music will be sounded by the Chief Bugler.

Half an hour before Dress Parade the signal will be sounded for the Band and Field Music to assemble on the Regimental Parade.

At the same time each Company will turn out, under arms, on its own Parade for Roll-Call and Inspection by its own officers.

When the Band commences playing the Companies will march promptly to the Parade Ground and form on the Color Company, to go through Dress Parade as laid down on pages 51 and 52 of the Army Regulations.

Cooks called one hour before Revielle to prepare Breakfast.

Between Revielle and Breakfast the men in each Company will see that their quarters and streets are in a cleanly and proper condition.

BY ORDER OF COLONEL E. E. CROSS.

CHARLES DODD, ADJUTANT.

A soldier's daily activities. (New Hampshire Historical Society, no. F4280)

James Hopkinson's place on Edisto Island, S.C., provided New England soldiers an opportunity to observe the lives of slaves. Henry C. Glines referred to Edisto in his letter of June 13, 1862. (New Hampshire Historical Society, no. 3909)

the people down South are fearfully behind the times and sadly need christianizing." Certainly religious feeling was not unique to New England, but this type of Christian critique of Southern vices was quite common among those who had been nurtured in an atmosphere in which revivalism and abolitionism had been closely intertwined.

Sometimes this criticism of the Southern way of life extended to a critique of Southern slavery. William Walker not only denounced Christmas in Dixie but also railed against "Southern indolence," which for him was epitomized by a "great buck nigger" who lazily kept the flies off a white lieutenant. Occasionally a glimmer of a highly ideological antislavery sentiment, some old-fashioned New England abolitionism, does emerge in these letters. Robert Kellogg of Connecticut came closest to this brand of thinking—an unequivocal and moral commitment to end slavery—when he wrote in his letter of September 10, 1862, two weeks before Lincoln issued his Emancipation Proclamation, "We must free the blacks or perish as a nation." Yet even among New England soldiers such sentiments were extremely few and far between. In general New England soldiers were not the abolitionists they were made out to be, and many tried to place considerable distance between themselves and abolitionist thinking. According to S. H. Norton of Connecticut, "New England has disparaged itself, by pandering so much to

African-American soldiers learning to read. (Library of Congress Prints and Photographs Division)

Abolition." Like other Northern soldiers, many of the New Englanders in this collection in the end were willing to accept emancipation, but only as a means to expedite a Union victory. Edward Hall, of the Third New Hampshire Volunteers, fought first and foremost for his sense of union, not for the slaves. If the Confederates were to succeed, he wrote in March 1863, "no one can tell where disunion will end." Even New England, he explained, "may be left out in the cold."

Like most Northerners in the 1860s, then, these New Englanders were not abolitionists; and like most Northerners these New Englanders espoused the prevalent racial prejudices of their day. "I wish the devil had them all any way," declared John Riggs in reference to Southern blacks. George Turner not only wrote of his antipathy for black slaves, he also described the cruel torment that he and his comrades imposed upon the contraband slaves who fled to Union army camps. Turner, like a number of other correspondents in this volume, was especially animated on the subject of black soldiers. But at least in this regard his views underwent an interesting metamorphosis. In June 1862 Turner wrote in reference to blacks in general, "I despise them more than dirt," and two months later he claimed his "opinion of 'nigger' soldiers has not risen very high." By July 1863, soon after the attack on Fort Wagner by the Fifty-fourth Massachusetts (Colored) Regiment, Turner saw things a little differently and remarked that the Massachusetts Fifty-fourth "is as good a fighting regiment as there is in the 10th Army Corps Department of the South." Yet Turner's conversion was apparently not all that thorough, as one year

Slaves at James Hopkinson's place on Edisto Island planting sweet potatoes. (New Hampshire Historical Society, no. F4083)

later he proclaimed, "I am not willing to fight shoulder to shoulder with a black dirty nigger." Clearly some impression had been made on Turner by the heroic efforts of individual black soldiers, yet this white Rhode Islander still clung to his personal philosophy of white supremacy.

Other soldiers also changed their opinions in the course of the war and through their firsthand experience with either slaves or black soldiers. Unlike Turner, some may have developed a more heartfelt respect for African Americans. Meschack Larry of Maine claimed that he now looked at slaves very differently as the result of his experiences. "Instead of thinking les of a negroe," he explained to his sister in February 1863, "I have sadly learned to think them beter than many wight meen that hold responsible positions."

Thus, the white New Englanders whose words are collected here reveal a wide range of attitudes in regard to race relations—including extreme and ugly prejudice, patrician nobility toward an "inferior" people, and a growing sense of equality for the human condition. New England blacks, of course, viewed Southern slavery and black soldiers very differently. Thomas Freeman, an African-American soldier with the Massachusetts Fifty-fourth and a free man of Worcester, expressed deep resentment of the treatment accorded black troops by the Union army. "Let me say," he wrote to his brother-in-law in March 1864, "we are not Soldiers but Labourers working for Uncle Sam for nothing but our board and clothes . . . we never can be Elevated in this country while such rascality is Performed." For Freeman the war experience brought racial oppression into sharp relief. For Charlotte Forten, a young black woman educated in New England who helped establish schools for freed slaves in the South Carolina Sea Islands, the war experience offered a unique opportunity to address long-standing problems of racial injustice.

"We believe that the slavery existing in these United States is a gross violation of the laws of God and of the fundamental principles of our government." Ladies Anti-Slavery Society, Dover, February 9, 1835. (New Hampshire Historical Society, no. F608)

The changes in party names, symbols, and slogans on these ballots illustrate the changes in public thinking during the course of the war. (New Hampshire Historical Society, no. F4279)

Forten's communication, which appeared in the *Liberator*, had a more public and political focus than Freeman's, and she used her experience to offer a more hopeful vision of the changes wrought by war. The blacks, she maintained, "seem to be . . . an honest, industrious, and sensible people. They are eager to learn; they rejoice in their new-found freedom. It does one good to see how jubilant they are over the downfall of their 'secesh' masters, as they call them."

In Forten's view the Civil War had begun to revolutionize Southern race and class relationships. As other writers in this volume suggest, the war had also begun to revolutionize certain New England relationships as well. On tranquil farms and in peaceful Yankee villages, sites far removed from the bloody Southern terrain, certain traditions and accepted forms of behavior seemed to be breaking down. In this regard one of the most important aspects of this collection of Civil War correspondence is its focus on the home front. In the letters that explore political and personal affairs at home, we gain a keen appreciation of just how much the war altered every aspect of New England life, including family and financial matters, women's roles, local elections, and the local economy. By revealing some of the domestic repercussions of the sectional conflict, this collection of letters represents an initial effort to fill a vacuum that has long existed in Civil War scholarship.[12]

Economically, the Civil War proved to be a mixed bag for the New England home front. Some producers and manufacturers, even some workers, enjoyed noticeable financial gains. One Massachusetts man, writing to his son, observed that the "tanning business is quite good now" and "shoe makers are getting better pay than they have had before for years." For John Norton, a Hartford purveyor of

12. In *People's Contest*, Phillip Paludan observes that historians have for too long overlooked the war's impact on the Northern homefront (p. xi).

clothes and textiles, business was booming. "We have got an order from the state for one Thousand overcoats," he told his sister, "and are running the Tailors shop night & Day & Sundays besides." Of course, such demands could and did take their toll on industrial workers who had to keep up with this breakneck speed. In addition, most unskilled industrial workers generally experienced a decline in their standard of living during the war years.[13]

In fact, for most of the correspondents in this collection, the war apparently entailed more financial hardship than benefit. When a soldier enlisted, a family often lost the income of a primary breadwinner. To some extent a soldier's salary, along with the benefits that many New England towns gave to soldiers' families, helped fill the void. But, as many letters reveal, army salaries and town benefits often failed to materialize on a consistent basis. Certainly the economic hardships suffered on

13. Ibid., 182.

This envelope decoration was printed after the assassination of Abraham Lincoln. (New Hampshire Historical Society, no. F4290)

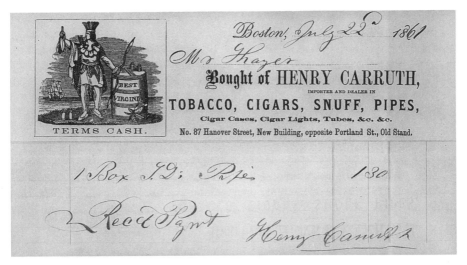

A receipt for the purchase of pipes. (New Hampshire Historical Society, no. F1770)

the New England home front do not appear to have been nearly so serious as those in the South; the financial commitment to soldiers' families on the part of New England states offers a striking contrast to the impoverishment and starvation in the Confederacy. Nonetheless, most New England families experienced the financial instability of the wartime economy and were forced to explore new income-producing options.

And, as many men realized, some of those new economic options entailed a greater reliance on women's labor. One Northampton correspondent obliquely observed how the war brought change to women in his own community. "There are many very pretty girls here now," wrote L. Lyman, "lots that I don't know, working in some of the Factories I presume." The Northern wartime economy did draw many women into active employment, in agriculture, in manufacturing, and in running businesses. The change generally did not entail a shift from idleness to industry but rather a more visible manifestation of women's work. Mary Livermore, for example, remarked on the startling wartime appearance of women performing arduous labor in Northern fields. And, as some letters reveal, even where women did not experience dramatic changes in their employment, the war nonetheless imposed new burdens and demands, especially in terms of juggling limited, and shrinking, family resources.[14]

Yet the economic and other demands of life on the home front produced more than anxiety and frustration for Yankee females. Some New England women apparently felt a certain degree of empowerment and confidence as they successfully struggled against adversity. L. W. White of Massachusetts revealed an understated sense of pride when she described to her husband the various ways she had found

14. Livermore, *My Story*, 146.

to make ends meet. "So you see," she unobtrusively remarked, "I am getting along pretty well." And few wrote as triumphantly of their accomplishments as Anne Smith, the wife of the governor of Vermont, who faced a Confederate raiding party in St. Albans without her husband's assistance. "I hope you don't imagine I was one moment frightened," she told her husband. Smith held the governor's empty pistol, she recounted, "feeling enraged but defiant."

Most New England women would not be affected by the war as dramatically as Anne Smith was. Unlike Southern women, for whom the war front and home front often merged, most New England women seldom experienced the war so directly. Still, some New England women intentionally placed themselves near the scenes of conflict and chose wartime dislocation over the relative tranquillity of home. This, too, suggests a uniquely New England and Northern quality, specifically in terms of the willingness of Yankee women to demonstrate a greater degree of indepen-

My only support—both boys gone to the war. I wonder if they would take me?

This envelope decoration illustrates the sentiments of a mother whose sons have gone to war. (New Hampshire Historical Society, no. F4291)

Rebel and Yankee soldiers work together to bury their dead. On the battlefront political loyalties sometimes broke down.

dence from menfolk and from gender norms. Both Charlotte Forten and Katharine Wormeley left home for war-torn Southern climes; both responded to the wartime crisis with actions that would have been more difficult to carry out in the more tradition-bound Confederacy.[15]

But while Forten and Wormeley found in the war the opportunity for change, other New England women, especially those in smaller towns and villages, found themselves restrained and oppressed by traditions. The selectmen "of the town of Cornish," wrote New Hampshire soldier John Gilbert to a friend at home, "take the advantage of my wife because I suppose she is a woman." Town fathers had refused to provide Gilbert's wife with her husband's army pay. For Ellen Horton of Vermont, tradition manifested itself in a very different way. She had apparently become the victim of the type of malicious gossip that was "said about Soldiers wives," specifically that she had been "sasaing [sashaying] around all sorts with any one" available. Clearly both Mrs. Gilbert and Mrs. Horton found that their standing in the community changed considerably when their husbands departed.

15. A number of historians have suggested that Southern society imposed sharper restrictions on white women's autonomy and independence, before as well as during the war. See, for example, Drew Faust, "Altars of Sacrifice: Confederate Women and the Narratives of War," in Nina Silber and Catherine Clinton, eds., *Divided Houses: Gender and the Civil War* (New York, 1992), 171–99.

Still, in various ways mothers, sisters, and sweethearts coped with the loss of menfolk. They rented rooms, took in sewing, settled accounts, and performed innumerable other tasks which they had not previously been accustomed to. The women, and the men, were inevitably changed by this process, and many of the writers in this volume showed a new appreciation for women's work and women's sacrifices. Robert Hubbard believed that "the time has come when [the ladies] as well as the sterner sex must put a shoulder to the wheel," even going so far as to suggest that women "spit upon those" who subverted the war effort on the home front. Josiah Corban praised his wife as "the most Patriotic of women and willing to make any sacrifice in your power to save our Government from ruin." As both Corban and Hubbard implied, the war placed women in a more explicitly political role; it tied their work very directly to a political cause, and it compelled both men and women to evaluate feminine sacrifices in a political context. Mattie Blanchard of Connecticut pushed this reassessment of women's sacrifices to its logical conclusion. She wrote to her husband with visible excitement about the upcoming state elections and even slipped in her own demand for suffrage. "I think they had ought to let the soldiers wives vote while they are gone," she implored; "dont you."

Thus, in their own distinctive way, New England men and women fought the Civil War. But in the end the war was of course much more than a regional

A formal portrait of B. F. Morse. (Vermont Historical Society, Montpelier, Vt.)

This shot of the Wabash Minstrels of the USS *Wabash* is unusually candid for Civil War photography. (New Hampshire Historical Society, no. F2435)

conflict. And in the end the war compelled even the staunchest Yankees to look beyond their regional concerns and to see themselves as a part of a larger Union effort to win the war. New Englanders became a part of a monumental federal enterprise, following the demands and dictates of government and military policy. They joined the army and followed army regulations, they marched and fought in all aspects and phases of the war, they coped with the irregularities of the federal payroll, they grumbled about the first federal income tax ever imposed, and they endured the first conscription law in American history. Indeed, on this last point we find that the draft was a considerable source of concern in many parts of New England, especially in light of the July 1863 riots in New York City. Draft rioting in New England, however, was never as fierce as it was in New York, and this, too, may suggest New Englanders' willingness to adhere more closely to the national agenda. And so, this war that had been born as a regional conflict and that had been nurtured in the states and local communities indelibly became a national war that re-created and redefined a uniquely American identity.

THE LETTERS THAT follow have been organized into six chapters. Although many letters speak to several different themes, we have attempted to separate the correspondence by identifying the predominant theme of each letter. Chapter 1 looks at the war experience and how soldiers described their participation in military campaigns and other aspects of military life. Chapter 2 examines the meaning of the war, or the way soldiers and their correspondents interpreted the causes and the significance of the Civil War. The letters in chapter 3 consider the way New England soldiers viewed various aspects of the Southern experience, including their observations on the Southern landscape, Southern slaves, and the use of slaves as Union troops. Chapters 4 and 5 shift the focus to the home front, first considering the political effects of the war at home, then examining the financial and personal changes wrought by the war. Finally, chapter 6 presents an extended exchange of letters within one Vermont family. These letters offer reflections on various aspects of the war and suggest the subtle and not-so-subtle ways in which New England lives were gradually changed by the sectional conflict.

In compiling the letters we have taken pains to represent different aspects of the New England experience. We have tried to represent a range of occupations and economic positions, of ideological positions, and of geography, with letters from all of the states of the New England region. We have also chosen letters based on their quality and literary merit. Hence, some soldiers (and family members) have been represented by several letters because they wrote with such clarity and forcefulness on the issues. Occasionally, we have chosen to reproduce parts of a letter rather than the entire document; consequently, all ellipsis that appear have been inserted by the editors. We have left spelling errors, abbreviations, and capitalization as we found them. Only a very few changes have been made—repeated words have been silently omitted, and a few misspellings that might have been unclear to the reader have been corrected with bracketed insertions. Finally, we have done a minimal amount of annotating, identifying persons and events when such knowledge was critical for understanding the logic of the letter but also trying not to intrude upon the personal perceptions of the writers. Our aim has been to have New Englanders speak, in their own words, about their Civil War experience.

CHAPTER ONE

The Military Experience

IN THIS SECTION those who participated in the war at or near the battlefronts offer reflections on their military experiences, describing the scenes and carnage of battle, the monotony of picket duty, encounters with the enemy, and the death of beloved comrades. As these letters reveal, New Englanders were active in all phases of the Civil War effort, including the early battles on the Virginia peninsula, the successful campaigns on the Mississippi River, the extended siege of Petersburg, and Sherman's devastating crusade through Georgia and the Carolinas.

George H. Sargent of Manchester, New Hampshire, enlisted in Company C of the Second New Hampshire Volunteer Regiment. Sargent was wounded at Gettysburg on July 2, 1863, and was mustered out of service on June 21, 1864. In this letter to his brother, he describes his experiences at the first battle of Bull Run on July 21, 1861.

Washington, D.C.
July 28, 1861

Dear Brother:

Yours of the 18th is at hand. I was verry glad to here from you. In my last I told you we were to go father South. We have been and got back one week ago today. Today is Sunday. We had the hardest Battle ever fought in this Country. We started for the south. We went to Fairfax Court House as soon as we got there. It was evacuated and our Brigade was encamped the nearest the Court House. We were encamped in the yard.

The rebels left in such hast that they left there blankts and a few other small things which we boys soon found use for. Took all we could cary with ease but we had to throw them away when to the field of Battle. When we got there we had a tough time of it. Went to fighting at 11 o'clock in the forenoon and fought till 4 in the afternoon when we had to retrete. I will tell you how it was.

We were the first to go onto the field and the last to leave it. We had to fight hard. We were drawn up in line of Battle when a masked Battery began to play on us with great loss on our side. In a short time the Rifemen opened on us and we fell like hail. Soon other masked Batteries began to play on us, then our cannon began and we had tough and tight, but after 4 or 5 hours we gained an advantage and we kept it. We drove them from one of their Batteries at the point of the Bayonet. When they were reinforced by about 30 thousand fresh men and we had to retrete in hast. Our orderly of our Company and five others with about 30 of other Regmts. went through or part way through some woods, we went through when we were on the way to Battle. We had got part through on our way back when we surrounded by 200 hundred Rebels when we broke away and ran for life. I got home the first one of our camp and on the whole I went over sixty miles and fought over six hours in 30 hours. I call that a good days work, dont you. I guess that would have given out if you had been me. Some of the men were taken prisoners. Thurl Emerson is one, so I guess he will not write you very soon.

If you have not enlisted, dont you do it. If you do, you will wish you had not. Now don't you do it and if you have enlisted, get out of it as soon as you can. I shall come at the first opitunity. It is not the Cannon Ball or the Bomb Shells of which I come for, although we had a plenty of them. It not them but don't you enlist in a company. We had one Ball took the legs of three boys at one time. They marched right behind me.

As for Mother, I must see here. I think she is sick. Write me all about her. I want to see you all, that wood of the old house.

New Hampshire Historical Society, Concord, Letters of George H. Sargent, 1976-3 (m).

Daniel Burt Fox of Taunton, Massachusetts, served as a sailor on board a privateer. The Confederate schooner Brilliant *captured the vessel, and Fox wrote to his mother to inform her of the event.*

Richmond, Virginia
August 21, 1861

Dear Mother

It was just three months ago today that I left home, little did think that in six weeks time I should be a prisoner and instead of roaming on the ocean be confined in one room, but it is not like being in prison for crime which would leave a stain on my character for ever and which would bring sorrow grief to my parents, but on the other hand I can feel that I was doing my duty. I was taken on the 2nd of July while onboard a prize bound to Keywest but if we had not been taken we should have probably found a harborage on some good looking beach or rock for we wer three hundred miles out of our reckoning in less than three fathoms water within 6 miles of the shore and a comander so drunk that he did not know wheather he was stearing for Keywest or the Mississippi. But I have had a good chance to see the country and people of the south and am in good health and a safe place for the present   I am in the Hospital attending the sick and wounded of our men this is not a very pleasant job I assure you but I dont know of any better way to serve my country and fellowmen than to take care of her sick and wounded soldiers. How is the health of all at home.

Please answer this soon direct to me as prisoner of war.

Yours　　D B Fox

Massachusetts Historical Society, Boston, Letters of Daniel Burt Fox, H. Hodges Papers.

Enoch George Adams of Durham, New Hampshire, enlisted in the Second Regiment, New Hampshire Volunteers. Adams was able to satisfy the desire for promotion expressed in this letter, for he rose through the ranks from private to sergeant, then to second lieutenant, and finally to captain.

Bladensburg, Maryland

Oct. 21, 1861

Dear Mother:

I sit down to write you a few lines. it is very cool this morning. We have not left Bladensburg yet. General Hooker says we shall march this week, but it depends altogether on circumstances. I have changed my tent, but not my camping ground. I am in another tent, but it sits just where the old one did, beneath the tall poplar. It is a wall tent, that is with sides like those of a house. Roberts, who is to be 2nd Lieut. & myself alone occupy it. It has any quantity of room, and is very very pleasant. We shall soon go out on skirmish drill. I enjoy drilling very much. We have a splendid band to march by. When the music stops, it seems as if you were let down upon the ground much as a bird must feel when it alights. I try to learn all I can about the military art, for I feel exceedingly anxious to be promoted. The higher up one gets the greater pay, the greater show and the greater honor if they perform their part well. I always keep my equipments, gun & clothes looking well, and am very prompt in doing all business I have to do. If I could get a Lieut's place in the Volunteer Militia, I should try to get a position in the regular army for life. it is exceedingly cold today, and my fingers are blue with cold while I write. George W. Burleigh and wife of Lieut Falls were in to visit our Camp last evening. He was very glad to see me. My health is good, and I live on the best, so you need worry but little about me. Have they stopped paying the $25.00 per month to men at Durham. I feel sorry about it. I hope I shall get a Lieut's berth soon, if I did, it would be a great help to us all, or if I could get a Paymaster's situation with rank of Captain it would be still better. I am worthy of the places and I think it a pity I should fill the position I do when I could fill a place so much higher. I want you who are at home, if you can bring any influence to bear, to help me, for helping me, you will help yourselves and our standing in community as a family. I have not written to Arthur as yet. I send him, Mrs. Chase and [*illegible*] papers. I have many papers, envelopes postage stamps &c given me also books &c. The Chaplain and Surgeon both make a great deal of me. The report is the Enemy have evacuated Bull Run, and fallen back to Manassas Gap & our forces hold Fairfax court house.[1]

Your aff. son, George

University of New Hampshire Library, Durham, Special Collections, Letters of Enoch George Adams, Adams Papers Coll. 56.

1. Adams apparently had received inaccurate information.

Thomas O. Nickerson was a corporal in Company D, Third Regiment, Rhode Island Volunteers. In this letter Nickerson writes to Mrs. Ellen Bullock, informing her of the death of her son John, a soldier in Nickerson's company.

Fort Seward, Bay Point, South Carolina
January 19, 1862

From a Friend.

Dear Woman i now set down with a broken heart to inform you of your Dear unfortunate Son, which died on Saturday January 18th. 1862. he had been sick about three weeks and at the time we shifted our quarters a crossed the river we were oblidge to leave him on acount of his being so lo. but we took it very hard in leaving him for we thought every thing of him. he was as nice and as good hearted a young man as we had in our Regiment. and i do not think i would of missed one of my own Brothers anymore than i do him for he always was willing to divied the last mouthfull of any thing he had among his friends or even his enimys. he was a deedful good hearted fellow and our offesers thought every thing of him and i myself has roat him a great many letters to send to you. and he used to bring me his letters which he recived from you and have me to read them, and by the letters which i have seen that came from you i take you to bee a very nice Woman and it apears that you are a poor Woman as well as my own Mother and a great many others and therefore i made a motion last night for our Company to put in one dollar a piece and have a head stone put to the head of his grave and what ever there is left to bee sent to you and use it as you think proper. in the first place i made a motion to have a head and foot stone but our Capt. and the Col. thought as he was agoing to be buried so far from home that a nice board with letters painted in grand stile would answer full as well as if it were stone and it would not cost near so much.

now Mrs. Bullock i am agoing to tel you and i am a going to do just the same by your Son as i would if it was eather of my Brothers which i have got here. in the first place perhaps we shall raise to the amount of $75. dollars or more. well if we should send to New York or some other place which would bee far from here and get a head and foot stone it would perhaps take the most part of the Money, but if we get some man right a round here to make a nice head board and have the letters painted in good shape it would not cost more that $10. dollars and what ever would be left it would do you a great deal more good aspecialy such times as we are haveing at present. John was a great friend of myne and i would do every thing i could for him, and i hope that you will not take so hard as to make you sick, for i think and earnestly pray to the lord that he has got out of this hard life and got into a far better world. we have not got our pay yet and do not know how soon we shall but we are a going to draw up a paper and sign our names to it and when our pay day comes we are to let our Capt have one dollar a peice. it is true that the most of our own folks are poor and needy, but still we are willing to do all we can towards this matter and i for one am shure it will do me $50 dollars worth of good to put in the sum of one dollar, and i hope that nothing will happen but every man in the Co will put his dollar in when our pay days comes. Mr. Simmons is well at present and is one of our cooks. there is but few that are sick in our Co, and i hope that there will not be an other such a thing to occur in our Co or even in the Regiment while i am in the service for it creates a dredful bad feeling amoung us. and another thing it is impossible to send a corps from here to R.I.

my Father has turned out quite a number of soldiers out of his family and he has also come himself

i went out in the first R.I. Regt. and i had a Brother in the same Co. also one in the second R.I. Regt and three cousins and we were in the fight at Bulls Run. no one got hirt exsept my Brother in the second R.I. he had a small piece shot of the end of his finger. then i came home and took my Father and two of my Brothers and came out in the Co which i am now in at present. i have also got a Brother in law and a cousin in the same Co. with me. so you see if we have a battle that we stand a narrow chance to all get of[f] without some of us being hirt.

i am in hopes that this war will soon be over and we poor soldiers return to our homes where our folks are now sheding teers for us. i will now close by saying this is from a friend of your Son.

Mr. Thomas O. Nickerson

Providence Public Library Manuscript Collection, Providence, R.I., Letters of Thomas O. Nickerson, Misc. CW Letters, vol. 5.

George Bradley enlisted in the Twenty-seventh Connecticut Volunteer Regiment. His letter describes fraternizing with Confederate soldiers on picket duty.

Camp Near Falmouth, Virginia
February 20, 1862

Dear Friends at Home,

I see in the papers that Gens. Burnside and Hooker talk very strong about sending home 9 months and 2 years men.[2] They say that by the time that they get there plans ready to carry out our time will be out, which if they let us go home they think that most of us will re-enlist for 3 years but I can't see it.

The last time that I was on Picket down in front of Fredericksburg their was a Rebel Picket right oposite of where I was stationed. Just acrost the river they

2. Gen. Ambrose E. Burnside, a native of Rhode Island, commanded a Union division which in conjunction with the navy captured or sealed off all harbors in North Carolina except Wilmington. Gen. Joseph Hooker commanded the Union's First Corps. Both generals Burnside and Hooker would later command the Army of the Potomac. Because enlistment was carried out at state and local levels, enlistment periods were not standardized but varied from three months to three years.

would come down to the river side and we would talk acrost to each other. They said that they belonged to the 10th Georgia Regt. and that their time was out 6 months ago but they would not let them go home. They said that they was very short of coffee and salt and clothing. But as for the eating part they live just as well as we do if not better. They fixed up a little boat and sent it acrost with 4 Secesh papers in it and some tobacco and we sent it back with some coffee in it. I took 2 papers and give the other 2 away and the tobacco. . . . They say that they want to go home and they are just as sick of the war as we are and if we would string up some of our leading men in Washington they would hang Jeff Davis and his cabinet and shake hands with us and go home.

Yours truly,
George

Yale University Library, New Haven, Manuscripts and Archives, Civil War Manuscripts Collection, Letters of George Bradley.

No biographical information is available about the next author, W. H. Robert of Rhode Island. He was a sailor with the Union navy, and his letter describes the battle during which Union forces captured New Orleans.

Mississippi River
April 28, 1862

My Dear Wife,

Since writing you from Steamer Connecticut, I received orders to join this ship. We carry twenty two Heavy 8 in shell Guns, & 350 men & is the strongest ship in the Fleet. On the 18th Porters Mortar Boats commenced bombarding the Forts, and continued for five days, without doing any great damage. On the morning of the 24th at 2 AM the Fleet formed in three divisions, we being the third ship. We got close up to the Forts at a quarter of four they opened a tremendous fire upon us—we giving broadsides of shell & Grape as fast as we could load and fire. At this time we struck upon a bank, opposite Fort St Phillip, and lay ten minuets under a terrific fire, after getting off we continued up the river, when the celebrated "Hillins Ram" run for us, striking our port quarter   Our sides proved to thick for her, and she was unable to sink us. At this time our division attacked "the Confederate Navy" consisting of about ten Gun Boats, six of which we sunk & run on shore—the crews takeing to the woods—our Grape & shell killing about two hundred of them[3]—their killed & wounded are scattered along within six miles of the Fort (no one looking out for them) they in return sinking one of our Gun Boats (Verona)[4]   It was now daylight and most of our fleet had run

---

3. Soldiers frequently overestimated the number of men killed, wounded, and taken prisoner during battles.

4. He is referring to the gunboat *Varuna*.

by the Forts—with the exception of three Gun Boats, and the sloop of War Portsmouth which returned—At this time the "ram" which was astern run for us—when we went about & run for her—going at the rate of 12 knots—our intention being to sink her—she then run for the shore—when we run her on shore, boarded her & destroyed her machinery—when she floated down the stream & sunk.

Up to this time none of our ships had suffered as much as expected with the exception of the Gun Boat sunk. We had at least 30 shot holes through us, our Mizzen Mast shot away, rigging dammaged, and boats tore in Pieces, but most fortunately, only two killed & Eight Wounded, one man had his head shot off another was cut in two. We came upon the Forts unaware, as they had no Idea that we dare attempt it, and thought it impossible for us to do so, as besides the Forts, they had an impregnible Iron floating battery. We run into it in the dark, & fired Grape into one of the ports, killing the Capt (Mackintosh) & several more— & they fired one shot just above our water line going entirely through us. At the Forts they had their Guns elevated for a long range when coming upon them so suddenly—we escaped being sunk, as in the dark, they were unable to get a good range upon us. We were one hour and thirty five minuets under their fire—the majority of their shots going just over our heads—it was awful and past description, and was probably the most terriffic fire that mortal man was ever exposed to, and escape. Our Fleet done nobly—and is praised by the *"secesh"* who thought it impossible for us to succeed. I expected to be shot, but having five Guns to look after I had no time, to take that in to consideration. I believe I done my duty faithfully, at any rate I have heard as much since. At 9 oclock we anchored at Quarantine, 6 miles above the Forts—taking possession of a camp of 500 men— keeping the Officers & letting the men go—At 1 PM leaving three Gun Boats behind to Guard the river—we formed in two lines & proceeded towards New Orleans. We however met with no obstruction until the next day (25th) at 10.30 AM—when about 10 miles below New Orleans we came upon two Batteries one on Each side of the river—mounting ten Guns Each   At first they had an advantage over us—as they could rake us, while we could only bring our bow guns to bear, but after getting our broadside to bear upon them from our heavy ship—in 10 minuets they were driven from their Guns & we took posession—We then proceeded up the river—and at 12.30 AM the Fleet—consisting of the steamer Hartford 26 Gun (Flag ship) Brooklyn 24, Pensacola 24, Richmond 26 (Propellar) and side wheele steamer Mississippi with two 2d class steamers and 6 Gun Boats came to anchor in Front of New Orleans. The City along the Levee appeared to be in the Hands of a mob   They setting on fire cotton, tobacco, and all Northern ships which they had seized. I saw the ship Marshall . . . floating down the river soon after she had been set on fire—she burned to the water edge. There was at least 15000 people on the Levee as we passed along. Their no doubt was many Union people among them—but they dare not express their oppinion. Many women were waving seccession flags & men cheering for Jeff Davis & hooting at us—in return our Band played "Hail Columbia" & the "Star Spangled Banner." Lovell[5] with 20,000 men has evacuated, & the Flag Officer[6] is now negociating terms for the surrender of the city. The next day we returned to Quarantin—Just above the Forts—where we now are. Gen. Butler[7] is now landing his troops from ship island a short distance across & leaving them here—when we will go to N.O. Since I commenced writing this letter they have blown up Fort Jackson—probably St Phillip will follow. Get Leslies papers & save them as his artist was on board of us through the fight save them for me. When we have shore communication I will send the alotment papers they will be in time. Direct to me—Act Master U.S. Steamer Friggate Mississippi Gulf Squadron. Kiss William for me—tell Mother I write this letter for her to—my love to all. I will write her soon.

[illegible] Robert

Rhode Island Historical Society Library, Providence, Manuscripts Collection, Letters of Robert Kelly, Wilbur Kelly Papers.

Born in England in 1830, Katharine Prescott Wormeley moved with her upper-class family to Newport, Rhode Island, in 1848. There she organized a local relief society after the outbreak of war and then, in May 1862, joined the hospital transport service of the U.S. Sanitary Commission. As a transport nurse, Wormeley cared for the sick and wounded during the military campaign on the Virginia peninsula in the spring and summer of 1862. She returned home in August 1862 and continued her relief efforts in Rhode Island. After the war she worked mostly with charitable organizations. In this letter, written on an army transport ship, Wormeley describes the difficulties involved in transporting and caring for sick and wounded soldiers.

"Knickerbocker"
May 26, 1862

Dear Mother,—I believe my last words on Saturday were that I was "called off,"— and so effectually called that this is my first quiet moment since then. We were called to go on board the "Wissahickon," from thence to the "Sea-Shore," and run down in the latter to West Point, to bring off twenty-five men said to be lying there sick and destitute. Two doctors went with us. After hunting an hour through the fleet for the "Sea-Shore" in vain, and having got as low as Cumberland, we decided (*we* being Mrs. Griffin[8] and I; for the doctors were new to the work, and glad to leave the responsibility upon us women) to push on in the tug, rather than leave the men another night on the ground, for a heavy storm of wind and rain had been going on all day. The pilot remonstrated, but the captain approved; and if the firemen had not suddenly let out the fires and detained us two hours, we might

---

5. Gen. Mansfield Lovell was the Confederate commander in New Orleans.
6. David Glasgow Farragut.
7. Gen. Benjamin F. Butler commanded the Union troops that occupied New Orleans.
8. Christine Kean Griffin was another transport nurse.

have got our men on board and returned comfortably soon after dark. But the delay cost us the precious daylight. It was night before the last man was got on board. There were fifty-six of them,—ten very sick ones.

The boat had a little shelter-cabin. As we were laying mattresses on the floor, while the doctors were finding the men, the captain stopped us, refusing to let us put typhoid fever cases below the deck,—on account of the crew, he said,—and threatening to push off at once from the shore. Mrs. Griffin and I looked at him. I did the terrible, and she the pathetic; and he abandoned the contest. The return passage was rather an anxious one. The river is much obstructed with sunken ships and trees, and we had to feel our way, slackening speed every ten minutes. If we had been alone, it would not have mattered; but to have fifty men upon our hands unable to move was too heavy a responsibility not to make us anxious. The captain and pilot said the boat was leaking (we heard the water gurgling under our feet), and they remarked casually that the river was "four fathoms deep about there;" but we saw their motive, and were not scared. We were safe alongside the "Spaulding" by midnight; but Mr. Olmsted's[9] tone of voice as he said; "You don't know how glad I am to see you," showed how much he had been worried. And yet it was the best thing we could have done, for three, perhaps five, of the men would have been dead before morning. We transferred the deck-men (who were not very ill) at once to the "Elm City,"[10] and kept the others on board the tug till the next morning (Sunday), when they were taken on board the "Spaulding," all living, and likely to live. Later in the day the "Spaulding" filled up to three hundred and fifty very sick men.

No one who has not shared them can form any idea of the hurry—unless it is kept down by extreme quiet of manner—and the solid hard work caused by this sudden influx of bad cases. Dr. Grymes taught me a valuable lesson the night I was at Yorktown on the "Webster."[11] A man with a ghastly wound—the first I ever saw—asked for something; I turned hastily to get it, with some sort of exclamation. Dr. Grymes stopped me and said: "Never do that again; never be hurried or excited, or you are not fit to be here;" and I've thanked him for that lesson ever since. It is a piteous sight to see these men; no one knows what war is until they see this black side of it. We may all sentimentalize over its possibilities as we see the regiments go off, or when we hear of a battle; but it is as far from the reality as to read of pain is far from feeling it. We who are here, however, dare not let our minds, much less our imaginations, rest on suffering; while *you* must rely on your imagination to project you into the state of things here.

At eleven o'clock (Saturday night), just as I had collected the weary in the pantry for a little claret-punch or brandy and water, after getting on what we thought the last man for the night, Captain Sawtelle came on board looking very

9. Frederick Law Olmsted was the general secretary of the U.S. Sanitary Commission and the supervisor of the USSC's hospital transports.

10. The *Spaulding* and the *Elm City* were two of the main hospital boats.

11. The *Daniel Webster* was another hospital boat.

sad. He had received orders to send every available transport to Acquia Creek. He told us that General Banks had been defeated, with the loss of two regiments; and he presumed the present order meant that a force was to be thrown back to guard Washington, and that McDowell was recalled to support Banks. Sad, sad news for us![12]

Of course there was nothing to be done but to give up the "Elm City" and get the men and stores out of her and into the "Spaulding" at once. The transports were to sail for Acquia Creek at 3 A.M., and had to be coaled in the mean time. So we went to work again. Poor weary Mr. Knapp[13] was off at once; the weary doctors and the weary young men began once more the work of hoisting on board, classing, registering, and bunking the poor fellows,—ninety in all; while the weary women brewed more milk-punch and beef-tea, and went once more upon their rounds. The last things were got off the "Elm City" about 2:30 A.M., when a telegram arrived countermanding the order!

I can give you no idea of the work thus accumulated into one day. But there were cheerful things in it after all. One thing I specially remember. A man very low with typhoid fever had been brought on board early in the afternoon, and begged me piteously to keep the bunk next him for his brother,—his twin brother,—from whom he had never been parted in his life, not even now in sickness; for his brother was sick too, and had come down on the same train. But, alas! in shipping the poor helpless fellows they had got separated. Of course I kept the next bunk empty, even taking out of it a man who had been put in during my absence; and all day long the painful look in the anxious eyes distressed me. Late at night, as the last men were coming off the "Elm City," and I was standing at the gangway by Dr. Draper, receiving his orders as he looked at the men when they came on board, I heard him read off the name of the brother! You may be sure I asked for that man; and the pleasure of putting him beside his brother cheered even that black night. Nor shall I ever forget the joy of a father who found his son on board, and, though ill himself, waited on him with infinite tenderness,—only, alas! to lose him soon.

What a day it was,—and a Sunday too! So unlike Sunday that I had forgotten it until we were asked to go ashore and be present at the funeral of five men who had died on board. Mrs. Griffin went; but one lady was all that could be spared. What days our Sundays have been! I think of you all at rest, with the sound of church-bells in your ears, with a strange, distant feeling. . . .

A good many wounded are now coming on board and filling the cots on the main-deck. I am writing in the upper saloon, listening to the typhoid moans of a poor fellow at my elbow. But I am too inexpressibly weary to keep my eyes open a moment longer. I need not tell you that I am well as ever, only so sleepy, oh, so

---

12. On May 25 Gen. Nathaniel Banks's troops were defeated by Stonewall Jackson's men in Winchester, Va., thus leading President Lincoln to order Gen. Irvin McDowell to divert some of his men away from Richmond to back up Banks.

13. Frederick N. Knapp was a Unitarian minister assisting in the transport effort.

sleepy! Yesterday, Captain Murray, of the "Sebago," and General Van Vliet came to see us; but of course we could not see them. Oh, these Sanitary Commission men, how they work,—early and late, sleepless, unflagging! Even as I write, come Dr. Ware and David Haight,—dragging a bed-sack which they have filled with fresh straw for me, because they found out that the one I have was last used by a patient with typhoid fever. Kind friends! Oh, how well I shall sleep to-night!

Reprinted from Katharine Wormely, *The Other Side of War: The Army of the Potomac* (Boston, 1889).

Henry C. Glines was a corporal with Company K, Seventh Regiment, Connecticut Volunteers. Glines died of bronchitis on February 27, 1864, while a prisoner at Richmond, Virginia. Glines describes the marching and picket duty that took up a great deal of the soldiers' time.

James Island South Carolina
June 13, 1862

My Dear Parents,
   I fear you have felt a great deal of anxiety in not hearing from me in so long a time, but after I tell you the scenes we have been in you will see the reason for my not writing   we left Pulaski the 1st of June and had a very pleasant sail in the Steamer Cosmopolitan to Edisto Island a distance of eighty miles or more, I thought of you being at Church and myself far out at Sea, we arrived at Edisto about three in the Afternoon landed and left our knapsacks then went on board the Steamer crossed over to Johns Island about three in the morning, we started from the beach about noon and marched six miles we encamped on a large Cotten field, Tuesday morning it commenced raining very hard we had no tents nothing but our ruber blankets, we took some rails and set them up put our blankets over them and made us quite an house, it rained so hard in the night that the Blankets came down and let the water on to James Howard, I took and held them up the best I could   Jim was about half asleep he began to cry, pretty soon down they came again and Jim cried out youl strangle me youl strangle me, how I laughed at him. Wednesday afternoon we passed in review by General Wright. we laid down on our arms at night and one in the morning we commenced our march by Legareville, we had not gone a great ways before it came poureing down and wet us all through the mud and water was half way up to our knees and once in a while we forded a stream we marched twelve miles in this style. and at little after noon came in right of the villiage we were put in one of the Houses, wasnt I some glad when we stoped, my feet were blistered and I dont believe I could have marched a mile further, we left the Villiage Friday Afternoon and crossed the Creek in the [*illegible*] to this Island, (James Island) we marched about a mile and camped on this field. I should think it was planted last year with corn and cotten, we only saw a few fields planted on our March, I saw some cotten growing it looked like white beans growing. Saturday afternoon we started out

on a skirmish we marched two miles and came to a piece of woods, our Skirmishers were put out and we started through they woods pretty soon bang went a gun on our left we kept on and in a few minutes fireing was heard on head, we halted came to a [*illegible*], fireing was heard all around us, in a few minutes a Corporal came down the line the blood runing off his hand, he was shot right above the wrist, one of the boys in our Company fainted a way, we marched on as far as the fort where we drove the Rebels from, it looked as though they left in a hurry, after our officers had seen all they wanted to we retreated back to camp in the evening dureing a terriffic Thunder Shower, we had one man wounded and one taken prisoner, Sunday some of the other regiments took four prisoners, they were smart looking fellows, Sunday Afternoon we went on picket, I was on one of the outpost we had to stand with our gun all ready to fire all night. the Rebel picket was only fifty rods from us, it was the hardest night's work I have had since I came out, the rain pored down in torrents and it was so dark we could not see but a little way and expected every minute to be attacked by the Rebels, thier were occational shots fired through the night and one volley on our left but none troubeled us, Monday forenoon the Rebels commenced fireing on our pickets from a battery of English Rifle guns and at short range the shell's cut off the tops of trees and ploughed up the ground. one shell struck in the ground in the center of a group of our boys and exploded it covered them all over with dirt but did not hurt them, a part of our Camp and two others with a few Caval[r]y went up towards the battery to recoinate its position, the pickets fired and put a couple of buck shot through the arm of a fellow in Comp G and then the Rebel battery opened on them the shell burst all arround and they retreated double quick, nearly the last shell that was fired came over my head and if I had not droped to the ground it would have hit me it went beyond a little ways and buried in the ground, it was the greatest wonder that nobody was killed, at night we were relieved and I was glad enough to get away from that place, It was the hotest hole I have been in, I had picketing enough for one day, we are makeing a battery of Barrels and James Rifle guns right under thier nose, we will show them soon that the fun aint all on one side, yesterday Afternoon we were called out and went up near our pickets staid there awhile and came back again. Monday night when we came in from picket we found our tents pitched and our knap-sacks had come, we were out from the first of June untill the tenth with nothing but our ruber blankets it rained steady from the 3d untill the 10th, I began to think we were soldiering it in earnest, I stood it through well only took a little cold, I found I was as tough as they made them, I spoilt my diary getting it wet so much, but if you will send me out another one I think I can copy it off. I would not loose it for any thing, while our knapsacks were at Edisto some one stole what Postage stamps I had and I have to borrow one to put on this letter, when I was up on picket I saw the flag on Fort Sumpter, if it will be convenient for you to send me an 1862 diary and a few postage stamps I would be very glad. I hope we will be paid off soon so that I can send you some money. I am geting so that I

dont mind the shells as I used to   it dont seam any different than if I was going to
do a days work, I see my paper is most full and I will close, give my love to May
and the little boys and lots for yourselves,

good bye   Henry

Ezra is not very well excuse all, write often

Yale University Library, New Haven, Manuscripts and Archives, Civil War Manuscripts Collection,
Letters of Henry C. Glines.

---

*Charles E. Jewett, of Gilford, New Hampshire, served with the Second New Hampshire
Volunteer Regiment. He was killed at the second battle of Bull Run on August 29, 1862. Here
he recounts his experiences with General George McClellan's Army of the Potomac during
the Seven Days battles (June 25–July 1, 1862) in which Union forces unsuccessfully attempted
to capture the Confederate capital of Richmond, Virginia.*

Harrisons Landing, Virginia

July 18, 1862

Dear Brother & Sister

Once more I take my pen in hand to answer your kind and welcom letter
which I received in due season and was very glad to hear from you though sorry
to hear that you was slim   I wish i was thare to help you   I think i should like to
swing a sythe first rate   we have to use Shovels and picks out hear   we have had
to either be marching, shoveling, or Fighting about every day since we left Camp
Beaufort the 5 of April and I tell you we have got pretty well used up   as for my
health it is as good as could be expected

I suppose you have heard all about the great movement with the armey, before
Richmond we have fell Back near the james River whare we can be protected by
the gun Boats   we are building fortifications clean acrost the peninsular to hold
our position until we can have Reinforcements and i hope it wont be long before
they will come for i have got about worn out myself in fact thare aint a man in
the Regiment that is fit for duty   you spock about John   tell him that i should
advise him by all means to stay whare he is if he knows when he is well of   if he
thinks it would be any Benefit to his health tell him to try it at home first   tell
him to go out dores and sleep on the ground through two or three rain storms
without any thing to put over or under him   if that dont disharten him put half
Bushel of corn on his back and march all day then take a Shovel and shovel all
night without any thing to eat or drink   but enough of this for i cant give but a
faint idear of our work   tell John to pay that money to Mrs. Shaw   I dont think of
much more to write just now   I don't think you get all of my letters and I dont
know as i get all of yours   I have written three or four times within the last four
weeks and i have received but one from you for five or six weeks   tell John
Bennett to write i have written to him and Sam but they dont seem to take pains

to answer me   Frank sendes his best respects to you and telles me to say that he is
well as usual and I shall have to draw to a close for want of room so good by for
this time

write as soon as you get this and dont delay

From Chas. E. Jewett

University of New Hampshire Library, Durham, Special Collections, Letters of Charles E.
Jewett, Coll. 123.

---

*Marshall Phillips of North Auburn, Maine, enlisted in the Fifth Maine Volunteer Regiment.
These two letters to his wife Diana discuss sickness in the army, Phillips's personal anxieties
about being away from home, and the pressure he feels to be a good soldier.*

Harrison's Landing, Virginia

July 25, 1862

Dear Wife
    I received a letter from you this morning mailed the 21 was very happy to hear
from you but am very sorry to hear that the babies health is so poor   if he has got
the direar try evry thing you can think of   take all the care of him that you can
my health is improveing but I have got so tired of war and am so anxious to get
home once more that I cant feel contented and cant enjoy myself atall but if I am
well must stop untill I am discharged   the papers call the health of the potomac
army good but we call the health of the army in this vicinity very poor more
sickly than it has been since we have been in the survice   there is one or two buri-
als in this regt and in the brigade evry day mostly of tyfoid feaver and direar   one
of co E men is to be buried to day of this regt   I see that Auburn and Lewiston
has offerd a big bounty for volinteers   I am glad to have them volinteer instead of
being drafted   I think I have done about my part   should like it if they could
come out and let me come home but if I am well must stand my chance with the
rest   keep up good courage it will do no good to worry although it is hard to
keep from doing it. when I lay down I think of you and the family   I feel some
times as if I done wrong by inlisting and leaveing you with a family of small children   I want you to take good care of your self and family   you dont write anything about how Florances ear gets along of late, I hope the next time I hear from
you to here that Lincoln is better[14]   do all you can for him   give my respect to all
Diana I never was in any place before but what I could come [home] if I had a
mind to and hope if ever I get out of this that I never shall be again   I have been

14. Florance and Lincoln were the Phillipses' children.

here so long and our living the same thing day after day very poor and at that this
with evry thing else to think of makes me sick of war

from your anxious husband
M.S. Phillips
write often

Virginia
June 2, 1863

Dear Wife
   A few lines to you privately   we have been paied off today two months pay
I think I shal send what I send by mail   dont open my letters before any one as
there is likely to be money in them at any time, I would not open them before
our children as they might speek about it   I shal not send but a little at a time
Diana you sed to me dont go in to another battle for my sake   dear Wife I will do
any thing that I can do to permote your happiness that will not disg[r]ace me nor
my family, but you dont want me if we are called upon to go in to battle to leave
the ranks and fall back in the rear if I am able to go with them   there is two or
three in this regt that has got to be courtmarseld for leaveing the ranks at this last
fight   one from our com[pany] but he has since diserted   Diana all that I can
think about wen I am about going in to a battle is you and the family but I suppose I have only about eleven months longer to serve   if I am permitted to live
that length of time I hope I may come home. . . .

Maine Historical Society, Portland, Letters of Marshall and Diana Phillips, S-166mb 6/3-6/8

Henry B. Gill served with the Seventh Connecticut Volunteer Regiment. This letter to his
brother hints at the opportunities the war made available to the shrewd businessman.

Hilton Head South Carolina
October 24

Dear Brother
   I received your letter just two minutes since and was very glad to hear that all
was well and that business was so good   would like some of your apples down
here   could get ten Dollars for Bbl[15] & retail for five cts a peice   one Bbl was sold
from our company at retail for 22,25 all cash   very good Profit   very good profit
when you can retail three Bbls per week   if I were sure of apples coming straight
through would order some but it is to risky   if the freight is not more than three

15. Barrel.

four dollars you may send two or three Bbls   also one Bbl dried apples an ten pair good undershirts   there has been some business here since I wrote last   have sent you a paper with full accounts, there is another expedition filling out we think will send paper if there is any news here but just ten minutes to write and have to write to Aunt May; will try and live as you would like me to   I remain your Afft

Brother HB Gill

PS have sent 50 dollars to you by mail if you do not receive it let me know   as soon as you receive this it is an order on our Chaplain payable to you or order will send as you direct if you think this is not safe

with much love to all
HB Gill

Yale University Library, New Haven, Manuscripts and Archives, Civil War Manuscripts Collection, Letters of Henry B. Gill.

George A. Spinney served in Company D, First Massachusetts Cavalry. In this letter to his sister, Spinney expresses the feelings of many soldiers toward the men at home who needed large bounties to induce them to enlist or who attempted to avoid enlistment altogether.

Washington, D.C.
November 19, 1862

Dear Sister

I am now in Washington again as you will see by the head of my letter. . . . All the Companies have been filled up with new Recruits which, you may think would make it easier for us but they are not the style of men we first had. Nearly all who attend the "sick call" are new Recruits. We have the credit of having "so many men" and have to furnish details that are made wether they have so many sick or well. The Bounty tempted them to enlist and now the Dr. is giving them their Discharges only being in service about 2 ½ months, getting 2 or 300 Dollars and then go home. Recruits are looked on as poor trash that came for the Bounty. Allowing that they are good men, they have only ½ the time to serve and get twice the amount we do who have probably seen more hardships and done more than they ever will be called on to do. This bounty business has turned out to prove poor business. It makes bad feelings between the men. I thought at one time that men who were willing to go ought to be well paid for it. I said if you have to pay a little more tax for staying at home don't grumble. Now I say if a man will stay at home when he *knows* he is needed, let him be drafted. I don't care about the talk of Drafted Men not fighting so well as Volunteers; Don't suppose they will, but then when they are placed where they have to fight the greatest *coward* will fight like a brave man . . . this paying the 9 months men Bounty as they did was poor policy. After the war is over, the Public does not distinguish the 9 months, 3 years, Drafted or Bounty men one from the other. This self-satisfaction is poor pay for an arm or a leg. . . . I have very little worth writing about.

They plough here with horses, 2 or 3. They place the horses 3 a breast . . . sometimes 4 horses are used, a string team as they call it. The ground is to rocky North to be so particular about geting the rows so straight as they do here. A piece of white rag is put up on the fence at the end opposit the one they start from and the Niggers will strike as straight a line as an Engineer. The corn is always as straight and *even* on top, the land being the same on all parts. Farmers who raise thousands of bushels of wheat have the poorest looking houses and barns you can find any where North. Log homes are all the go here. Love to one and all, good Bye, write soon.

Ever your loving Brother,
G. A. Spinney

Boston Public Library, Rare Books and Manuscripts, Letters of George A. Spinney, Ms.Am.1754.

John H. B. Kent enlisted in Company G of the Forty-fourth Massachusetts Volunteer Regiment. He writes here to a Sunday school teacher and students, describing the day-to-day conditions of life in the Union army.

Camp Stevenson, Newbern North Carolina
Dec. 29, 1862

Mr. Baxter, Teachers & members of the Hasret Place Sabbath School;

I take my pen at this time to write you a few words, descriptive of where we are, & what we do, & how we get along. In the first place we are in No. Carolina, and to-day is *so hot,* I am sitting in the sun while writing this, with flies in large numbers to bother me, while the *trees* are filled with *robins & sparrows* making the air sweet with music: it is not the music of cannon, or drums, & I like it much better. The Country where we are, & have been, is all sand, not a stone as large as a hens egg, have I seen since coming out; the inhabitants are all tall, lean, sallow, ugly looking fellows, *for men,* and the *women* are *the same,* only better *fighters;* you should see some of them defend their homes from our foraging parties, their husbands & brothers being in the Southern army! *It was fun.* . . .

We have no bell here to summon us to the place of worship, or splendid organ to give us the time, or pitch, still if we are disposed we can worship God here, as well as at home. The 44th has been on 2 Expeditions, marching some days 28 & 30 miles, others 15 & 18, & laying down on the cold ground & sleeping soundly, get up in the morning, drink a pint of coffee eat 2 or 3 hard tack, & march off 30 or more miles, fight 1 hour or more, and lay down again to sleep. The 44th has been in 2 skirmishes, & 2 battles, losing 13 killed, & 32 wounded, in all. I have had a man killed *beside me* & one wounded, the other, at the same time   I felt myself in the midst of Death, but the fear is all felt while moving *to the fields,* & not *after you are engaged.* then excitement takes the place of thought   A battlefield is a horrid sight; for the wounded are helped off, while the dead are left till the day is won then we go on, & find, & bury, all of our Regt, the rebels carry off their dead &

wounded while fighting & retreating so we do not know their loss so well. On these marches through the country we forage, or clean every house out of every thing we can find to eat, drink, wear, or carry away—even to mules, horses, wagons, dresses, books, &c. On our first we found large quantities of nice honey & it went well on hard tack. Some of the Cities we took were very fine, houses made for comfort & convenience; splendid gardens of all kinds of flowers in full bloom. In Newbern roses may be seen to day in their prime: while your ground is covered with snow ours is open, & no signs of freezing. The water when first drawn from the well is very warm, but becomes ice cold in ½ or ¾ hour, while the exposed water is cold, but becomes warm after being in our canteens a short time. Nearly the whole Regt are suffereing from colds contracted on the last march, while some are troubled with rheumatism which is my principle trouble together with a severe cold so I feel quite stupid, and I must offer that as an excuse for the stupidity and lack of interesting matter in this letter. To-day we are expecting the *Pay master,* and no one ever received a more hearty welcome than will be given him, & his *$26.00* in *green backs.* I would like to look in on you of a pleasant Sunday morning and I live in hopes to, at some future time. I have altered my mind with regard to its being every mans duty to do what he can to stop the war and further I do not think bullets will settle it; nothing but foreign interference. The manner of taking & disposing of prisoners is really amusing, on our last march we took some 600 prisoners   took their guns & threw them in the river; then paroled the men, many said they were tired and sick but would be forced to fight again, some of them we captured 3 weeks before on our first march, Here we have Barracks as in old Readville & I am nearly used to sleeping on boards; once in a while we turn the boards so as to find the *soft side* but we *seldom find it.* Our rations in Camp are very good consisting of Stewed Beans for Breakfast, Boiled Corned Beef (or Salt Horse as we call it) & Potatoes for Dinner: Boiled Rice & molasses for Supper. *Co*ffee without milk for Breakfast; and Tea for Supper. It is varied some times by the Cook getting up a mess of Fried Potatoes, or Hashed Meat or Fish. We have Fresh Beef & soft Bread every other day. Our Butter & Gingerbread we buy ourselves. The negroes here do our washing for sixpence (5 cents) a peice: and bring pies & cakes, all for 5 cents each. In the evenings we get 2 or 3 negroes in the Barracks & make them dance & sing. My letter is longer than I intended at first but if it interests any of you enough to answer I shall be very glad & will try my hand again. Accept my best wishes for the success of all & hoping to hear from you all that you are all well I remain

Your sincere & interested friend
John H.B. Kent

Massachusetts Historical Society, Boston, Letters of John H. B. Kent, George H. Baxter Collection.

Reuben F. Thornton, of Warwick, Rhode Island, served in Company C, Eleventh Regiment, Rhode Island Volunteers. Thornton's letter gives an indication of the hardships the soldiers tried to bear with some degree of good humor.

Camp Distribution, Alexandria, Virginia
March 15, 1863

Friend George

Well george i am a soldier in the armey of the lord and haveing a gay old time. We are in camp near Alexandria Va and have been garding prisoners for six weeks but we are under marching orders and expect to leave tomorrow but we hint going fir. I left home last october to spend the winter down south but it is a rough place to come for it cold one day and hot the other and a pretty muddy place When it rains we can lay in our bunks and se the water run through the tent this is rougher than hoeing corn for charles. Last christmas night i was on picket at falls church and we had a pretty good time There was a house whare the gard stayed and the boys went to work and stole a man's fence and burnt that up then set fire to the house this is the way we do business out here. A solders life is a rough one for when we lay down at night we dont Know whare we will be in the morning for when we was encamped on miners hill they had us up every night One night they called us up at 11 oclock and had orders to pack up our knapsacks and be ready to fall in line at 12 oclock that night so we was their. Their was the 40th mass and the 22 con and the 11th RI numbering about three thousand men the line moved at one oclock for [*illegible*] cross roads we got there at five the next morning pretty well tired out Stayed there the next day and then went back to camp There is plenty of salt pork floating round out here and we got a pretty good surpley of it soup for dinner and government pies for supper. we hint got but three months longer to stay. We leave here the 15th of June for home. Send me word whare gideon spencer is and the direction whare he is. Well george how do you get a long farming [*illegible*] and how do you and lidia get along. I suppose you have got married for i hint seen or hear anything of you for a long time Ask your Mother if she has used that raged coat up yet that she used to talk so much about. We are on gard to day, and it looks like a storme so i must draw this letter to a close by bidding you good by Give my love all your folks and to H.H. Gorton and Mary Lidia and all the rest of the folks.

Write soon From your friend
Reuben

Write soon I am well and happy as a clam

Providence Public Library, Providence, R.I., C. Fiske Harris Collection on the Civil War and Slavery, Letters of Reuben F. Thornton and Henri Eugene Bacon.

James Edward ("Ned") Holmes was a soldier from Maine. He writes to his sister in Boston,
telling her of his participation in the battle of Chancellorsville, part of which took place
around Fredericksburg.

Camp near White Oak Church, Virginia
May 21, 1863

My dear Sister Abbie;

Your favors came to hand about the same date. I should have written ere now
but that my connections with the Adjutant's office was such that it left me no
opportunity until the present moment.

Well, I suppose you would like to have in detail our exploits in the last battles
of Fredericksburgh. Probably you have learned by the papers before this the general movements of our army.

The light division were underway at 11 o'clock AM., April 30. We marched
about six miles and then rested until dark. We were marched about one mile to
where the pontoon train was the then and there were ordered to remove them
from the wagons and carry them to the river, all of which we did successfully.
After we launched the boats, the 119 Penn Vols were ordered on board and were
taken across the river from whence they advanced in line of battle up to the rifle
pits and carried them with scarcely the loss of a man, in fact we had been successful in surprising the rebels completely.

On the 3rd May we moved up in front of the works of Maray's Hill[16] and
there laid in line of battle until about 12 M when we were ordered to charge the
enemies' works which we did successfully but at a fearful cost to my reg't in
particular.

In my company the killed were Cap'n Gray, Serg't Holmes (a Cousin of mine)
and privates Fogg and Krive. We had eighteen wounded. On the 4th of May we
lost two taken prisoners. Our loss now foots up eighteen wounded and missing.
And in all probability we shall lose permanently sixteen who were wounded so
seriously that it hardly probable they will ever be fit for military duty again. At
least during their term of service.

Our loss in the two right Co's was much heavier than it would have been if it
was not that two Rng'ts on our right broke and fled ignominiously which exposed
us to an enfilading fire from the enemy in the rifle pits on our right.

I thought I had become callous having witnesses so much suffering, having
seen so many dead and dying of the past years, but I never in the experience of
the whole of my misspent life, felt so bad as I did on the ever memorable 3rd
of May.

Associated as I have been with many of the men for two years, we had become
as one family, we had become endeared to each other by the strong ties which our
dangerous occupation will not be likely to weaken.

16. Marye's Heights.

To see lying around you, your warmest friends and companions, some in excruciating pain from severe wounds, others in the cold embrace of death, who but a few moments before were in robust health, to see them . . . caused me more pain than anything I ever before experienced in life. God grant I may never witness the like again.

With many apologies for this senseless letter and promises to try to do better in my next, and with love to all inquiring friends of which please to take a good share to yourself. I will close.

Write soon and oblige, your aff'te Brother, Ned

Massachusetts Historical Society, Boston, Letters of James Edward Holmes, Holmes Family Papers.

Calvin M. Burbank, of Boscawen, New Hampshire, served as corporal in Company B, Second New Hampshire Infantry. He was mustered in on June 1, 1861, as a private and was promoted to corporal on May 1, 1862. He was wounded at Gettysburg on July 2, 1863, discharged June 21, 1864, and died April 13, 1866, in Manchester, New Hampshire. He recounts his experiences at Gettysburg in this letter.

Philadelphia, Pennsylvania
Aug 10, 1863

Dear Cousin,

Once more I am able to wield the pen myself. The two last were written one by a comrade, and the other by one of our Commissioners. What I have suffered for the past three weeks I hope I never shall again be called to experience.

Owing to exposure after I was wounded, I took a severe cold, which fastened upon my lungs, before I could get medical treatment. This was attended with violent headache, at first, then severe pain in my side, &c, but these troubles are fast disappearing, and I am feeling pretty well again.

My wound is doing nicely.

Your letter of yesterday, with the money came safe to hand this morning. Your other two letters also came to hand the second morning after they were written and the paper & pamphlet in the afternoon. That letter I received from you after reaching the Hospital was the first one that I had received from you since leaving home and all the one, save one, that I received from anyone.

I will give you a little account of my adventures in and after the late battle. Our regiment was ordered some distance across an open plain to support a battery on an [*illegible*] adjoining We went across the plain on the double quick, and reached the point with comparative safety There we lay for an hour, exposed to fierce cannonading but with few men hurt. At the end of an hour the batteries were relieved by others, and the torrent of iron hail poured upon them was so fierce that they could not withstand it and they left.

This left us sole defenders of the position which we were now resolved to maintain. A brigade of rebel infantry was hurled against us which by well directed fire we succeeded in heating up and dispersing. Next two brigades were thrown against us which if they had not executed a flank movement we should also have beaten. but as it was we were forced to retreat. It was just at this moment and when the order to retreat had been given, that I was struck. The Captain seeing me fall ordered one of the boys to assist me off the field. I soon began to grow weak & faint and finding that we were falling behind, requested him to leave me and save himself which he did. This was about 5 P.M. from that time till dark I was exposed to the severest fire that I ever saw. How I escaped I know not. I lay on the field that night, and the next morning crawled to an old barn where I spend the day and the next night and was taken off the field the next morning. . . .

The weather here is extremely warm and I have wet this sheet with sweat repeatedly, as to getting a furlough I shall get one if possible but it looks rather doubtful. With kind regards to all, am about tired out I remain

Yours as ever
C.M. Burbank

Dartmouth College Library, Hanover, N.H., Letters of Calvin M. Burbank, MS 861611.

Edwin Horton of Chittenden, Vermont, served in Company C, Fourth Vermont Regiment. Horton began his period of service in a less-than-exemplary manner; he was placed under military arrest for attempting to avoid conscription. However, despite this bad beginning Horton was promoted to corporal in January 1865 and successfully completed his term of service. In this letter to his wife he gives a complete account of his capture and incarceration.

Camp near Culpepper, Virginia
September 28, 1863

Dear wife

it is with the greatest pleasure I now seat myself to inform you that I am well and hope this may find you the same I wrote to you on the 25th and enclosed you five dollars and I also enclose you too dollars to day I havent drawed any pay yet but you know I have a great faculty for making money so I dont know as it makes any differents whether I get any pay or not I sold my watch for Eight dollars and I owed a feller too dollars out of that and the next knight I had sixteen dollars so you see how I am getting along all right I told you in my last letter that I would give you a description of my journey here when I left home on the 2nd I went direct to Mendon and from there to Rutland and I was arrested in a few moments after I arrived there by Sheriff Simons I was put under guard and kept untill the next morning and then I was sent to Brattleboro and there I was locked up. . . . I was taken out of there in the morning of the fourth and carried to Long Island I was placed in the guard house there and remained there too weeks it was the most dismal place I ever was in there was about thirty roughs from Boston and New York imprisoned there John Noyes was with me there about a week and then he was taken out and I have not seen him since while John stayed the roughs dident dare to trouble us much but when he was gone they picked into me and took every thing I had away excepting my watch and that they smashed all to peaces so they thought it wasent worth taking I dident dare to report them for fear of being killed myself I was taken out of there at the expiration of too weeks and placed on board the boat was put on the upper deck with to guards over me and in about an hour it commenced raining and I asked the guards to take me under shelter and they wouldent do it and I stayed there until about ten o'clock that night and it was raining awful hard and the wind blew and I was completly wet through and I commenced to swear and curse when the sargent of the guard came and put the shackles on me and chained me up to a post where I remained all night I caught an awful cold but I was released from the irons in the morning and put down in the hole of the boat where I stayed four days with too guards over me excepting they took me out once a day to clean the decks of the boat after the other soldiers run over them all day when I arrived in Alexandria they called me out and released me to go with the other conscrips I stayed in Alexandria one day and then was marched to the cars and was brought out to Culpeper where we got of [f] and had to march about three miles to the fourths camp I was put in Co C whether there is agoing to be any thing more to it I do not know but you know the old saying is a bad beginning makes a good ending so I think to take the whole thing into consideration I ought to have glorius good luck from this time out this is the whole journey please write soon and direct to the fourth Vermont Co C Washington DC this from your true and ever loving old friend & husband

Edwin Horton

Vermont Historical Society, Montpelier, Letters of Edwin and Ellen Horton, MSS 21, no. 16.

Thomas D. Freeman of Worcester, Massachusetts, was an African American who enlisted in the Fifty-fourth Massachusetts Volunteer Regiment. In this letter to his brother-in-law, Freeman details many of the difficulties African-American soldiers faced in the Union army.

Jacksonville, Florida
March 26, 1864

Dear William

I will devote some spare moments I have in writing you a few lines which I hope may find you and all your family the same, also all of my many Friends in Worcester Since the Regiment Departure from Morris Island I have enjoyed the best of health. the weather here is Beautiful it is warm here as it is home in July. the Regiment in general are in Good Health but in Low Spirits and no reason why for they have all to a man done there duty as a soldier it is 1 Year the 1st Day of April since I enlisted and there is men here in the regiment that have been in Enlisted 13 Months and have never recieved one cent But there bounty and they more or less have family, and 2 thirds have never received anny State Aid, and how do you think men can feel to do there duty as Soldiers, but let me say we are not Soldiers but Labourers working for Uncle Sam for nothing but our board and clothes . . . we never can be Elevated in this country while such rascality is Performed Slavery with all its horrorrs can not Equalise this for it is nothing but work from morning till night Building Batteries Hauling Guns Cleaning Bricks clearing up land for other Regiments to settle on and if a Man Says he is sick it is the Doctors Priveledge to say yes or no if you cannot work then you are sent to the Guard House Bucked Gagged and stay so till they see fit to relieve You and if you dont like that some white man will Give you a crack over the Head with his sword. now do you call this Equality if so God help such Equality there is many things I could relate on this matter but I will say no more I want You to consult some counsel in Relation to the Matter and see if a man could not sue for his Discharge and get his views on the Subject and let me know immiedeitely for I am tired of such treatment Please answer soon as you can and Oblidge Yours

T.D. Freeman

American Antiquarian Society, Worcester, Mass., Letters of Thomas D. Freeman, Brown Family Papers.

George Upton, of Derry, New Hampshire, enlisted in the Sixth Regiment, New Hampshire Volunteers, in October 1862. He was promoted to the rank of sergeant in March 1862, then to first lieutenant in October 1863. On July 30, 1864, he was wounded in a mine explosion that created "the Crater" at Petersburg, Virginia. He died the next day. In this letter to his wife, Upton offers his assessment of what must be done for the Union to win the war.

Petersburg, Virginia
July 10, 1864

My Dear Sarah—

We are in the second line of intrenchments to day, consequently not quite so much exposed as when we are to the extreme point, yet there is danger anywhere around here when one gets above the ground. I am now occupying a *hole* that is in dimensions about six feet by three, and three feet in depth; in one end toward the enemy the bottom part is dug under two feet, for the purpose of getting one's head under, in case they go to throwing thier confounded mortar shells. No one can be too carefull in such a place as this, and it is no mark of a coward to keep protected whenever we can in a seige operation. but on the other hand it is our *duty* to be cautious, and save ourselves as much as possible from the deadly missles of our enemys. Yes, we owe this duty to our *families*, our *country*, ourselves and our God. *Many* of the now dead and wounded, would of been alive & well to day, had it not of been for thier carelessness.

The weather continues about the same as when I last wrote, dry, hot and *awfull* dusty.

We never had such a time lying round in the dirt as we are now having, but it would not be so bad if we could get a little sprinkling of rain now and then.

The latest news from Maryland is indeffinate but one thing is certain, a portion of Gen Lees Army is penetrating that section of the country, and wherever they go, depradations of all sorts are committed.[17] I suppose the North will think *now* will be a chance for success in this quarter, but in this I think they will be doomed to disappointment. They are *strongly* fortified, and for us to attack, one of thier men would be equal to three of ours, and we have not the men to spare.

Truly this sabbath morning is a dark day in our nation, especially when we look at the circumstances. It has been claimed by all the Press that Gen Grant moved down the Peninsula in the manner which he did, in order to prevent the Rebel Army from going North.[18] In so doing we lost at least 75000 men in getting here, and notwithstanding all this the tread of the Confederate Army is heard in the free states to day.

This may awake the people of the North to the fact, that if they are going to put down the Rebellion, by the Sword & Bayonet, and *ever* get through it, they have got to lay aside thier work at home, and come in person to the rescue. Money & *such* substitutes as they send are of no avail. In order to do anything successfully we must have men come that are willing to march to the canons mouth. The Soldiers feel that every man that is drafted should be obliged to come, and they also think the Government is slow to send us the necessary amount of men.

I was thinking this morning that I have served seven months of my last "muster in," and the last two has seemed the longest I have ever experienced since being in the Army, but as I have said before, I am willing to work hard this year, provided they will give us men enough to wind it up. Many at home think we like the business—that its easy—good pay, and the like of that, but to all such I would say, come and try for yourselves, and I will warrant them to cry enough before six months have passed over thier heads. Men should come here for *true* patriotism for this blessed country, and not for the love of gain. My ever dear Wife I should like to be with you this holy sabbath day, but this cannot be, circumstances have placed miles between us, but let us *hope* that there will be an end to such times as these—that peace & prosperity shall e'er long dawn upon our distracted Nation. May we ever be thankfull to God that it is as well with us, as it is, to day. Sickness and disease have thus far, mostly, been kept from this family, and both at home and abroad we are under circumstances of great mercy.

17. Upton refers to Confederate general Jubal Early's raid into Maryland, which brought him within five miles of Washington, D.C. Facing fortifications at Washington manned by the Union army's sixth Corps, with other Union forces gathering in his rear, Early returned to Virginia after stealing and destroying the property of many Northerners.

18. Upton refers to Ulysses Grant's campaign in May and June 1864, which led to 65,000 Union casualties.

I am in my usual health, and hope this will find my family the same. This makes the second letter I have written since last monday, none from you have reached me during this time.

Affectionately Yours

Geo. E. Upton

New Hampshire Historical Society, Concord, Letters of George Upton, 1963–29.

In this letter Edwin Horton of Company C, Fourth Vermont Regiment, compares his life as a Union soldier with the soldier's lot in the Confederate army.

Harewood Hospital, Ward 4

Washington, DC

August 19, 1864

Dearest Ellen

it is with pleasure I now seat myself to inform you that I am well and hope this will find you the same   I have written you one letter since I received any from you   I hope this will find you enjoying yourself firstrate   I have been feeling real lone some but I begin to get over it some now. . . . what a pitty it was nell that I couldent had luck enough to have got hold of one of those big bounties so you and me could have flourished a little   when I think of it nell it almost makes me think that I will not do much more good down here. . . . I know you said that you was a union woman when I was at home and I want to please you so I play union but really I am getting a good deal sesesh feeling about me   I think if it wasent for you I should go over to them   they use a private soldier with more respect than they do in our army   when they get so they use the best blod of the north worse than they do the mules and keep them on worse fodder a fellow ought to get a thousand to come out here and stay three years but when a fellow has to come out for nothing while others that never has been out get the spoil it looks to me rather tough   but enough of this. . . . please write soon and tell me all the news you must be shure and take up my note that Mrs Porter holds when it becomes due   I suppose you will have to get the mony of some one else for a while   now Nell I must tell you I have been writing to another gal in Masschusetts to day   I had a work bag full of little trinkets give to me by the sanitary[19] and it had a letter in it which contained the address of a lady and a requist to write   so I rote her a line to day but I dident put any love in it   now nell give my regards to all of the folks

yours with much love

Edwin Horton

Vermont Historical Society, Montpelier, Letters of Edwin and Ellen Horton, MSS 21, no. 16.

19. The U.S. Sanitary Commission frequently distributed among the troops bags of clothing and food that had been made and donated by Northern women.

Samuel Augustus Duncan of Meriden, New Hampshire, enlisted as major of the Fourteenth New Hampshire Volunteer Regiment in September 1862. In September 1863 President Lincoln commissioned Duncan, who was white, as colonel of the Fourth U.S. Colored Regiment. Duncan was wounded at an engagement at New Market Heights, for which he was brevetted brigadier general. In this fragment of a letter to his future wife, Julia Jones, Duncan explains why he believes Sherman's destructive march through the South was necessary.

NorthEast Station, Above Wilmington, North Carolina
March 15, 1865

. . . for the last two days we have been marching to the roar of Sherman's guns. We have now joined the all-conquering army that is now sweeping like an avalanche over the domains of the rebellion—like that engine of destruction, marking its path with ruin & desolation. South Carolina, especially, has been most sadly torn by the ploughshare of war. The vengeance which our warworn veterans have been nursing against that nestingplace of traitors has vented itself to the full.

Our columns have blackened a path 100 miles in width,—cattle are driven off, the supplies consumed or destroyed, the mansions burned. It seems a terrible retribution to befal a people, but in its corrections I believe it a mercy. This inhuman war will not cease until the arrogant South is brought under the rod, and made to *feel* that the North is *a power, to be respected and feared*. This fearful destruction of property is one of the legitimate fruits of the rebellion. Call me not unfeeling, call me not inhuman, when I say that it is with a sort of triumph—not unmixed of course with sadness—I see the heavens blackened with the ascending smoke of some rich planters house. "Whoso soweth to the wind shall reap the whirlwind." Is *rebel property* more sacred than the *lives* of our *loyal soldiers*? Yet so the braggart miscreants of the South & the too tender hearted people at home would seem to assert when they raise their hands in holy horror because a rebel's house or cotton has been given to the flames. . . .

New Hampshire Historical Society, Concord, Letters of Samuel A. Duncan, Duncan/Jones Collection.

John Peirce of Beverly, Massachusetts, enlisted in the Twelfth Unattached Company, Heavy Artillery. Peirce gives an account of the effects that President Lincoln's assassination had on the army's activities and morale.

Fort Lincoln, Washington, D.C.
April 15, 1865

My Dear Wife

I have just come into Camp   we have been out scouting   we have captuered five prisinors, Rebs   we have them in the gard house   the order was to take all rebel deserters or any suspicious persons in the afternoon we were orderd to take all persons coming from the city   the guard are stationed all around the fortifications near enough to make one another hear   all our men are on guard detailed men and all the gratest excitement that every was known prevals here no one can leive the City   last nite about two oclock all the men in the defences were turned out with arms   at daylite we were sent out   what a tarable murder we all felt as though we had our father murdered   it is the worst thing that could have happened at this present time   how different from last thursday nite   the City was illumanated and look handsom i can tell you   three men from each Co went to fix up our Gen quarters   surly we cannot tell what a day will bring forth we were telling yesterday about taking off one of our picket posts now all are on picket except the detailed men and we shell go on in the morning. it has rained all day and a gloomy day   if an army of rebs had marched into the City we should felt half so bad becaus we could have fought them and drove them out but our presiden we can not replace at the pre[s]ant time   what a wreach that commited the deed   we should not have asked a reb to halt a grate many times to day i can tell you   one of the rebs that we took to day seemed to be glad that the President was dead   the people out are a most all Rebs at hart   after Lee gave up they were sulkey and would hardly give one a civel answar   you at home have no idea of how the old slave holders feel   they hate a Northern man and would quick tell him so if they dard to tell one so. . . . it seemed very solemn to hear the Bells toling when we were in the woods scouting today   if we could get the scamp that killed our President we should have felt better   I recieved from you and John and was glad to hear that you are all well at home   i suppose you have herd of the muder of the presedent before now rite and let me know what time you herd of it and if you believed it at first. . . . I hope this will find you all well at home now my love to you Clara

Yours Ever   John

Peabody Essex Museum, Salem, Mass., Letters of John Peirce, John Peirce Papers.

Dr. Henry J. Millard from North Adams, Massachusetts, was a surgeon with the Thirty-fourth Massachusetts Volunteer Infantry. He writes this account of General Robert E. Lee's surrender at Appomattox Court House.

Richmond, Virginia
April 26, 1865

Dear Sister Hattie

Although our camp is 1 ½ miles out of the city I think I am justified in dating it Richmond, and it affords me pleasure in so doing, in view of the perfect fredom both of body & mind which I am privileged to exercise, in sight of the Libby[20] & other Buildings where so many of our brave men have from time to time been confined and obliged to suffer from wounds and starvation & have consequently died most horrible deaths, but noble defenders of their country whose names will live as long as memory lasts. But those from whom they have recd such cruel & brutal punishment will be dealt with according to thier just deserts for their Rebellious & Barbarous course by the strong hand who conducts and rules the armies of both Heaven & Earth. I recd a Letter from you last Eve, & also a bundle of papers and another paper today containing a Heandkerchief, all for which I am a thousand times obliged and will compensate to you in some *way* for them. We arrived here where we are now in camp yesterday having been on the march since we left camp Holly (March 25th) working almost dayly and fighting nearly every day up to the surrender of Genl Lees army since which time I can lay myself down at night with the satisfaction, and a *mighty agreeable feeling* of the command not being obliged to rally into line of Battle during the night, for a good nights rest is essential when we are obliged to march 30 miles during the day in the hot sun & dust. The campaign has been short, but a very active one. I doubt not whether our noblest commanders in the field anticipated so much and was looking for so great a reaction in our national affairs so soon. Indeed, the surrender of Genl Lees army was a big thing and the day was the happiest day of my life. and glad that I was that I had lived to see it after a continued chasing and fighting for several days; and to be an Eye Witness of such an important event and one rather looked for by the north, was a blessed privilege. and the privilege of riding through Genl Lees army while they were all yet in posession of their arms (which I did immediately after the surrender) was a privilege I expected to have never had. All the officers of high rank were very well clad & Equiped, but all others were looking very shabby. The whole army was evidently in a very disorganised and demoralised condition, and were glad enough to give up the ship. The terms of surrender (doubtless) you have already read. i did not see Genl Lee but saw many other Genls of whom his son was one. I think I dropped you a few lines in pencil while on our march to Lynchburg and handed it to a Col. who was going to return to Washington and I suppose you refer to this in speaking of hearing from me. I wrote you very hastily when assuming a painfull position on the ground, it being the best I could do under the circumstances. Our whole marching has been when we could not either receive any mail or send any as the Rail

---

20. Union prisoners of war were kept in the Libby Prison in Richmond.

Roads were all cut, Bridges burned &c. We remained at Lynchburg one & a half days, long enough to put the city under Marshall law, and destroy confed. Gov. property. Col. Robbin of this Regt was Provo Marshal, & the Regt done Provo duty while there, the men being Quartered in the court house yard and all the officers in the court house. Lynchburg is of 12000 inhabitants, and a wealthy city, many splendid private residences, new England style, was evidently a great Tobacco market previous to the war.

Massachusetts Historical Society, Boston, Letters of Henry J. Millard, Millard Papers.

CHAPTER TWO

The Meaning of the War

IN THIS SECTION soldiers and their correspondents examine the war in terms of its broader meaning and significance. In particular, they consider questions of union and slavery and the underlying principles of the American political experiment. Through their reflections they comment on the conduct of the war, often voicing complaints about specific politicians and government policies. Given the spiritual orientation of nineteenth-century New Englanders, it is not surprising to find a number of writers interpreting the war in a religious context.

In this letter Fred Spooner, a resident of Providence, Rhode Island, writes to his older brother, Henry Joshua Spooner, who was studying law in Albany, New York. In 1862 Henry was commissioned second lieutenant in the Fourth Regiment, Rhode Island Volunteers. He was promoted to first lieutenant after the battle of Antietam in September 1862. Mustered out of the service in 1865, Henry Spooner went on to a career in the U.S. House of Representatives between 1875 and 1881, serving as Speaker from 1879 to 1881. This letter conveys a sense of the enthusiasm with which Northerners at first greeted the war, as well as some prevalent Northern beliefs about the South and Southerners.

Providence, Rhode Island
April 30, 1861

Dear Henry,

Your letter was received, and I now sit down in my shirt sleeves (as it is warm) to write in return.

For the last few weeks there has been great excitement here, and nothing has been thought of scarcely except that one subject which now received the undivided attention of the whole loyal North,—war.

And well may war, so hideous and disgusting in itself receive such attention when carried on for such noble and just principles as in the present case.

Traitors have begun the conflict, let us continue and end it. Let us settle it now, once and for all.

Let us settle it, even if the whole South has to be made one common graveyard, and their cotton soaked in blood. let us do it *now* while the whole North is aroused from the inactivity and apparent laziness in which it has been so long.

There are plenty of men, an abundance of money, and a military enthusiasm never before known in the annals of history, all of which combined will do the

work nice and clean, and if need be will wipe out that palmetto, pelican, rat-
tlesnake region entirely. The holy cause in which our volunteers are enlisted will
urge them on to almost superhuman exertions. The South *may* be courageous but
I doubt it, they can *gas* and *hag* first rate; they can lie and steal to perfection, but I
really do believe that they cannot fight—"Barking dogs never bite." Southern sen-
ators can bluster, bully and blackguard, but I believe them to be cowards at heart.
As for instance there was the case of Potter and Pryor.[1]

Besides the very nature of their country and their manner of living, have a tendency, I think to make them otherwise than brave.

But granting them to be brave (wh[ich] I dont believe can be proven) they
have no chance to overturn this government. They havent the resources, the
"almighty dollar," that powerful ally, or formidable enemy,—is against them.
They have no money—their property has legs and will be continually disappearing.

They have prospered dealing in human flesh,—let them now take the results
of it.

They have had what *they* consider the *blessings* of slavery,—let them now
receive the *curses* of it.

They must be put down, conquered and thoroughly subdued if need be. They
have no earthly hope of overcoming this government. The fifteen weak states of
the South can stand no chance against the nineteen powerful states of the North.

What *I* want to see done is, that if Baltimore makes any *farther* resistance
to the passage of troops through her streets, that bloody "Plug Ugly" city
cleaned up![2]

Well,—do you think I'm crasy? I find that I've been steaming on here at what is
sometimes termed "a great grist," and that I've written a page and half on war,
the South, Baltimore, "Plug Uglies" &c, &c.

When I began I did not intend to give a lecture or write a composition on the
"crisis," and I had not as Mayor Knight[3] would say "made preparations for a
speech," but unconsciously I got on the all-absorbing topic at the very commencement, and it was hard work to let go of it.

there hasent been much studying lately, and it is very hard work to think or
write concerning any other subject than that on which I've paused so long.

So therefore excuse my "crisis" beginning.

---

1. Roger Pryor was a Virginian who had advocated that South Carolina attack Fort Sumter in
order to convince Virginians to support the Confederate cause. The Potter reference is most likely to
John Potter, a delegate at the Alabama seccession convention, who urged a course of moderation after
Lincoln's election.

2. On April 19, 1861, residents of Baltimore, Md., rioted in response to the passage of the Sixth
Massachusetts Regiment through that city on its way to Washington, D.C. Maryland was a slave state
that remained in the Union, but in the early stages of the war strong secessionist sentiment existed,
creating a volatile situation in that state. "Plug Ugly" was Baltimore slang for a street ruffian.

3. The mayor of Providence.

The volunteering still goes on, although the first regiment have left us for the scene of battle.

You now know by the papers of course who have gone so there will be no use of my naming them.

A great many that I know have gone, and many more with whom I'm acquainted have enlisted.

Some twenty fellows I should think have gone from the Gymnasium. Bowen was one of the first to enlist, so your society is represented.

I'm much surprised at some who have enlisted, persons whom you would have supposed would have shrunk from the fatigue and dangers of war.

Only think of Mose Jenkins set to work throwing up a breastwork! Or that big bull-headed Goddard getting his muscle up on salt junk and crackers! I'm afraid "Mose" will want to know what the last style of coat is before the three months are up, and that Goddard will miss his accustomed drinks; but never mind, it shows patriotism in the right place, and I say "Bully for them."

Mr Brown you know has gone as captain of the 2nd company of the Infantry, he left home very unexpectedly. the troops departed in the "Empire State," at three separate times, and at each time rousing crowds (the largest I ever saw,) gathered to see them off, and to Bid them God speed on their holy errand.

The departure of the first detachment was very imposing. The deck was all covered with the soldiers dressed in their neat and easy uniforms, while the wharves were literally jammed with human beings, and the vessels swarmed with persons all eager to bid them good bye. Cheers after cheers rent the air, while the band played all the national airs. Greene played on his bugle beautifully, he surpassed himself, and I dont believe he could be beat.

And as the steamer slowly moved from the wharve the strains of "Auld Lang Syne" were wafted back to the friends whom they had left behind,—friends mournful that they had left them, yet rejoicing that they went to "fight the good fight."

It was truly imposing, and the Providence soldier in his dying hour, will look back with pleasure upon the scene wh[ich] met his eyes at his departure from Fox Point.

"Hughy Johnson" stood there with his short rifle in his hands, waving his hat as fast as his muscular arms would permit, and cheering to the extreme of his lungs.

The regiment was composed of a mighty fine looking set of men, and doubtless will do work. You see what compliments they have received from the papers dont you?

Flags are flying in every part of the city, not those dirty pelican, palmetto affairs, but the good old stars and stripes. Sayles is here now, but he came out in a strong Union speech from the Post Office, where he had taken refuge from a crowd who threatened him violence.

About the same time the office of the Post was threatened, since wh[ich] they have put out the American flag, and came out *very strong* in favor of the Administration. . . .

Your letter reached here for Father to night. All are well.

Shall expect to hear from you soon.

Affcnly   Fred

Rhode Island Historical Society, Library, Providence, Manuscripts Collection, Letters of Fred Spooner and Henry Joshua Spooner, Henry J. Spooner Papers, MSS 732.

Samuel Hinckley was a well-to-do Massachusetts businessman who owned two silk facto-ries: the Glasgow Company in Boston and the Northampton Silk Mill. These two letters were written by Hinckley to his son Henry. Henry Hinckley was attending school in Berlin, Germany, when the war first broke out, but he returned to serve as a lieutenant in the Fifth Massachusetts Cavalry. In his letters Samuel Hinckley expresses his opinion of the Union's chances for victory and the effects he believed the war would have on the nation.

Boston, Massachusetts
May 1, 1861

My dear Henry

Your letter 7th April was rec'd announcing your intention to leave Berlin 1st May today. . . . You have some idea from the papers of the state of our country. But you can have little idea of the actual excitement & unanimity of all parties in the North, East, & West in putting down forcibly the gigantic Southern rebellion. It will be put down. It may be by a great effusion of blood if thretened resistance is attempted. There are indications of backing down on the part of the South & it is possible the leaders forseeing what must be the issue of battle will retire & flee for their lives. No one can foretell. The clouds are lifting, & all looks brighter for the safety of our country & the perpetuation of the Union. for ten days great fears were entertained for the safety of the Capitol & if Davis had at once sent on his army after their capture of Fort Sumpter they would undoubtedly have taken Washington. They were well armed & we were not. Now we are preparing & prepared for them Washington is safe. Traitors in the Army & Navy are well sifted out & if more appear they will be summarily dealt with, hung or *shot*. Scott[4] is to make his headquarters at Phil'a. Mass'tts had done nobly & we have all the free States, you I hope will live to see the U.S. a stronger Gov. than ever before. The attack & capture of Fort Sumpter roused the whole North East & West & the slaughter of Mass'ts soldiers by the mob in Baltimore started a more intense demonstration.[5] If any recurrence of mob violence in Baltimore takes

4. Gen. Winfield Scott was at that time the commander-in-chief of the Union army.
5. Four soldiers were killed in the riot that ensued when the Sixth Massachusetts Regiment passed through Baltimore on April 19, 1861.

place she will be a bed of ashes & New Orleans a fish pon & three cheers for the Union. These events however are having a surprising effect on general business But I trust it is only temporary & that another year we shall be on the high road to greater prosperity than ever before. . . .

The South are sorely disappointed in the unanimity of the North. They counted on a general rising in their [the South's] favor by all not of the Republican party & that the Republicans were craven & would not fight. How grievously mistaken.

From S[amuel] L[yman] H[inckley]

Boston, Massachusetts
March 11, 1862

[My dear Henry]

The Union cause will prevail, though at an awful cost of blood & treasure, more of treasure than of blood for modern implements of war speak more at a distance than the ancient mode of hand to hand when the eye spoke to eye & kindled the spirit of the devil within. Henry Hoppin has gone as 2nd Lieut. in Green's 14th Reg. & writes in good spirits about camp life & discipline & prospects of sudden call to glory. We are marching on & the rebels are every where impressed with superior power & are retreating, but it will be a long time before they will be humbled to unqualified submission. They are too much like ourselves & will not acknowledge beat when routed & whipped. Power and might will do it but mortification will rankle & it may take a generation to restore fraternal feeling. Taxes are & will be enormous for long years to come. We must not flinch from meeting our duty in this trying conflict. I am disposed to do all I can in the way of taxes & gratuities. My income is reduced, but I am thankful to find in the years (1861) experience I "hold my own." That is if I have not made anything in business I have not lost to any considerable amt. nor at all in depreciation of some kinds of property, real estate at the West particularly. The silk factory comes out about even. . . .

This civil war will work good to the young men of this age & land. Money making & peddling give place to higher aspirations and this war is marking a distinctive manly character in our young men. We have a country & government not to be assailed by foes within, or foes without with impunity cost what it may of blood, life & treasure. It is hard for me to be patriotic. I am coming to it for though practical abolitionists behaved badly, slaveholders have behaved worse. Now they must cave or die & slavery with them. Slavery is doomed at all event. We have had a few days of great excitement The rebels have spent a year on the Steamer Merrimac to make her impregnable & destructive to our entire navy &

but for our preparation was likely to do it. She has just tried her power & though she did great damage proved not invulnerable.[6]

[From Samuel L. Hinckley]

Isaac Austin Brooks from Providence, Rhode Island, served in the Second Brigade, Second Division, Third Army Corps, Army of the Potomac. He explains the meaning of the war in this letter to his children.

Camp Caldwell
October 13, 1861

My Dear Children,

As there are so many of you in the nest at home, I cannot write to each one, and therefore send this to you all. I think you will be glad to hear from me, in a letter to you all, as well as to hear of me through Mothers letters, for I never forget you, even if I do not write to you. Mothers accounts of you are very gratifying to me, for I think you are all trying to be good children, to give Mother as little trouble as you can, & to improve yourselves. My life here, is not very pleasant, but I submit to it because I think it is for the best and it is the duty of us all, to do what we can for our country and to preserve its integrity even to the sacrifice of our lives, if that is necessary. It is a glorious country, and *must* be preserved to our children. It was given to *us entire,* and *we* must give it to you, entire and *you* must give it as you receive it, to those who come after you. Remember your *country* is next to your God, in love, and never see it injured, or disgraced, if you have a hand, or a mind, to put forth in its defense. I hope to return to you in due time, safe and well, and find *you* are well and happy, but should it be so ordered that we do not meet again on earth, remember to love, and serve your country in whatever way it may be your lot to do so. To do this, many things are needed, which you will all learn in due time, but one of the *foundations* will be, to be sober, honest, and industrious. . . .

So be good children all of you, & remember I *think* of you all, *daily,* even if I can not see you.

Your Affectionate Father

---

6. The Confederates converted the USS *Merrimac* to an ironclad vessel and on March 8, 1862, she sank two U.S. vessels. However, on March 9, 1862, the *Merrimac* fought her famous battle with the Union ironclad USS *Monitor,* and although both crews claimed victory in this indecisive battle, the *Merrimac* sustained heavy damage and did not fight again. When the Union army captured Norfolk, Va., where the *Merrimac* was harbored in May 1862, the ship's crew blew up the vessel.

William Augustus ("Gus") Walker, from Northampton, Massachusetts, was captain of Company C, Twenty-seventh Regiment, Massachusetts Volunteers. Walker's comments indicate that for some Americans a desire to end slavery did not coexist with a belief in racial equality.

Batchelder's Creek

Newbern, North Carolina

July 11, 1862

You must excuse my writing you, dear sister mine, on such very unfashionable paper, my commercial note is all gone & I have nothing on hand but such as government furnishes, so if I write now as I feel just like doing, why you must put up with my necessities.

We are again out here in the woods, trying our best to kill time, last Monday two companies of us came out to relieve other two in doing picket duty, we are quartered on Capt Clark's plantation now in the rebel army & are very comfortably located. The officers occupy his house so that we live quite like christian people, it seems odd to lodge beneath a wooden roof & sit at an open window or on the piazza, when one has dwelt in tents so long. There is one advantage in being out here, which I fully appreciate, we can get fresh vegetables, eggs, milk, apples, chickens, berries &c all we want & at less cost than in town, to one so fond of everything in its season as I am, this is a great advantage & a very good thing for our healths. My men are well contented here & I like it pretty well for a change, but it is growing terribly monotonous, there is literally nothing to do for officers, every night at 7 o'c we station twenty seven pickets at nine different post, at 7 o'c in the morning these come in & we station six others at three posts for the day, I drill my men about an hour each day & this is all we have to do. I read & write & sleep & smoke & walk & manage to get through the day feeling very tired, doing actually nothing. This would be jolly for a lazy man, but I am not a lazy man & so prefer a little more activity. The past few days has been fearfully hot, thermometer 95° to 105° in the shade in the sun it was almost insupportable, we could only sit in our quarters in the scantiest of costumes & by the aid of iced claret punches manage to get through the day. While I write a scene is going on in the opposite room, highly characteristic of Southern indolence. A Lieut sits writing, near him sits a great buck nigger, very black & very fragant, bare feet, tattered shirt & knotted hair, with a stick in his hand a rug tied on one end of it waving it to & fro with a very sleepy air, to keep the flies from said Lieut. The flies are really tormenting & the heat is intolerable but I had rather endure both, than to have one of those confounded dirty niggers anywhere within twenty feet of me. As a class they are lazy, filthy, ragged, dishonest & confounded stupid. There are exceptional cases & if I could find a decent bright mulatto boy I would take him & bring him home with me but the boys learn mischief & wickedness so early that a respectable specimen is as scarce as hens teeth. I have the same boy that came with me from Annapolis, he is faithful & honest as the sun, smart, spunky, yet respectful & quiet. I could not find a better one anywhere.

Monday July 14

We received a mail to-day & learned of some fighting near Richmond, the 10th I see has again suffered severely.[7] My friend Maj Miller was killed, a brave, true, nobler man, never wielded a sword. Is not this war becoming more & more horrible, the valuable lives daily sacrificed to the fury of these infernal rebels, are worth more than the whole Southern population & shall it ever be said when so many thousands of our bravest & best men offer up their lives for their country, that the savage *curse* which caused all this misery, shall be allowed to *live*. No! let slavery *die,* let our armies sweep over the South & destroy from off the face of the country every vestige of this enormous crime. We can have no *peace* until slavery is *dead.*

I send remembrance to all the family. For Frankie, darling, kisses & much love & for you Sister dear the old, strong & true love of

Brother Gus

Historic Northampton, Northampton, Mass., Letters of William A. Walker, W. A. Walker Papers.

George Upton of Derry, New Hampshire, a sergeant in the Sixth New Hampshire Volunteer Regiment, gives advice on running the farm as well as his views on the political debates of the day in this letter to his wife.

Newport News, Virginia
July 17, 1862

My Dear Sarah,

Letter No 11 from you came to hand day before yesterday about nine o'clock at night, and I was awfull glad to hear from you I can asshore you, but as it was written so long since I feel anxious to get another. It is of no use for me to say anything about the grass now for probably somebody's sythe has been in the field ere this, and if it was not too late I should lease it to Father & you to do as best you see fit. His judgement is as good if not better than mine, and whatever you, and him think for the best I shall feel *perfectly* satisfied with. If you are like to have any Apples this year you had better look out for some Barrels right off to put them in, as it is hard to get them when Apples are plenty unless they are got a long time before they are wanted. I dont know as you expect to have any as you have never written whether what the prospect was. I have heard from other parts of the state by the Boys, and they say the prospect is for a large crop, but it may not be the case there in Derry & vicinity. The crop of Babies seems to be quite good, and if

7. Tenth Regiment, Massachusetts Volunteers.

Wheeler's folks keep on "Sir Franklin" will be Grandfather of a large flock before he dies if he lives eight or ten years more. I should be inclined to think the *oven* was not left empty long, well perhaps it held the heat, and they concluded to bake another batch before it yet coolled down, ha! I got a letter from Henry the same time I got one from you, and he says Jenny is not very well, and I conclude he has been doing like all other married folks, and I mistrust he will have something to call him Pa some day. Well Women that have Husbands in the Army will have a chance to rest in this respect—so there is no loss without some small gain. In regard to that Bill it was Holes fault—he paid the money but did not notice but what it was marked paid—he carried the Box to the office and done the business, and I had nothing to do about it, but it must pass now, and I must learn wisdom by it for the future—though I guess you will be inclined to think it costs *considerable* to learn me wisdom. I am glad to say that my health is improving fast, and if it continues a few days longer I shall be as well as ever, so you can tell Mother & Grandmother that they wont see me at present, but if it was necessay for me to go home on account of my health it would be allmost *impossible*—they wont discharge Men untill in many cases death stares them in the face—in fact there is only two ways as a general thing by which Men get their discharge one is by death, and the other by being severely wounded—not a very pleasing fact to be shure. I dont think justice is done by the sick in a large share of cases, but I am not allowed to be judge—if I was I would send home *every* Man that was hanging round, and of no use to the Army whatever. Every Regt has more or less sick which they are in hopes will be better, so they keep them till at last they send them home on the verry brink of the grave. . . . It dont seem hardly possible that it is now haying season for nothing looks like it here—there is no grass and we hear nothing but the tramp of War. Capt Putnam went over to Norfolk the other day, and he reports the Navy Yard totally demolished—one grand ruin—thus it is that desolation marks the footsteps of war. Every where in these parts dessolation stares one in the face—the blow falls with great severity upon the South. . . . I expect the taxes will be high soon. I see a picture yesterday of the United States Officer taking the invoice, and I thought I would tell you so you might not be taken by surprise when they get along as to what they was going to do as it might frighten you *te te ho ha*. There was three of them in the picture I see—one was looking at the Mans Watch—one was looking *under* the Bed to take the value of the *thunder jug,* and the other was down on his knees feeling up the outside skirts to see the value of the *hoop* or at least that was the *pretense,* but he *might* of been *thinking* of *something* else for ought I know—so you had better look out *haha!*[8] Wel I think I have written nonsense enough at this time. Aside from the Milatary we dont see much in the shape of humanity but Niggers, and the worst wish I have for any one North is that all that think so much of them was out here to fight—*especially* if they turn this warfare into fighting for the Niggers only. I came

---

8. Upton is referring to a political cartoon commenting on the extensive taxes levied by the U.S. government to fund the war effort.

out here to help support the Constitution & Laws of our land, and for *nothing* else, and if it is turned into some other purpose—then those that do it may do the fighting for all me, and if I had my say, in case of an abolition war—*every* abolishonest should be *compelled* to come out here, and when here to be in the *front rank*—then we would see how long their love for the Darkies would continue. Demagogues are found in all parties, so they are found in the war department, and some are *determined* to have this war continue to the longest possible extent, but the hand of God may cut short their wicked designs. We have not seen anything of the Paymaster yet, but I think we shall soon. I shall send you a certificate for two months when this month is out.[9] . . . I hope Ann will be able to stay with you the most of the time for I dont like to have you there alone. It has been a source of great comfort to me to know she has been with you so much. Is there to be any Berries for Eddie & Mary to pick this season. Oh those dear little ones how glad their father would be to see them. Keep up good spirits—put your trust in God, and all will yet be well. Ask me any questions you like and I will *gladly* answer them. Regards to all & love to the family.

Most Affectionately, Yours   George

New Hampshire Historical Society, Concord, Letters of George Upton, 1963-29.

Samuel B. Shepard from Madison, Connecticut, served with the Sixth Regiment, Connecticut Volunteers. In this letter Shepard offers a detailed critique of the Union's conduct of the war and his analysis of the cause of the war.

Beaufort, South Carolina
July 30, 1862

Friend Thomas, Dr. Tom, D.D.S.

Your letters always do me good. There is always something in them which goes right to my spot, & which I find nowhere else. When I rec'd your letter this morning, I said to myself, as soon as I had read the first line, "that is from Tom." So Madison has really found out at last that her young men are called upon to do something to save a Gov't & a Union, to which they owe their existence, contemptible as it is! I am glad of it, & wish some chaps there, who are good for nothing else, who acknowledge no law, no decency, & no morality, just like two thirds of *"our brave soldiers,"* were obliged to come out here, & pass through a course of military discipline; it is what they want. But I dont feel as if such a family as yours, bound to me as it is by a thousand precious recollections, ought to be broken up, for any call that at present exists. This war ought to have been over by the middle of last Jan, & could have been, & might have been, & the country restored to its original condition. But I will just go over the actual state of

---

9. Instead of receiving all of their pay themselves, soldiers were able to send certificates of payment to their families who could then redeem them.

affairs with you, & let you judge for yourself about coming to the war, as for what is necessary when you do come, I will tell you when we get to it. The people, last fall, rose up in their might, against secession & rebellion, & expected to have it put down. Is it put down yet? No. Will it be put down, as long as Messrs So & so, among the politicians & contractors, have a chance to make money, or gain fat offices out of it? No. The people expected when they poured out their money, & their life in the shape of their sons, that the authors of this Rebellion should be punished. Are they punished? How! & who punished them? Our soldiers are, a great proportion of them, employed to guard the property of Southern planters, whose sons are in the rebel armies, & whose slaves are going about over the field of battle, knocking in the heads of our dying soldiers. Our bravest officers & soldiers are starving & languishing in Southern jails & negro pens as prisoners of war while Messrs Mason & Slidell are quartered awhile in Fort Warren, treated with the utmost attention & courtesy, & finally allowed to depart for England in triumph.[10] Gen. Scott, the greatest soldier but one, the world has ever known, is set aside, Because mr Somebody or other thinks he is too old.[11] Gen. Fremont, who was sweeping down the Missippi valley, & driving the rebels before him like chaff, is forced to resign,[12] there & in Virg. because he is accomplishing something, & likely to carry out the principles on which this war is waged, & the consequence is, that the Western States are still ravaged by guerillas & ruffians, Richmond is still holding us at bay, England is threatening to interfere[13]—Washington is hardly safe—Baltimore in the same condition—& the war no nearer an end, than it was a year ago. It has hardly begun yet, & when it ends, the probability is that Jeff Davis & Co, will occupy the chief seats in the nation, that they did formerly, for *"are they not our dear Southern brethren?"* "Would it not

10. James Mason and John Slidell were Confederate envoys traveling to Europe aboard a British steamer in an attempt to gain foreign support for the Confederacy. The Union navy intercepted the British vessel and arrested Mason and Slidell on the pretext that the diplomatic dispatches they carried were contraband of war. Great Britain demanded that the Union release the Confederate diplomats, and President Lincoln, unwilling to take any action that might lead to British recognition of the Confederacy, complied.

11. Gen. Winfield Scott, general in chief of the U.S. Army when war broke out in 1861, was seventy-four years old and plagued by various health problems. Pressure from Republican congressmen and other military officials led to Scott's retirement in November 1861, when Gen. George McClellan succeeded him as general in chief.

12. In the summer and fall of 1861, Gen. John C. Frémont was commander of the Western Department, fighting against Confederate supporters in Missouri, a slave state which remained loyal to the Union. In August 1861 Frémont declared martial law in Missouri and issued an edict emancipating the slaves of Confederate activists. Anxious to retain the support of Missouri slaveholders, President Lincoln revoked the edict. In March 1862 Lincoln appointed Frémont to command the Department of West Virginia, where he unsuccessfully pursued the army of Confederate Gen. Thomas ("Stonewall") Jackson. Frémont resigned his command in July 1862 in response to the promotion of a junior general over his head.

13. The Confederacy had been attempting to gain British recognition and perhaps intervention on its behalf since the beginning of the war. Although this recognition never came, British support remained a critical factor in the South's strategy for much of the war.

be a wicked thing to take a cent of their property, or a drop of their blood?"
"Wont some of these Northern contractors & politicians want fat offices & fat
jobs by & by when the Union is reconstructed, & wont it be well to conciliate the
Southern leaders?" We deplore the shedding of blood. It is an awful thing. It is
terrible to see these happy Southern homes ravaged by plundering Northern soldiers,—yes! & in those very houses (oh! they are perfect paradises I have seen
them with my own eyes, & been through their marble halls, & inhaled the orien-
tal fragrance of their gardens, & heard the chorus of their mocking birds,) in
those very houses, I say, we have found footstools made of the skulls, & pipes of
the thigh bones, & purses made of the skins of Northern mechanics & farmers,
who enlisted under the miserable delusion that they were going to fight for their
country. Yes, & in this very village of Beaufort, where we now are, I myself have
found a Constitution & Bylaws of the Beaufort Lyceum,[14] A Lyceum founded just
like our old Lyceum at home, only having for its sole object the contrivance of
plans to break up the American Union. So the blackest treason is sucked in by
Southern children with their mother's milk, & yet you can see an universal howl
about the loyal people of the South, & how they ought to be protected, & all
that. Where are the loyal people of the South? How do they show their loyalty? I
can answer these questions, from my own personal observation. Why dont they
stand up & show themselves, & help the Northern troops? When we have driven
the rebel soldiers away, & these beautiful, angelic, loyal people are perfectly free
to act as they choose, do they hoist the American flag, & welcome the American
troops? No, they send a message to the General, saying, "We are Union men. We
have not dared to own it before; but now, we hope that the soldiers will not be
allowed to molest our property.["] And, forthwith, a guard is stationed about the
estate. This very guard composed of men who have eaten nothing more than
rotten pork & mouldy hard tack for a week, & whose families are starving at
home for want of the paternal support. And in the meantime, these *"Union men"*
are stealing our cattle, horses, everything they can lay hands on, shooting our
men on the outposts, enticing them into houses by the promise of a tempting
meal, & butchering them in cold blood before the last mouthful is swallowed. I
myself have been left in charge of the sick, with only one commissioned officer,
& one hospital attendant, in a region entirely surrounded by secesh, between
them & the only Federal reg't within 20 miles, & that reg't half a mile off, when
all three of us have been obliged, pistol in hand, to leave our beds, night after
night for weeks, & patrol the deserted camp, & hunt along the edge of the
woods, to guard against spies, who might bring the emissaries of these same
"Union men" upon us, to cut our throats in the night. I dont tell half I can, nor half
I experience, because I know nobody at home sitting at his ease after his day's
work is done, & slandering his neighbors, & reading the *"On to Richmond"* newspapers, would believe a word of it. I except *you,* however, from the slandering part

14. A lyceum was either an academy or a more informal association providing public lectures, con-
certs, and entertainments.

of it, because I know that is business you are not addicted to. When I became old enough to understand the workings of such things, I posted myself thoroughly on the history of our country & the principles of our Gov't. I have kept myself posted ever since, & I mean to continue in the same course. I have only given you facts so far, & expressed no opinion. Now I will give you my opinion. The deeds & words of our Revolutionary fathers are the principles on which our gov't was founded, & on which the Republic has reached its present prosperity. Since the days of Jackson, those principles have been gradually yielding to a pro-slavery aristocracy, founded on the eternal nigger. The Constitution of the U.S. acknowledges no such aristocracy, as I understand it. Every man has his own understanding of the Constitution. Every man has his own understanding of the Bible. The religious creed which every man professes, is his understanding of the Bible. The political platform to which each man subscribes, is his understanding of the Constitution. I subscribe to the Chicago Platform,[15] & I have yet perfect faith in the men whom the people have elected to carry it out. But I have not so much faith in some of the agents & underlings who work the political & military wires. Abe Lincoln & his Cabinet, Gen. McClellan, Burnside, & others, I believe in yet.

But these scheming war horse politicians & military editors, & political generals, I don't believe in. Are they going to carry out these principles? Are they going to bring back the country to its original prosperity? I can't see it. These men who broke down Scott & Fremont & will break down McClellan if possible, now hold public meetings & spout. Let 'em spout. They talk about drafting, let 'em draft. But if I was out of the army, I wouldn't stir a peg to enlist until I could perceive some guarantee that these principles for which we are contending are to be carried out. I say guarantee. I mean a guarantee. I mean the promoting of such men to fill the innumerable offices & contracts, such enforcements of the Laws, both military & constitutional, as shall let the people see that the North is in earnest [illegible] the scales off the eyes of the Secesh, so that they will see it, too. And a guarantee that this shall be done as it ought to be, before the nation is so riddled & racked & ruined that what is left of it wont be worth fighting for. When this guarantee is given, they wont need to draft, there will be men enough. They wont need to take mr. So & So by the button hole, & whisper in his ear, "You give us money to carry out our plans,—we will give you patronage to carry out yours." There will be money enough. The people will rouse up as they did at first. The young men wont need any such inducements to enlist as they offer now. England wont interfere. France will rather aid than oppose us. We shall gain the respect of other nations, & our own confidence, when this is done, & not till then. What extraordinary people the Secesh must be. Here the newspapers have been telling us for a whole year, how their coast was blockaded, their internal communications all cut off, their supplies of every kind completely exhausted. And yet they hold out, & are likely to hold out. No doubt we shall eventually beat

15. The platform adopted at the 1860 Republican party convention held in Chicago.

them. How? Just as you would beat a child you was playing with, & didn't want to hurt. When? At a time which you & I will not live to see. With what result? This I have already stated. The whole thing (at present appearances) is just like a firm, composed of honest, upright, sagacious, thorough-going business men. They employ a great many laborers, a great many clerks & superintendents. The laborers do their work, take their pay & ask no questions. The clerks have a certain responsibility & a certain authority over their laborers. The superintendents are set above the clerks, & are responsible to the partners. The firm intend to carry on a great transaction, in which the cooperation of all hands is necessary. The customers of the firm yield them unlimited confidence. They expect the completion of the business within a year. But for some reason unknown, it drags on without any prospect of being completed. The customers pile on their confidence, furnish renewed supplies of money & means without stint. Parents think it is a great privilege to get their sons employed as laborers in the establishment. But the business drags. Finally they want to hire more laborers; they cant get them. Extraordinary inducements are offered. The laborers come in slowly. They come because they are attached to the firm, & dont want to see it fail.

My letter is not ¼ finished, but I must send it. Will continue. Keep the different parts, & you will have the thread of the story.

S.B. Shepard.

Connecticut Historical Society, Hartford, Letters of Samuel B. Shepard, Ms Stack.

William Augustus Willoughby of New Haven, Connecticut, served with Company A of the Tenth Connecticut Volunteer Regiment. This letter to his wife Nancy hints at some possible financial motives for his enlistment as well as motives of a more patriotic nature.

August 1862

Dear Wif

I have not time to notice your letter of July 15th in all its details in be in time for the mail for I am just informed that the mail closes in half an hour. You speak of the probabilities of my return home   I do not expect to come home under one year from now. I made another effort to get a furlough for 30 Days after Col Perdee returned to the Regt   he said he would use what influence he could for me but he says its impossable to obtain more than two furloughs at a time from one company and there C[on]valesents enough to occupy and fill the chance for gitting home

You make some allusion in this and in your letter of the 11th to soome persons who seem to gather satisfaction from our seeming defeat. Whatever satisfaction they take they have got to take now for the time is not far away in which all thier hope will be swept away like a fog before the Sun   And I wish it distinctly understood that whoever says I want the war because I was out of work or that I was from necessity obliged to go falsifies the truth and I do not thank them for such an Apology no matter who they are and what is still more if when my three years is up I will prove their courage by another (if the war is not closed) three years enlistment and they may enlist with seseshs and they may prove their courage and loyalty at the same time. I was always a law abiding citizen and joined the Army to sustain the Govermunt and Laws under which I was willing to live and obey. And if nessesary will join for 3 Years more to fight any rebel "north" or "south" who seeks to break down either. One word more and I must close for now and that is this

You seem to fear that I may become hardened by being in the army, and while passing the trying scenes of a Soldiers life. I think to many and perhaps to most such will prove true. Yet so far as I am concerned I am in hopes to turn these scenes to some good account and return a better man than when I left home. As to what is said in your letters respecting mother I shall leave intill I come home. I have no time to notice Celias letter for the want of time and room now. I send her my kindest regards and will try to say more in answer to her in my next. I send her my kindest for now and Remember me to all others relatives and friends. Tell Father when I get my mind a little settled I shall write him a letter. Write me how he is situated: And now Nancy accept my warmest love for yourself and dear little Raymond and answer this as soon as you can, while I remain Your true and Affectionate Husband

W. A. Willoughby

It is almost impossable for one to write about any thing for some is dancing some playing cards others reading loud enough to be heard ¼ of a mile So you must excuse all mistakes

William

American Antiquarian Society, Worcester, Mass., Letters of William A. Willoughby, W. A. Willoughby Papers.

Robert Hale Kellogg enlisted in Company A, Sixteenth Connecticut Volunteer Regiment. He was promoted to sergeant in November 1862. In April 1864 Kellogg was captured at Plymouth, North Carolina, and was sent to Andersonville Prison. After the war Kellogg served as a witness in the Union military commission's trial of Andersonville's commandant, Henry Wirz. The commission found Wirz guilty of war crimes and executed him—the only Confederate official to be executed after the war. In this letter Kellogg attaches religious significance to the war and the issue of emancipation.

Leesboro, Maryland
Sept. 10, 1862

I mean to express my mind a little in this letter in regard to the conduct of the war. We have, I think, plenty of troops but lack leaders. What has been loudly called in the papers *strategy* is merely what we have been *forced* to do, by a well disciplined and well *generaled* rebel army. This nation has trusted too much to

McClellan & Halleck[16] & too little to that only source of help in trouble—God. We *must* free the blacks or perish as a nation. I have long held this view and have been sneered at & called an abolitionist, but i am content to wait. I think I'm *right*. We have got to fight *now* to save our northern states from invasion! What a digression! Here a few months ago we were "driving the enemy to the wall"—it was a "mere question of time" in regard to the taking of Richmond and it seemed as if the whole South lay at our feet conquered—I honestly think it is because the nation has disregarded God's voice   we've not let the enslaved blacks go free when we had the power. many if not most of our Gens are profane, wicked men—and as a nation we have been proud and corrupt. Are we not now receiving a just rebuke? It certainly seems so to me—I don't like Prest. Lincoln's last letter at all. I dont think the Union as it *was* is desirable.[17] *Conquer* the rebels first, effectually *subdue* them; let their slaves go free and *then* talk about *Union*. . . . I will now close till my next letter. I am as ever your aff. son

Robert H. Kellogg

Connecticut Historical Society, Hartford, Letters of Robert Hale Kellogg, MS 68013.

Samuel Storrow enlisted as a corporal in Company H, Forty-fourth Massachusetts Volunteer Regiment on September 12, 1862. He was mustered out of that regiment in June 1863 and reenlisted on September 22, 1864, as first lieutenant in Company G, Second Massachusetts Volunteer Infantry. Storrow served with Sherman's army in Georgia and the Carolinas. He died on March 16, 1865, at Averysboro, North Carolina. In this letter he explains to his father his reasons for enlisting.

Boston, Massachusetts
Oct. 12, 1862

My dear Father

   Before you arrive here our regiment will have reached Newbern to enter at once upon active service. I feel therefore that it is right and proper for me, before going, to state to you plainly and as well as I am able to by writing the circumstances under which I have taken this step in your absence and the various motives from which I have acted. It is very hard to do this satisfactorily and completely without a personal interview, which for a thousand reasons I hope may take place before long.

---

   16. Gen. George McClellan was commander of the Army of the Potomac and Gen. Henry Halleck was serving as general in chief of the Union army at this point in the war.

   17. Kellogg refers to President Lincoln's letter of Aug. 22, 1862, to Horace Greeley, editor of the *New York Tribune,* who had called on the administration to emancipate the slaves. Lincoln explained that his primary concern was to preserve the Union and that he would consider emancipation only as it related to his goal of preserving the Union.

On the 10th of August I left Fayal[18] to return home. I had heard no news later than that of the long continued and fiercely contested battles of the last week of June,[19] which resulted in a change in the position of our army before Richmond and the adoption of a new base of operations, which as it then seemed to me, was likely to result in the speedy capture of the rebel capital and downfall of the rebellion. During our homeward voyage we all felt certain that these joyous tidings would greet our ears as we again set foot upon our native shores. You who witnessed the gradual change from victory to defeat can scarcely imagine the sudden revulsion of our feelings on hearing from the pilot who boarded us that the scene of active operations had been shifted from before the enemy's capital to within a few miles of our own, that our troops were being beaten back upon Washington,[20] that 600,000 new levies had been called for by proclamation of the President, and that now, 14 months after the commencement of the war, thousands of armed men were rushing to the defence of the national capital. As soon as I landed I heard of the formation of the 44th and of Charley's[21] commission. I at once wished to join this, but Mother and Charley both opposed it, saying that it was your intention and desire that I should rejoin my class, at once, and expressed themselves so strongly against my enlisting that on the following Monday I went to Cambridge and resumed my studies with what zeal I could.[22] During that week we heard that the rebel forces were pushing forward and Northward in every point along our borders, and that the points at which they were now aiming were no longer Washington and Nashville, but Philadelphia and Cincinnati and St. Louis. Each day now brought with it new hopes and fears; hopes for the better, now that our gallant young chieftain had been recalled to the head of our armies by the unanimous acclamations of his own soldiers and the general voice of the people;[23] fears lest this step might have been delayed too long even for him to cause victory once more to perch upon the eagles of the republic. Already the enemy had crossed the Potomac and was hastening to visit all the dread horrors of war upon the fertile fields and quiet homesteads of Pennsylvania. Already, too, the sturdy yeomanry of that state were pouring forth by thousands and tens of thousands from the workshop and from the field in prompt obedience to their Governors call to oppose their strong arms, and many breasts to the further progress of the invader. The excitement and intensity of feeling, the daily agony of doubt and suspense is a thing scarcely to be appreciated in full by one who was not here at the time and who did not pass through it. I assure you, my dear father, I know of nothing in the course of my life which has caused me such deep and

18. An island in the Azores.

19. During the Seven Days battles, June 25–July 1, 1862, Union capture of Richmond seemed imminent, but instead of capitalizing on his victories, General McClellan retreated from Richmond after each battle.

20. Second battle of Bull Run, Aug. 29–Sept. 1, 1862.

21. Storrow's older brother Charles.

22. Storrow was a student at Harvard College.

23. General McClellan took command of the defense of Washington, D.C.

serious thought as this trying crisis in the history of our nation. What is the worth of this man's life or of that man's education, if this great and glorious fabric of our Union, raised with such toil and labor by our forefathers and transmitted to us in value increased tenfold, is to be shattered to pieces by traitorous hands and allowed to fall crumbling into the dust. If our country and our nationality is to perish, better that we should all perish with it and not survive to see it a laughingstock for all posterity, to be pointed at as the unsuccessful trial of republicanism. It seems to me the part of a coward to stay at home and allow others to fight my battles and incur dangers for me. What shame, what mortification would it cause me years hence to be obliged to confess that in the great struggle for our national existence *I* stood aloof, an idle spectator without any peculiar ties to retain me at home and yet not caring, or not daring to do anything in the defense of my country. It was impossible for me to carry on my studies with any degree of interest or of profit to myself. I would read in Tacitus of the destruction and dismemberment of the mighty empire of Rome by internal feuds and civil dissensions, and my mind would be brought to the thought of another nation equal in magnitude and power to that which issued its decrees from the seven-hilled city, which was to be saved from a like fate only by the timely aid and support of every one of its sons. I felt that if I remained at College I could derive no benefit whatever while my mind was so entirely interested in another quarter. The only reason which could at all deter me from enlisting was your absense. I felt reluctant to take so important a step without your advice and consent, and yet I felt that had you been here you would have given me your blessing and have bade me go. Here was a regiment formed and commanded by friends and kinsmen & far surpassing all others in the material of which it was composed. If I embraced this opportunity I should be among friends and equals instead of being forced to accept as my associates any with whom I might be placed. If I did not make my decision quickly the chance would be lost, and I knew that if I went you would agree with mother in much preferring that Charley and I should be together in the same regiment. At that time, too, a draft seemed almost certain and as several thousand were said to be wanting to complete the quota of Boston the chance of being drawn was by no means small. (James thought it sufficiently great to get up a kind of Mutual Insurance company for providing substitutes.)[24] I confess that the thought of leaving mother alone while you were away was very unpleasant to me, but in reality, since I was at Cambridge all the time, with the exception of Sunday, she would be left alone very little more, and since we have received the letter in which you say that you will sail on the 11th I feel much more easy about it, as you will arrive a week after our departure. Poor mother. She has had a hard time during your absence, especially in coming to a decision about me,

24. Under the terms of the 1862 militia law, states could enact a draft in order to meet state militia quotas required by the federal government. It was possible, however, to avoid the draft by hiring a substitute. The insurance company Storrow mentions was a scheme for raising money to hire substitutes.

and the burden has been increased by the entire withholding of any expression, of sympathy or condolence on the part of her family, Uncle Frank and the rest all thinking it horrid that she should have given her consent to it. She has longed for you and felt the need of your advice and consolation more than she ever did, and says that if you are satisfied that she has done right she shall be perfectly happy. Assure her fully of your approval of the course she has taken and I shall be happy too. Everybody outside of mother's family sympathizes with her and thinks that she has acted nobly and that you have reason to be proud of your wife as we have of our mother.

I have tried as well as I can, and I find that it is but poorly, to give you some idea of my feelings on this subject. I feel well satisfied that I have done what, upon careful deliberation, has seemed to me most in accordance with all my duties. I have looked at the matter from every point of view, and if I shall seem to you to have arrived at a wrong conclusion, believe me, it was not from any hasty impulse of the moment but from the sober dictates of my best judgment. If I have unwittingly made the wrong choice, God forgive me, I did what I thought was for the best.

Ever your affectionate son
Samuel Storrow

Massachusetts Historical Society, Boston, Letters of Samuel Storrow, Samuel Storrow Papers.

John Harpin Riggs of Seymour, Connecticut, enlisted in Company F, Seventh Regiment, Connecticut Volunteers in August 1861. He reenlisted in January 1864 and was promoted to corporal in October 1864. He was mustered out of the service on July 20, 1865. In this letter to his father, Riggs expresses the pro-Union, antiabolition sentiments common to most Northern Democrats.

Beaufort, South Carolina
January 2, 1863

Dear Father

I received your letter yesterday and one about 5 days ago which I delayed answering on account of being on picket for ten days out to Port Royal fery we have hard duty out there bacaus the rebels are just on the others side of the crick only about a hundred yards distance we had no trouble with them yet they fired two shots on chistmas night but did not injure any body I have not received any box yet but I expect I shall before long. Well, Father I have arrived at the age when It becomes me to think about politic some and they think of letting the soldiers vote and I want to have you post me a little they send nothing but abolition documents here and I should like to see some old Democratic papers and some speaches there ought to have one to match Parson Bronlows that man aught to

have his head shaved and be drumed out of the country[25] pleas send me some
papers and if you can find a good union democratic speach send it as soon as posable[26] if the news you sent is true there will be no more fighting and I hope there
will not be I hope it will be settled before long by . . . injenious method by the
people you know that the war can not go on mutch longer if you do think so I
do not I guess that . . . burnside has not resigned[27] but I hear a report that there
has been an cesation of hostilitys till the new congress meats but I can not see
that I wish I could come home for a few days but I can not yet you must settle
this thing up and then I shall be home to help you I do not want to fight any
longer when I enlisted I came to defend the flag and to keep the union as it was
but they have turned this war into a niger war and I want to get out now as soon
as posable the first that was yesterday our military Govener had the black devils
turned out and told them that they wer all free men could do and act as they
choused and that if they worked they could demand pay and all sutch things[28]
now you neavr not expect soldiers to like this mutch to have them black whelps
lying around if they get in my way I shall poke the boyonet through them that is
so. the thing is played out with me if ever one of them comes to get in on me I
will send him back double quick or kill him. you wanted to know about Frank
Lewis death he and I slept in the same bed and eat together and he died in the
tent when I was on guard but one of the other boyes held him in his armes and
he died in pain he had a very bad throat and he was sick a long time with it but he
would not give up the last wordes he sayed was never mind I shall be better in
the morning

New Haven Colony Historical Society, New Haven, John Harpin Riggs, MSS 77, Civil War
Collection, box 2, folder 0.

---

*S. H. Norton was, most likely, Simeon H. Norton, a businessman of Southington,
Connecticut, who apparently lost his only son at the battle of Chancellorsville in May 1863.
It is somewhat ironic that in this letter Norton expresses the views of some Northern
Democrats, who believed, especially after the Emancipation Proclamation, that the Union
should come to terms with the Confederacy and end the war.*

25. William G. ("Parson") Brownlow was a former clergyman who became the editor of the
Knoxville Whig and worked for the Unionist cause in Tennessee, speaking out strongly against seces-
sionists and slaveholders.
26. Most Northern Democrats supported the war to preserve the Union as it was before the secession crisis. They were opposed to the abolition of slavery and believed that Southerners should continue to be able to own slaves in a restored Union.
27. After the disastrous Union defeat at Fredericksburg in December 1862 and the humiliating
"mud march" in January 1863, President Lincoln removed General Burnside from the command of the
Army of the Potomac and replaced him with General Hooker. Burnside did not resign but was transferred to the command of the Department of the Ohio.
28. The Emancipation Proclamation had taken effect on Jan. 1, 1863.

Plantsville
Saturday Evening
Febry 21, 1863
A.P. Plant Esq.

Dear Sir

Your much esteemed favor of this date, was received early this evening. I
hasten to reply very briefly. I regard it as a gentle reproof to me, for advocating at
the present time, peace and conciliation. Our present National difficulties may be
compared to a great family Quarrel, the bone of contention being slavery. A small
number of the members like it, think it humane, right, and beneficial.

A larger dislike it, consider it inhuman, wrong, and injurious. Some are very
sensitive, easily irritated, and extremely tenacious of their rights. Others, take
great pleasure in stirring up all the bad blood of their more sensitive and irritable
brethren, by taunting them and pointing at them the finger of scorn.

The smaller number complain to the heads of the family that their rights are
trampled upon. The family government changes and they are told to shut their
mouths, that they have always had more than they deserved &c, And assert most
positively, that their former privileges must be curtailed. Then the majority clap
their hands, and triumphantly exult over them. Some of the more irritable, and
refractory members, fly into a passion; defy the family government, and actually
go at fighting. They continue fighting for a long, long time. Some lose their eyes,
some their limbs, some get killed &c &c until it seems as though the whole
family must inevitably be destroyed. Now the question arises, what shall be done,
what course does reason and common sense dictate? Go in for continued fighting,
or for peace & reconciliation?

For some time past, I have been of the opinion, that a strong, persistent, stren-
uous, effort should be made, to stop this family Quarrel, of states by conciliation,
and extending to each other the hand of friendship, in order to restore the "Union
as it was" giving to Slavery all the guarantees & privileges it ever had. The
Democratic Party stand upon that Ground, which I think to be tenable, and therefore I am with them.

It may be we shall not succeed; but we will try. This Union never could have
been formed without tolerating slavery, and I sincerely believe it never can be
restored without guaranteeing it. If I mistake not the tone of public feeling in this
country it is for the cessation of hostilities between the north & south, and a settlement upon the best attainable terms. This feeling is said to be almost universal
among the Federal troops. Now please mark my words. It is my opinion that the
Republican Party will lead off very soon for a cessation of the war, by a dissolu-
tion of the Union; that is, by letting the South separate; while the Democrats will
cling to the Union of all the States. Now Mr Plant *I am not a Traitor.* I am not dis-
loyal to the Government and Constitution of the United States. In political matters it has always been my principle to act conscientiously, and not be so swayed
by party feeling, as to act contrary to my settled convictions of right; and I assure
you, if I ever acted conscientiously in my life, it is in doing all I can consistently to
stop this war, and restore the "Union of these States as it was" and to re establish

and re affirm the "Constitution as it is" but whether such a thing be possible, I am unable to say, but war, war, war, has been tried so long, and so unsuccessfully, that I have become quite satisfied that the longer it is continued the worse will matters become. I thank you for your letter. It is on the whole very temperate in its tone. I have no other feelings towards you than those of Friendship & Respect.

I did not intend to inflict a long letter upon you although a crowd of though[t]s presses upon my mind but I will tell you frankly that the R[epublican] Party is impalatable to me, because it is so strongly tinctured with Political Abolitionism. In my humble opinion, this party never will prevail to any great extend, in this country.

New England has disparaged itself, by pandering so much to Abolition, but enough of this.

Now my dear Sir the circumstances of our Country have sadly changed, since the time I addressed you upon the occasion of your Flag Raising nearly two years ago. There I spoke the true sentiments of my heart. I do the same now.

Then we had hopes of crushing the Rebellion in 90 days, with 75000 men with trifling loss of life & treasure. Now we are surrounded by circumstances of extra-ordinary solemnity. We are now standing amid the new made graves of 200,000 northern men whose lives have been given up for the cause of their Country. The groans of the wounded & dying fill the very Atmosphere. Whole families in almost every town in these States are clad in the habiliments of mourning, for the loved ones who went down to the war and are dead.

Great Calamities and disasters are weighing us down. National Bankruptcy stares us in the face. Under all these circumstances, and many more which might be mentioned, can you say that we are traitors, for quietly, calmly, but firmly resolving to make a determined effort to stop this gigantic family Quarrel, by conciliatory measures but I said that I did not intend to inflict a lengthy letter upon you, so I will stop. I sincerely thank you for the very kind gentlemanly feel-ing you have always manifested towards me.

I have always endeavored to reciprocate this feeling, towards you, in my poor humble way.

I have written in haste, & have scrawled rather than written but I trust you will excuse every error, as coming from your friend

and I Remain
Yours with much Respect
S.H. Norton

Connecticut Historical Society, Hartford, Letters of S. H. Norton, MS 72.622.

Edward F. Hall of Exeter, New Hampshire, enlisted in Company B of the Third Regiment, New Hampshire Volunteers, in July 1861. He was wounded on August 16, 1864, at Deep Bottom, Virginia. He lost an arm and was discharged on October 28, 1864. In this letter to his wife, Hall explains his positions on the war, emancipation, and conscription.

Pinkney Island, Port Royal, South Carolina

March 22, 1863

Dear Susan—

Yours of the 11th inst I received last night and very glad was I to learn that you and the boy was well, I mailed a letter to Ned yesterday and have nothing new to add today, for 3 days we have been having the equinoxial storm. it has not rained very hard except a part of the day yesterday but it has been cold raw and disagreeable. we have been obliged to lay a bed to keep warm it has not cleared off yet, and as I write my fingers are numb with cold, hop it will be warmer soon, I suppose you had rather exciting times in N.H. lately, it being election times, and according to reports the democrats have very nearly carried the state, but not quite. There is the same difference of feeling and opinion here as there, and we hear every day the same kind of talk as is reported in the N.H. papers. the same cursing of abolishionists, and the same swearing at the "copperheads"[29] and I am afraid these party differences, both at home and in the army, will be the cause of our failure to conquor this rebellion, I think there is only two roads to peace, one is to conquor the rebels and force them to submit the other is to let them go, all the talk about compromising with them is mere nonsense and is not worth the thought of an intelligent man, and if the democrats could have the controll of government placed in their hands today, I think they would find themselves obliged to carry on the war—no doubt they would change the abolition pollicy somewhat, though they don't all agree, a good many of their prominent men support the Presidents proclamation for freeing the slaves. I don't though, it was altogether unnessessary in my opinion but I have no respect for those who find more fault with the administration than with rebellion itself, we hear a great deal about the draft, conscription &c is it any worse to draft now than in the war with England? if the country is in danger it has the right to the services of every able bodied man for its defence, no matter where the enemy comes from, every country has its conscription laws, and when men will not vollunteer they are made to fight, and I think it is fairer than paying such large bounties as were given last summer and fall,[30] and all this talk about resisting the draft is rank treason, and those who counsel it are no better than Jeff Davis and all his friends, thems my sentiments, and all those who think the abolition of slavery of more consequence than the Union are as much traitors as anybody else—they have no love for the constitution or the country, and have been disunionists for years, and I am very sorry their counsels have prevailed, and wish all mere party feeling might be laid aside, and all unite to put down this unholy rebellion, very few I think are ready to say divide the Union and let the South go. Gov Seamore of N.Y. will not

---

29. "Copperheads" was the name given to those Democrats who wanted the Union to come to terms with the Confederacy and end the war.

30. In March 1863 Congress passed the first national conscription act, which gave the federal government the power to implement the draft. State and local governments had frequently offered cash bounties to induce men to enlist and to help meet the state quotas specified in the 1862 militia law.

consent to that and he is no friend to the administration[31]—then I think the only way is to fight it out, and the only way to fight successfully is to unite—when we are as ready and determined to fight as the rebels are, we shall have some prospect of success, but if half the people north think, and are free to say so, that the administration is worse than the rebels, I am afraid the government will be upset, the Union divided, and all go to smash, and let me tell you that when this Union is divided, no one can tell where disunion will end, instead of *two*, there may be several different governments established on the ruins. "New England may be left out in the cold." the great west may strike for independence, and so with the middle states, and party feeling will do it all, wo to the country when it sees that day, I don't want to survive long enough to witness such a state of things. Give my love to all and write again soon. From your absent and loving husband,

Ed F. Hall

New Hampshire Historical Society, Concord, Letters of Edward F. Hall, 1977–89.

W. H. Cudworth was a soldier from Boston, Massachusetts. He writes here to his friend, and possibly his minister, the Reverend Caleb Davis Bradlee of Boston. Like other soldiers, Cudworth believed the war had religious implications.

Falmouth, Virginia
May 9, 1863

My Dear Brother

I have received four letters from you since able to write one being engaged in duties connected with the fiercely contested battle of Chansellorsville.

The army of the Potomac has failed again although supplied with everything to make it irresistible and apparently in splended condition.[32] It was God's will. I bow to it. Our national pride is not yet sufficiently humbled nor our great and greivous sin against the Indian and African races sufficiently atoned for, nor our greed for gain sufficiently rebuked. The condition of our cities, the confidence and boastings of our people, the abundant supplies of our armies and the fullness of our treasury all show that we have not begun to suffer as the rebels are suffering. The multitudes of our strong men at home *reading* and *talking* about the travail of their country, which they should be in the field to relieve, show it.

So I fear that the bitterest portion of our cup remains yet to be drained and hope that people in New York, Boston, and all our sea board cities will prepare to

31. New York's Governor Horatio Seymour was a leading Democratic spokesman against the Lincoln administration's emancipation and conscription policies. However, Seymour supported a war to preserve the Union.

32. The Army of the Potomac was defeated at the battle of Chancellorsville, May 2-6, 1863.

take their part. The rebels intend to enter all our harbors, if they can. They will enter some. What will our credit be worth when they succeed and without credit, where are we? . . .

God forbid that foes at home again open a fire on our rear, by trying to distract and weaken Government. The fierce onslaught of rebel hordes upon our front last Sunday morning was honor and manhood in comparison with such cowardly back striking!

Cordially Yours
W.H. Cudworth

American Antiquarian Society, Worcester, Mass., Letters of W. H. Cudworth, Civil War Papers Collection.

In this letter Samuel B. Duncan writes to his son Samuel, who served as major with the Fourteenth New Hampshire Volunteer Regiment and as colonel with the Fourth U.S. Colored Regiment.

Meriden, New Hampshire
July 15 1863

Dear Son

Yours of the 11 ins was recd last night and informed us that you was yet at Washington and we were rather glad than otherwise and especially Mrs Rowe, but I see that men are ready to expose themselves to certain danger and death even rather than endure such a dul monotonous life as the soldier is obliged to endure in camp without a change of employment or objects. I have just been down to see Mr Collins he is not able to join his regament though he expresses a strong desire to, sores in his head yet continue to collect, he is some better and sends his compliments to you rejoice, much that Dr Thayer is acquitted says he is a nice man and good Surgeon   he said he would see Abbot soon   it is a wonder that he was not killed. As to the story about your cruelty to the soldiers it has not troubled me at all and the thing like a thousand rumors has passed away. we or the boys celebrated the taking of Vixburg the second time also burnt powder on the 4 of July.[33] the world is full of agitation and excitement as to the enrollment it is about to begin   I mean the draft in this state, I hope no such scenes will be enacted as experienced as in N York city but that has been for a long time a rebellious city in the full sense of the word.[34] in Boston and vicinity the Draft went on quietly and John D. Bryant Esq is one of the drafted soldiers   John was here with

33. Gen. Ulysses S. Grant captured the Confederate stronghold at Vicksburg, Miss., on July 3, 1863.
34. Crowds in New York City rioted on July 13–17, 1863, in response to the beginning of the draft in that city.

Mr Reynold his wife & daughter and staid 3 or 4 day and went to the copperas work[35] the mean time to attend their anual meeting Mrs Bryants health is tolerable good at this time. Helen Tichenor is with us but will leave this week for the Doctors   she has been here 3 or 4 weeks and is in good health. We send the articles you directed in your letter by express   the boots are nearly through at the toes but may stand you a while   Mrs Bryant may send something to William   she will have an invitation and a chance   We have very rainy weather here of late and no chance to get hay   the crop will be increased by the wet which has been more than a week after a rather severe Drouth, the weather has been remarcable dry in the vicinity of Boston but not so bad here. Now as to this wicked and unholy war I will say I believe it is a judgment upon us for our great national and individual sins and although grievous we must be submissive to the divine will, there is mourning all over the land for there is scarcely a place but what some one has lost a friend or an acquaintance either in battle or the Hospital   we are waiting with anxiety for the result of the present opperations on the Potomac[36]   may God in mercy grant us victory and put an end in his own good time to the Rebellion. Helen and your mother and all desire to be remembered to you. tell William I hope he will not be sick   tell Mr Rowe that his family are well   Mrs Rowe is pretty well but was very tired for some time after she got back. we expect Henry tomorrow or next day   Helen say she shall expect a letter from you direct to East Lebanon

Your afft father
Saml B Duncan

Dartmouth College, Hanover, N.H., Letters of Samuel Duncan, Duncan Papers.

In this letter to his wife, John Peirce, a resident of Salem, Massachusetts, and a member of the Twelfth Unattached Company, Heavy Artillery, gives some indication of the financial motives behind his and other soldiers' decisions to enlist.

January 3, 1864
Dear Wife
I recieved your letter last knight and was glad to hear you i have just come off guard   it was a little chillie on the beat last knight but i stood it very well we have hade a littel excitment here this mornning   the mess room cought fire on the roof   it was put out with a few buckets of water if it hade cought in the knight it wold have bur[n]t down   i and Add went to the camp togeather   the day we went back we hade a tip top dinner newyers up to the Essex house   Stephen C phillips made a speech and Capt Richardson but we could not raize a one from

---

35. Copperas is a crystal used in fertilizers and inks.
36. This refers to Gen. George Meade's unsuccessful pursuit of Robert E. Lee's Army of Northern Virginia after the battle of Gettysburg.

our Lieutanants the capt made a good one he said he was like Burnside he was willing to allow somthing to the rank and file mr. Phillips giv us a grate prare in behalf of the Citizens of Salem he said we behaved like Soldiers and men and the citizens of Salem hoped we stay here ontill we was dischard he thought we should he said the city was proud of us he said the Capt hade us under good disipline or we like the Capt the Capt got up and said it was both we gave cheers for Salem and our Capt and our four Lieuts the Capt told us to leve out the tigar this morning the Capt came in to the gurd house and said the citizen said we behaved better then any Soldiers that ever went into the Essex house what do you think of that the capt says he feels proud of us after we hade our dinner we all went on Wash St and hade a dress Parade we hade the band to play for us so much for new yers you say you did not get the state aid i wold get it every month certin you say you can spend the money I want you to spend all you want that is what i came here for nothing will pleas me better then to have you enjoy it i hope you will Clara remember i do not want to you to deny your-self of any thing i want you to live well and to dress well and the childrin to so long as you are provided for i can content myself and you will be so long as i am in Unkel Sams servis that makes me content the capt says we shall get our US pay this week the rest of the bounty is not due till we are musterd out of the servis i did inspection this afternoon at for at half past two we have got to go out with our knapsacks on tell John the next letter i send will be to him his name on it it is eving we are a going to signe the pay roll to knight we are a going to escort the nineteenth Reg when they come home we think they will come tomorow good knight Clara when i say good knight it makes me think of old times in 1847 and 1848 darling Clara the story in the papers that we are a going Newburn the capt he dont know any thing about it do not believe any storeys our going away i gess the capt will know as soon as any one

    i am well and i hope this will find you the same

my Love to you   John Peirce

Peabody Essex Museum, Salem, Mass., Letters of John Peirce, John Peirce Papers.

Meschack Purington Larry, a soldier from Maine, gives another indication of the financial motives behind the enlistment of many New Englanders.

Camp Bullock near Brandy Station, Virginia

January 26, 1865

Dear Sister Phebe

    Yours of the 17th and 19th came to hand in due time I now take the opportunity to inform you that I am in the best of health and also have had the pleasure of seeing Daniel who came over to our camp last Sunday I think he has changed much since I last saw him but is as full of schemes and speculations as ever. I ast him what started him out here again he very honestly said for the big Bounty and to escape for the draft   he thought that New Englanders would fight beter for Big bountys than they would from patriotic motives as for himself he could bost of not having a might of patriotism   one to hear him talk would think him half crazy but there is no one that thinks more corectly or has a better idea of the war than he does. . . .

M P Larry

Maine Historical Society, Portland, Letters of Meschack P. Larry, S-293mb 11/4.

CHAPTER THREE

Views of the South

IN THIS SECTION New Englanders at the warfront reflect on the South, writing about a variety of scenes and situations that reveal distinctive features of the Southern experience. Not surprisingly, the writers here pay considerable attention to slaves and contrabands (the name given to slaves who ran to Union lines), often revealing deeply held prejudices toward African Americans. This section also includes soldiers' observations on black troops, the majority of whom were former slaves. Included here as well are the views of an African-American schoolteacher who taught the former slaves in the Sea Islands of South Carolina. Aside from their frequent comments on African Americans, New Englanders were also struck by distinctive aspects of the Southern landscape and contrasted the ramshackle appearance of Southern farms with the orderliness of the New England scene.

In this letter to his cousin, Calvin M. Burbank of Company B, Second New Hampshire Infantry, criticizes the South for lacking many of the elements of the New England countryside.

Camp Baker, Charles County, Maryland
Nov. 11, 1861

Cousin Sarah,

Yours of the 6th inst was received this morning, being five days reaching us, instead of, as formerly, but two, and as we are somewhat unstable in our habits of late, somewhat given to moving about, I take this present opportunity to answer your letter. As I have just written to Henry, we have changed our location, and have moved somewhat further south. If you have a map of the seat of war, from the description I gave him, you can easily trace out our present position.

We have all read in glowing verse of poetry charming accounts of the beautiful, sunny South. Either I am mistaken, or else that exists only in the fevered imagination of the poets head. *Charming South,* indeed. No roads, no bridges, no towns, or villages, no Churches, or Schoolhouses, no beautiful, and tasty country residences, to meet the eye, no well cultivated farms and gardens, no orchards, and nurseries of fruit, nothing but poverty, and sterility meet the eye, at every point. and this too in a country, which in its original state, was far superior to our own New England. O! the curse of human slavery. We at the North do not know, or realise, nor can we till seen with our own eyes, the absolute degradation of everything connected with it. Shame on the man who will uphold it. The very slaveholders themselves are ashamed of it. They feel that it degrades them, more than it does the enslaved. I had quite an interesting conversation with a man last night, and he mourned over its existence, and owned that it was a curse to everything concerned with it. but it was entailed upon them, having been handed down to them by their Fathers, and it is fostered, and kept alive by scheming, corrupt politicians. the people of the South as a general thing are not great readers, and they have a very wrong view of the feelings, and intentions of the North.

We miss very much our pleasant situation at Bladensburg. We there had some communication with the *visible world,* receiving our mail daily and seeing men from Washington. But here all is ignorance. What few residents there are about here, know comparatively nothing, in fact they are in point of intelligence, hardly on an equality with the plantation slaves. . . .

All Yours
C.M. Burbank

Dartmouth College Library, Hanover, N.H., Letters of Calvin M. Burbank, MS 861611.

George M. Turner, a sergeant in Company A, Third Rhode Island Artillery, wrote these five letters to various family members. The letters demonstrate Turner's evolving views on the abilities of African Americans. Turner's attitudes change from racist ridicule and disgust to a grudging appreciation of the bravery and competence of African-American soldiers. However, as the final letter demonstrates, Turner did not completely overcome his belief in African-American inferiority.

Hilton Head, South Carolina
December 15, 1861

Dear Cousin,

Yours of the 28 of November received with great pleasure and I will try to return one to you equaly as good. . . .

You write that you think of me often, and so do I of you, and the rest of the dear ones at home; but not as a homesick person would, for I am in too glorious a cause to be homesick; No, Sir, you will not find this child homesick, if he does have to endure some hardships.

The curley headed contraband is here, in great quantities, male and female, old and young; I can tell you honestly that if our army stays he[re] much longer there

will be more niggers than soldiers for they are coming into our camps every day.[1]
. . . Now us soldier boys have a great deal of sport with these contrabands, and
nearly every night after we have had our supper, we get a crowd of them together
and they sing and dance until our sides are nearly bursting with laughter and then
to draw the exercise to a close an empty barrel is brought before the audiance, we
then offer one of the niggers five cents, to butt the head in with his wooly pate,
no sooner is the offer made than some one of them accepts, and lets fly his head
at the barrel head, and in goes barrel head, nigger head and half his body. Then
goes up a shout of laughter and we close by singing the 459 Hymn, Long Metre,
another item of interest is their prayer meetings, which is equal to any Minstrel
Concert I ever attended at home. . . .

Yours truly
George

Hilton Head, South Carolina
June 19, 1862

Dear Father:
　　Yours of the 9 inst came to hand last evening, also a letter and a newspaper
from cousin Ursula. . . .
　　Sunday I attended divine service, the services were conducted by some abolitionists who came from the state of Massachusetts and there was so much talk
about the confounded niggers that I came out disgusted and by the way if any
one comes to you asking for contributions for the niggers, tell them you have a
son in the army who needs your help much more than they do. The niggers are
used much better than the soldiers, and there is not a soldier who does not hate
the sight of a nigger.
　　Father I once did respect a negro, but my respect for them has vanished, I
despise them more than dirt.
　　My health is good in fact perfect and I can say that this life agrees with me. . . .
　　Please write very soon, give my love to mother and cousin John Trask and take
a share of the love sent to yourself.

Good Bye
Your loving son
POP
George M. Turner

---

　　1. When Union troops occupied the South Carolina Sea Islands, they found that the plantation
owners had abandoned their property and left their slaves behind. The Union army allowed the slaves
to continue to work the plantations and to keep or sell the produce. Wherever the Union army went
in the South, slaves from the surrounding areas would escape to Union lines and offer information on
Confederate army whereabouts, services such as laundering, and goods such as eggs and vegetables to
the Union troops. Union soldiers referred to these escaped slaves as contrabands, and in March 1862
Congress passed an act forbidding the return of these escaped slaves to their masters.

Hilton Head, Port Royal, South Carolina
August 13, 1862

Dear Aunt Susan:

The rebels have not driven us into the sea yet and I hardly think they will right away.

Your received yesterday and was pleased to have a line from you again. . . .

It is with feelings of sorrow and sympathy that I learn of the continued severe headaches that dear mother is subjected to.

My opinion of 'nigger' soldiers has not risen very high, when the U.S. Government gets so hard pushed, that she feels compelled to take these confounded niggers to fight her battles, it better sell out to the first bidder. . . .

Aunty I hardly know what to write, it is so very dull here, we have a plenty of shoveling to do.

The weather is a great deal warmer than last month, so you must excuse my short letters.

Good Bye
George

Beaufort, South Carolina
July 28, 1863

Cousin Ursula:

Your kind a[nd] loving, and welcome, and long, and sweet and interesting, and and and and—letter came to hand this morning, and I have just lighted my tallow candle, taken my position in the middle of my small cloth house, on a seat made of a hard tack box, with a company clothing book for a desk to write upon. . . .

Forts Wagner and Gregg are still held by the rebels; but I think they will not hold them much longer, and when we get them in our pocession Fort Sumter is as good as in our hands. . . .

When you hear nay one remark that nigger soldiers will not fight, please request them to come down here and judge for themselves.

The 54th Mass Infantry "colored" is as good a fighting regiment as there is in the 10th Army Corps Department of the South.

This was proved July 18 at the charge on Fort Wagner.[2]

Col. Shaw in command of the regiment was killed, many of the officers and men were taken prisoners, the rebels will not exchange them, they want to keep the nigs and their officers in Charleston on exhibition.

My opinion is that they will not have that privilege very long. . . .

Give my love to Father, Mother and all enquiring friends. . . .

From your loving cousin,
Cor'pl. Pop Turner

2. On July 18, 1863, the Fifty-fourth Massachusetts Colored Regiment led a frontal assault on Fort Wagner, which guarded the entrance to Charleston harbor. The Fifty-fourth suffered tremendous losses, and the attack failed; however, the bravery demonstrated by this African-American regiment was responsible for many Northerners' change of attitude regarding black soldiers.

Jacksonville, Florida
May 2, 1864

My dear aunt Susan:

Please do not be offended at my being so tardy in answerin very welcome letter of April 3rd; but when your letter came to hand my company was being mounted as a battery of light artillery, and as soon as we were in readiness we were ordered to Jacksonville Florida, and I have not had time to write before this afternoon. . . .

The troops at this place are most all colored soldiers, two regiments to white soldiers and our battery make up the rest of the array.

The white soldiers feel pretty owly over the situation, the Brigade commander, of this Post and the Chief of Artillery are officers of colored troops and they are inclined to place the niggers above us. . . .

The plan of having negro soldiers is very well in some cases; but when it comes to putting the whites and blacks on the same footin, I come to the conclusion it is about time to quit soldiering, in fact I do not have any very great love for a nigger, for they are the 'bone' over which the Northern and Southern dogs are quarreling, it is rather hard for us white boys to have to bow to them, when we are fighting for them and have left everything that is near and dear to us on their account. I want to see the war come to a close, this rebellion crushed, and the Stars and Stripes waving over a united country once more, and I am willing to fight for it, but I am not willing to fight shoulder to shoulder with a black dirty nigger. . . .

Give my love to Father, Mother and all the rest of my friends, tell them I am well and happy, enjoying myself hugely away down South and Florida.

Yours truly
George M.

Rhode Island Historical Society Library, Providence, Manuscripts Collection, Letters of George M. Turner, George M. Turner Letter Books, MSS 763.

In this letter to his wife, Edward F. Hall of Company B, Third New Hampshire Volunteer Regiment, compares what he calls Yankee "industry" with Southern "shiftlessness."

Port Royal, South Carolina
Mar. 9, 1862

My dear Susan,

The appearance of Hilton Head Island has altered some, since the great expedition came, the difference between Yankee industry and the shiftlessness of southern Chivalry can plainly be seen, every where, before we came the indolent southren only fixed a place just big enough to squat on, build a little sand fort, mounted some twenty gunds, and sat themselves down content to wait for the coming of the Yankees, with the full confidence that they could sink every vessel that came within range of their guns. How they were wofully deceived, when the fleet came, is published to the world no sooner had the hardy and industrious northerner affected a landing than he went to *work,* clearing up large fields, for camping ground, smoothing off large spaces for drilling grounds, building large store houses, for the storage of provisions and amunition, large stables for the horses, a long wharf for the unloading of vessels, it is 1500 feet long from the Bank to the end, with a cross, across the end 350 feet long, same as you would cross a T, it is built by driving spikes 20 feet into the bottom of the river and fraiming and planking on the top ends, the timber being cut in the woods near by, and the work done by the army a large entrenchment has been thrown up, 60 or 70 guns mounted on it, four or five magazines built at regular distances along the works, to keep the amunition in. a large general Hospital has been built, or nearly so, capable of accommodating one thousand sick and disabled soldiers, it is built one story high, in the form of a hollow square. 325 feet on each side on front, and a piazza all around it, about one acre of land inside the square, which is to be made into an ornamental garden traders have come and put up litle stores which can be taken down again in parts and packed up and transported to some other place when nesessary, two or three long blocks, for Barracks for the negro's have been put up, a large bakery has been built, where good soft Bread is baked for the army, and a Steam saw mill is being built, close to a heavey growth of hard pine timber. in fact industry has taken the place of indolence, in everything to be seen, it is likely to be quite a town here some day I think, it *looks* like quite a town now in the vicinity of the Fort. it is an excelant harbour here and would be a good place for a Navy yard and a City which might rival Charleston, and perhaps will some day. labor, work, industry, has done all this, and in this lies the superiority of northerners over southerners. this *labor* is what the southerner is too proud to do himself, and too aristocratic ever to be a Base Carpenter, or mason, or overseer of his farm or plantation as they call it here. there are some splendid plantations on this Island, but the buildings are poor affairs, no large barns and store houses to keep their crops in, as in New England, and their houses to live in are old, small, and ill contrived and not so good as are built in NE for the mechanic to live in. they dont need very warm houses but I should think they would want them more tasty and neat looking. I suppose they are in their towns and cities. what they want is Yankee energy and thrift, and a little less arristocratic pride. I see by the papers, that the cotton sent from here, has sold as high as 63 cts per pound, some of at least, in NY. I will send this in my next letter to you,

E F Hall

New Hampshire Historical Society, Concord, Letters of Edward F. Hall, 1977–89.

John Henry Jenks, a sergeant with the Fourteenth New Hampshire Volunteer Infantry, describes the ways in which several slaves freed by the Union army were exercising their freedom.

Camp Parapet, Louisiana
May 22, 1862

Dear Wife

Sabbath has once more dawned upon me in all its loveliness. But o, how warm. I never knew before what intense heat was. In the middle of the day it is almost impossible to endure the scorching sun. Even to sit in the shade is enough to satisfy me of its warmth, there I perspire freely, not withstanding we have a breeze from the river. If we shd be called into action, the men could do but little I fear from 11 to 4 o'clock. For the past week the nights have been much warmer, but not uncomfortable, only the missquitoes are so very thick. I now have a misquito cover over my bed which keeps them out entirely, so that I rest in peace and quiet all night. . . . Two of our men run into an Aligater last week 7 feet long, he began to swell up like a toad, and show them two sets of long teeth, and they thought it best to leave him to his own reflections as all he desired was "to be let alone," as do the Sesech at the South. But we cant see the point of leaving *them* alone, for their hands are already red with the blood of those who have stood up for their Countries flag, and there are millions here, anxiously looking us to redeem them from bondage, worse than that of the Children of Isreal. I was talking with a colored woman and her *almost* white daughter last night upon the subject of slavery and her desires for freedom. When the war first broke out she was living in N. Orleans, and her Master fearing for the safety of the city sold them both to go up the river some 80 miles. She brought $1000 and her handsome daughter brought $1750. Soon after N.O. was taken a Steamer went up the river within 16 miles of where they lived, and one of the officers with some soldiers scouted through the country & came to the plantation where she was. The officer knew her Master, as he was formerly from the North, and gave him a terrable talking to, and told him he ought to be killed for being down here owning slaves, and even told him he *shd* do it, and the poor fellow put down in the dust on his knees and beged for his life; finerally he told him if he was any where in these parts tomorrow he should do it, but when the morrow came he was not to be found. The Officer told the slaves to take his carriage, horses and anything they could get and meet him at the boat, and he would carry them to N.O., and they did so, and came up here soon after to cook and wash for the Officers. After the Officers left, they built them a little shanty, and surrounded it with a high fence, where they now live as happy as can be. They take in washing for a living and have a little yard where they raise vegetables; close to their back door are two noble fig trees, under which they sit when evening shades warn them of nights approach, and tell of the past, sad past, and the golden hopes of the future, which they can see in the distance, with no fears mingled with their joy, when this war shall be over, and they know they are no longer to be slaves. I could but feel that amid all the desolations of war, the sundering of family ties, the deserted hearthstones, the vacant chairs the intense solicitude for absent freinds—and the deep settled grief for those bourne on the list of dead, there are many hearts made happy—many ties made sacred, and many a hearthstone surrounded with happiness and love through this same monster, war. P.M. Have just been out in the grove to a meeting. You dont know how good it seemed, and I hope it will result in good—he spoke (the minister) to all classes, those who professed to be Christians, the Sabboth breaker, the drunkard, the profane swearer and I hope all will profit by what they heard. I feel for one I ought to live a far differant life from what I do, I make resolutions that I will, but how frail I am, how soon do I forget them. It is hard to live a christian life when at home, under the influence of a christian wife and family, under the preached gospel, and surrounded by many christian friends, but oh how much harder in the army away from all these influences, but I pray God I may be kept from sin. . . . Love to you Flora and Henry and Mother and all others who inquire after me.

Your Affectionate Husband,

J. Henry Jenks

University of New Hampshire Library, Durham, Special Collections, Letters of John Henry Jenks, Coll. iii.

Edward F. Hall, of Company B, Third Regiment, New Hampshire Volunteers, expresses his opinion on how to make use of the many runaway slaves that fled to the Union army in this letter to his wife and son.

Hilton Head, South Carolina

July 15, 1862

My dear Susan and Eddy

Here are some of my "Idees" on the great question   A great deal of trouble has been caused in this country for 15 or 20 years by the Negro question—it has been the chief question in most all elections—the chief topic of discussion in Congress and in the newspapers. the great theme of letter writers, and newspaper correspondents—it has created a great deal of bad feeling and has had a great deal to do in preparing the way for this war and some think it is *the chief* cause— and now the war is going on—it is as much cause of contention as ever—what to do with the Negro is the cheif trouble in the war pollicy. The President seems to hold the power in his hands, to do about as he pleases—so he says—but he dont seem to have made up his mind exactly what to do—but lets it run along any way—some are for making a clean sweep of Slavery—as far as our army can penetrate—and issue proclamations, declaring all Slaves free, as an inducement for them to escape from their masters. others say, carry on the war vigorously, and let the institution of Slavery alone entirely—and a good deal of warm discussion has been going on, for a long time, in congres, and in the News Papers—without however settling the question—some are for arming the Negro, and making a soldier of him. others say no—some say employ him for fatigue duty, to cook for the soldiers—dig trenches—throw up breast works for us—thus saving our men a great deal of hard—and often very disagreeable work. Now I dont believe in "Abolition" but in the progress of the war, as our army penetrates the Southern country—of course we shall find a great many Negros who have been left behind by their masters—and many more who have run away from their owners—now *something* must be done with them, what shall it be? they are strong robust and healthy—used to work—and are perfectly at home in the climate—now when we have batteries to build, roads to make through malarious Swamps, large lots of commissary, and Quarter Master's stores to move—to put aboard ship, or to carry ashore from ship—cooking—getting wood to cook with—and such like hard and disagreeable work to do—I say instead of taking soldiers from the ranks—set the Negros at work to do it—and give them enough to eat—and if they have families—give them rations—there was a case happened in this division when if they had been used instead of soldiers—a good many lives might have been saved— that was the case of the Maine 8th building batteries in those Swamps and mud holes around Fort Pulaski—they caught the Swamp fever—and the regt was about ruined—when we left for James Island, it was said that over 200 of the regt was in the Hospital here—and less than 200 of the whole regt was fit for duty

I have seen in the papers, that McClellan's men were obliged to work building roads in the Swamp where the mud and water would come up to their arms   I say use the Negros, instead of using up the soldiers by such work—that army has had *fighting* enough to do since they started on the road to richmond—without being obliged to use the Spade—in addition to all their severe fighting—they have had a great deal of Picket guard duty to do—and I dont know of anything more wearing than that—especially close to the enemy—and their duties in the ranks is enough—but when you add to it all these severe *fatigue* duties—it is tough for the soldier and the Negro might just as well be used as not—but as to *arming* them I dont believe in it—I dont believe they would make *good* soldiers—they have been educated to *fear* the white man from their earliest infancy—and if they were to be brought up face to face with their former white masters—they would break and run—I think—what would they be good for, to put into such close, hand to hand fighting as they have had near richmond lately? they would run like Sheep—they might do to shoot, if they could be hid—where the enemy couldn't see them per- haps—but we dont *want such* soldiers in this war—we want men who will face anything—another thing I should like to see altered I want to see a little less respect shown for rebel property—when we come to a place which has been deserted by the rebels—and a lot of fruit and vegetables are growing—I want the soldiers to have some of it—without buying it—instead of allowing the Negros to take possession of it, and sell it at enormous prices to the soldiers, as was done on this Island when we first landed on it—and as seems to be the government policy everywhere—there are or have been some of our men sick lately with scurvy caused by eating government rations—mostly salt provisions without any vegeta- bles—and now we are right among green stuff fruit and vegitables—the officers say to us you must eat a lot of new potatos, green corn—Tomatos and such things—but they don't furnish it for us as rations—but if we get it we must *buy* it with our own wages—here are men *made sick by living on government rations—and we are to cure ourselves by buying with our money, what will cure us*—now I don't believe this is right. I say whatever is good for the men to eat in the enemies coun- try—and on an enemies plantation—*take* it and *give* it to the men as rations—the Negros sell the stuff to us, and take our money, and go down to the sutler stores at the fork and spend it for flashy dresses—and pay them two or three times as much as they are worth—and thus the speculating Jew sutlers reap all the benefit.

EFH

New Hampshire Historical Society, Concord, Letters of Edward F. Hall, 1977–89.

Justus F. Gale of Elmore, Vermont, enlisted in Company A, Eighth Regiment, Vermont Volunteers, on September 23, 1861. He died of chronic diarrhea on September 19, 1863. In this letter to his sister Almeida, Gale argues for arming the slaves to fight against their masters.

Algiers, La
August 26, 1862

there hasent been much of great importance a going on with us since I last wrote except there are any amount of darkies a coming into camp here every day; they come in, in squads from 5 to 75 at once; since Sunday morning I should think there had at least 200 colored people come into our camp, they are enlisting the blacks up the river 8 miles from here. I expect they will send these up there to enlist, they have already got up nearly two regiments of them & I dont know but more. I wish they would arm all the slaves there is in the south and set them on & spat their hands and holler ateboy. they are ready to go at the rebels like a mess of blood hounds. I dont see any appearance of an attack on this place but cant tel what will come round before the war is closed. I heard they had had another battle at Verginia and that Gen Jacksons army was all cut up.[3] I am glad to hear that spunkey boys of Vermont are still enlisting to put down this black unprincipaled rebelion, I am sorry that it is nesicary to call so many to the battlefield; but the more that go the quicker it will be over with. . . .

Vermont Historical Society, Montpelier, Letters of Justus F. Gale, Gale-Morse Papers, MSA 50.

Charlotte L. Forten was born in 1837 into a prominent black Philadelphia family. During the 1850s she spent considerable time as a student and teacher in Salem, Massachusetts, and became actively involved in the antislavery crusade in Massachusetts. In 1862 she traveled to the Union-occupied South Carolina Sea Islands where she became the first black teacher assigned to instruct the former slaves. After the war Charlotte Forten returned to Boston where she did relief work for the freed people. After her marriage to Francis Grimké, she remained active in civil rights work for the rest of her life. In this letter, published in the Liberator on December 12, 1862, Forten describes some of her critical reactions to the Sea Islands and their inhabitants.

3. This is possibly a reference to the battle of Cedar Mountain in which Jackson's army eventually was forced to retreat.

St. Helena's Island, Beaufort, South Carolina
November 20, 1862

My Dear Friend: You will doubtless be surprised to receive from me a letter dated from South Carolina. I cannot tell you how glad I am to be here. My coming, at the last, was very unexpected. I did not know until the day before we were to sail that there was a certainty of my coming. There was a good opportunity for me to go, in case of an elderly gentleman, a friend who, with his daughter, was coming to open a store for the freed p[eople] on the island. I left Philadelphia on the 24th of October, and arrived here on the 28th. . . . St. Helena's Island, on which I am, is about six miles from the main land of Beaufort. I must tell you that we were rowed hither from Beaufort by a crew of negro boatmen, and that they sung for us several of their own beautiful songs. There is a peculiar wildness and solemnity about them which cannot be described, and the people accompany the singing with a singular swaying motion of the body, which seems to make it more effective. How much I enjoyed that row in the beautiful, brilliant southern sunset, with no sounds to be heard but the musical murmur of the water, and the wonderfully rich, clear tones of the singers! But all the time I did not realize that I was actually in South Carolina! And indeed I believe I do not quite realize it now. But we were far from feeling fear,—we were in a very excited, jubilant state of mind, and sang the John Brown song with spirit, as we drove through the pines and palmettos. Ah! it was good to be able to sing that *here,* in the very heart of Rebeldom!

There are no white soldiers on this island. It is protected by gunboats, and by negro pickets, who do their duty well. These men attacked and drove back a boatload of rebels who tried to land here one night, several weeks ago. Gen. Saxton is forming a colored regiment at Beaufort, and many of the colored men from this and the adjacent islands have joined it.[4] The General is a noble-hearted man, who has a deep interest in the people here, and he is generally beloved and trusted by them. I am sorry to say that some other officers treat the freed people and speak of them with the greatest contempt. They are consequently disliked and feared.

As far as I have been able to observe—and although I have not been here long, I have seen and talked with many of the people—the negroes here seem to be, for the most part, an honest, industrious, and sensible people. They are eager to learn; they rejoice in their new-found freedom. It does one good to see how *jubilant* they are over the downfall of their "secesh" masters, as they call them. I do not believe there is a man, woman, or even a child that is old enough to be sensible, that would submit to being made a slave again. There is evidently a deep determination in their souls that *that* shall never be. Their hearts are full of gratitude to the Government and to the "Yankees." Some of them have said to me, "We bress de Lord, ebery day we bress de Lord for sendin' de Union people to make us free. De Yankees has been good to us. We suffered bery long, missus, bery long. But de Lord will bring it all right at last." I think they are a truly reli-

4. Gen. Rufus Saxton was the Union commander in charge of the occupied South Carolina Sea Islands.

gious people. They speak to God with a loving familiarity. He seems nearer to them than to most people. They are very grateful—almost too much so, for in return for the least kindness that is done them, they insist on giving you something—potatoes, eggs, peanuts, or something else from their little store.

And they would think it unkind if you refused it. Another trait that I have noticed is their natural courtesy of manner. There is nothing cringing about it; but it seems inborn, and one might almost say elegant. It marks their behavior towards each other as well as to the white people. The plantation on which we live is called "Oakland's." The house is in a somewhat dilapidated condition, as are most of the houses on these islands—and the fields around have a very forlorn, desolate look—very different from our flourishing, richly cultivated Northern fields. But they are encircled by a belt of beautiful woods; and our yard and garden, though neglected-looking, are rich in roses, which bloom constantly, even so late as this, and in ivy, which creeps about the ground and under the houses. I send you some of this English ivy, which has found a home in the rebellious little Palmetto State. My school is about a mile from here, in the little Baptist church, which is in a grove of white oaks. These trees are beautiful—evergreen—and every branch heavily draped with long, heavy bearded moss, which gives them a strange, mournful look. A grove of them looks like an assemblage of solemn patriarchs. There are two ladies in the school beside myself—Miss T. and Miss M., both of whom are most enthusiastic teachers. They have done a great deal of good here. At present, our school is small,—many of the children on the island being ill with whooping cough, but in general it averages eighty or ninety. I find the children generally well-behaved, and eager to learn; yes, they are nearly all most eager to learn, and many of them make most rapid improvement. It is a great happiness to teach them. I wish some of those persons at the North, who say the race is hopelessly and naturally inferior, could see the readiness with which these children, so long oppressed and deprived of every privilege, learn and understand. . . .

C.F.

Reprinted from the *Liberator*, Dec. 12, 1862.

Henry Joshua Spooner, first lieutenant in the Fourth Rhode Island Volunteer Regiment, writes to his brother Frankey, commenting on the southern countryside and his African-American servant.

Opposite Fredericksburg, Virginia

Nov. 21, 1862

My Dear Brother Frankey,

Your very acceptable letter would have been answered long ago, had I found time in which to do it; but, as you must have learned from my letter to father, the position which I occupy is one which affords me but little liberty. When on the march it is of course impossible to write. When encamped, or in bivouac rather, (for we are never really encamped) my duties are multifarious. My first thought, when I catch an opportunity to write at all, is to write *home*—& I then generally write to father as the head of the family & the one to whom my first obligations are due. I wrote father just before taking tea—& now having smoked my first evening pipe I am able to dedicate a few moments to my *"little"* brother. . . .

The appearance of this country differs much from that of New England. Not that the face of the country itself is so different—but the works of man are widely so. The houses through the country are very generally built of logs—many of them wretched, decayed hovels—everything about them filthy & neglected in appearance. You miss entirely that taste & neatness in the building & surroundings which is apparent about nearly every new England dwelling. The logs are piled together rough hewn & the intervals between filled with mud. In very many instances the chimneys are built in the same manner of logs & mud. The chimneys are almost universally built on the outside of the house by no means presenting a neat appearance. Sometimes they are built of stone—mud being used for plaster. The mud here is extremely gummy & answers very well the purpose of cement—when hardened it is tough & solid.

My nigger boy "Tom" is quite a specimen in his way & deserves a line. I picked him up on the march from Washington. Was looking for a boy to carry my blankets. "Jourdan" a young contraband belonging to the other Lieutenant in my company brought in Tom for inspection. Tom was a stocky young fellow of 14, crisp & wooly as to the hair—a knowing leer to his eye & an extremely niggerish grin lurking about his mouth. Jourdan gave as his opinion that Tom was a "right smart boy." Tom passed muster & was duly installed as knight of the blankets. He has proved himself a pretty faithful boy. Has but little eye to the main chance however—has had no less than three blankets; but has thrown them all away rather than carry them!—*lost* them he says—but we all know *how* they were lost. He sleeps cuddled close up to the fire with no blanket through rain and storm. Last night he was drenched by the storm & today you might have wrung him out. How you would enjoy sleeping out every night my boy, with neither tent, overcoat nor blanket to cover you. So Tom does, & would rather than carry either, I believe. Niggers are shiftless rascals, & you must keep watch on them at all times—they never look forward—the present alone they care for—they remind me strongly of the scriptural "lily of the field"! Tom's ideas of religion are peculiar. He assured me tonight that he intended to get religion bye & by—couldn't get it he said, in war times. "Getting religion", he took it was going to church regularly. If he didn't get religion, he would go to hell when he died & the devil would throw him into a big fire on a pitchfork & burn him forever—continually pricking him up with the pitchfork. If he went to heaven, he would sit on a white throne & eat milk & honey! Quite as amusing was the remark of the Lieut. Colonels nigger "Dixie" who in discussing slavery said he'd "hearn the preachers say as how a man must live by the sweat of his *eye* brow"!

But I'm writing too long a letter. Wish mother very much love from me—tell
Fred I received his kind letter & will write him soon & believe me

Very truly yr. affec. brother

H.J. Spooner

Rhode Island Historical Society Library, Providence, Manuscripts Collection, Letters of Fred
Spooner and Henry Joshua Spooner, Henry J. Spooner Papers, MSS 732.

---

*John Harpin Riggs of Company F, Seventh Connecticut Volunteers, offers a negative opin-
ion of the effects that emancipation would have on the war and on African Americans in
this letter to his father.*

Beaufort, South Carolina

December 12, 1862

Dear Father

I received a letter from you to day for the first in about a month and was glad
to here you had good luck in gathering your crops and making your cider and
Brandy I wish I had a quart of the brandy to day but I live in hop[e]s of getting
some if I live long enough I see by your letter that the people are getting woked
up about the war holding out so long I think it is time something was done you
wanted to know what my ideas wer on the subject I will try to tell you altho I
am no partyman   now I am for the union as it was and let the south have there
negros and do what they pleas with them I think that they are a great deal better
of with there Masters than they are now if the government did not furnish
rations for them they would die, if they have a family and you give the old ones
any thing and they will eat it temselfs and the young ones may get them some or
starve   they get a shilling and they will keep it and beg for a living they do not
learn very fast the young ones learn slow but the old boy could not understand
them and hear them talking among themselfs I think that the President has got a
big thing to do if he fights till he frees all the black scamps I wish the devil had
them all any way give me union now and forever and if you take the negros away
there never will be union that is sertain   they are as incompetant of ruling themselfs as the small children at home   if you get a bi[g] club and tell them to go and
do sutch a thing they will do it but they will go so slow that you can not tell
which way they are going you may think as you are a mind and so will I   dam
the negroes I dont mean them abolitionist up north I am a Southern man myself
you can never expect to see me agane among the rocks of the north I have not
seen a peble stone since I left annapolis that is more than a year since I have seen a
stone   this is my views on the subject

From your Son

John H. Riggs

New Haven Colony Historical Society, New Haven, John Harpin Riggs, MSS 77, Civil War
Collection, box 2, folder O.

William Augustus Willoughby of Company A, Tenth Regiment, Connecticut Volunteers, discusses the war's impact on Southern society and offers his assessment of the Emancipation Proclamation in this letter to his wife.

Newbern, North Carolina
January 22, 1863

My Dear Wife

You will see that up to this writing that we are still at Newbern. Although I have written you that we expected to leave here severall days ago   And now we expect to leave to Morrow   Still we not leave in severall days yet and I may have an opportunity to complete this letter and perhaps mail it.

In your last letter you seem to be discouraged and as about to give up all hopes as to putting down this "Rebellion"   I think there is no necessity for that yet, and for many reasons. I cannot see why we have not been making gains pretty steadily in every place unless it may be in *Virginia* and even there in Virginia. notwithstanding the treachery of some in the Army, and perhaps some in Washington. I think we have fast been approaching a final victory.

If you could see the *ruin devastation* and *utter abandonment* of *villages. Plantations* and *farms,* which but a short time ago was *Peopled, fenced* and *stocked, Houses* once comfortable that are now either burned or deserted, barns in ashes all along the road side, fences destroyed for miles and over thousands of acres, No cows horses mules sheep or poultry to be seen where ever the Union army advances, and you would see conclusively that the destitution for the coming year is to be four fold greater than the past year. This whole country for all purposes of maintainance for man or beast for the next twelve months is a *desert* as hop[e]less as *Sahara* itself, If this *war* continues another twelve months this country will be little else than a "howling wilderness" and the "abomination of desolation" will be written on their very "gait post"   When I say this *Country* I mean this "Southern Confederacy" and then again if our *Government* follows up what it has already commenced and that is to carry out the Presidents proclamation[5] and then raise, as the Government probably will armies of contrabands in every available place, and they can be raised in all most any place and all most any numbers, and arm them, this rebellion is crushed out. I think there could be here in Newbern One thousand who formally were slaves but who are now free, enlisted into the Union Army, who would fight like *Tigers* to defend their rights as they now enjoy them   So on the whole I do not see any good reason for being discouraged or being in doubt as to final success. Another reason for hope is in the fact that we have at the head of this Army in Verginia a *General* who has an Eternal hatred to that Institution which is the "sum of all Villianies" "American Slavery."[6]

5. The Emancipation Proclamation, which went into effect on Jan. 1, 1863.
6. General Burnside.

Then again the Proclimation of the *President* will Inaugurate a new System of Laws and customs among the people in abolishing old ideas and establishing new ones among our Northern people which will encourage our arms and weaken the *Rebels* equal to three hundred thousands Soldiers in our favor

The first day of January *1863* should be classed with the fourth day of July *1776* as commencing a new Era, or rather as completing what our Forefathers began Eighty Seven years ago next fourth of July

Slavery is doomed and it is only question of time as to when it will make its last struggle. It may be this year and it may be the next but die it must there is not a doubt

American Antiquarian Society, Worcester, Mass., Letters of William A. Willoughby, W. A. Willoughby Papers.

In this letter to his sister, Meschack Purington Larry, a soldier from Maine, explains how a firsthand view of slavery changed his opinion of African Americans.

Feb 16, 1863

Dear sister

I have got the ring done that I spoke of   the figures are cut with a corn pocket knife and filled with sealing wax. It is nothing very presious but as it is made here it may be interisting enough to some one I wish I could make a beter one but as I never worked on fine work there will not be much expected. I must make one for Lois soon or I may get such a punch that I shal not be able to make any thing. I think things are improving under Hookers comand[7] but Barnum says there is no resarction to a dead curiousety, I think people talk to much about fighting for the negroe, for my part what I *believed* to be the curses of slavery has become knowledge and instead of thinking les of a negroe I have sadly learned to think them beter than many wight meen that hold responsible positions   Why blame the negroe for what he can not help   why speak of him with scorn and contempt when he does all he is alowed to do, god knows that a soldier life is hard, but I do not wish to exchange mine for that of a negroes bond or free. as for liberty I have all that a soldier could expect and sertanly feel as free as a king   I agreed to obey orders and therefore no one is to blame but myself if I do not like them   can a slave say the same

M.P. Larry

Maine Historical Society, Portland, Letters of Meschack P. Larry, S-293mb 11/4.

---

7. President Lincoln replaced General Burnside with General Hooker as commander of the Army of the Potomac in January 1863. Hooker was a popular general who helped eliminate corruption and improve conditions in camps and hospitals.

This letter of Justus Gale, Company A, Eighth Vermont Volunteer Regiment, to his sister Almeida offers evidence of the typical New England concern with temperance, a concern Gale found noticeably lacking in the South.

New Orleans, Louisiana
Feb. 22, 1863

Dear Sis,

I take my pen again this pleasant Saboth morning to spend a portion of this dearly prized day in writing to you; how many times I think of the many pleasant days I have passed in little Elmore in gone by days in going to the house of worship and there listen to the preaching of our Dear pastors, but such days are gone with me for the present. . . .

I have now been enlisted 17 months and during all this time have been cirrounded by many temptations hearing the most wicked oaths—having many invitations to play cards—take a drink of whiskey &c! but I have yet to play my first game of cards and to take my first drink of liquor Except when we were of [f] on marches last August when we were almost melted then I drank a little of the called sparkling good for you. I dont wish to boast of my good qualities but consider my carecter of just as much importance here as at home. This State is the worst place for drinking of any place I ever heard of. Liquor is just as common here as watter is in Vt; you can hardly go by a door in this City without seeing the glass and bottle siting on the bar. there is about as many women here that get drunk as there is men in the north that get drunk. . . .

give my love to Lyman & Mira and all enquiring friends, please write often and oblige. this from your brother who often thinks of you.

J. F. Gale

Vermont Historical Society, Montpelier, Letters of Justus F. Gale, Gale-Morse Papers, MSA 50.

John Henry Jenks of Keene, New Hampshire, served as a sergeant with the Fourteenth New Hampshire Volunteer Infantry. In this letter he describes meeting a group of slaves and offers his opinion of the condition of enslaved African Americans.

Poolesville, Maryland
March 10, 1863

Dear Wife,

Yesterday was a very exciting day in our camp. About 3 oclock P.M. news came to camp that one of our Soldiers was shot by one of the citizens, while in the act of getting some straw for his bed. . . . Our Adjutant, Capt Cowles, and many officers went immediately to the grounds in pursuit of the scamp—also about thirty Cavelry. They scoured the woods, and searched the houses in the vicinity, but could find no one who answered to the description the young man gave who had a full view of him and could tell him if seen. They came back to camp about dark, but was not willing to give the matter so, Col Jewett, Comander of this Brigade told Capts Cowles and Ripley to make further search, and investigate the subject according to the best of their judgment, they choosing such men as they saw fit to take with them. About 7 oclock Capt Cowles sent for Leyford, Sergt Stone and myself to come to his office, which we quickley obeyed he told us to arm ourselves with revolvers, knives, &c, and be ready to go with him on a nights expidition, in searching houses and gaining all information in our power. . . . we got our point of compass and started to go to Chissells.[8] It was thought the one who shot him might come there in the night, and perhaps others who was interested, in either party (I would here say Mr. Chissel had been arrested in the P.M.) and concluded to secreet ourselves and watch to see if any one come and arrest him, also to stop any disturbance should the soldiers come. . . . I tried to see and hear what I could but made no discovery of importance. When I got cold I went into a *Niggar* shanty close to the house, which was ocupied by a negro woman about 50 years old, her son who had fits, and a man about 35. They had a nice fire in the huge fireplace all night. I wish I could tell you my feelings as I sat there alone at the dead of night, (the man went with Captain as guide) in that negro shanty, talking to that poor ignorant slave. It brought impressively to my mind the reading of "Uncle Toms Cabin." Little did I then think I should spend a night with them. Her husband lived 4 miles distant she has had 14 children 7 of them have died, the rest are within a radious of 12 miles. Her daughter was in another shanty and had lots of little ones; her husband ran off 2 months ago; he did not live on the same plantation with her. The other negro *Henry* was married to a girl 12 miles off, had 5 children. After he gets through with the toils of the day for his Master he makes brooms chairs and baskets to sell to procure tobacco, Sunday clothes for himself and wife, and some of the luxuries of life, such as sugar. Dont you think such men can take care of themselves . . .? The Capt made an arrest of the other man who owned a part of the straw, and sent him into camp. They staid there all night to watch the proceedings, and came to where I was about 7 oclock, they then took horses and went two miles further to arrest a man they had suspicion of but when they got there the cavelry had arrested him, but as yet the true man has not been found. . . . I took no cold last night and very well except I am a little sleepy, and I will go to bed and dream of thee. So good night. Love to Flora kiss the Babe and hunks of love to you.

J. Henry Jenks

University of New Hampshire Library, Durham, Special Collections, Letters of John Henry Jenks, Coll. III.

8. The man who owned the property on which the soldier was shot.

Dr. Robert Hubbard of Bridgeport, Connecticut, was commissioned surgeon of the Seventeenth Connecticut Volunteer Regiment in 1862. He was promoted to medical director of General Davis's division and then to medical director of the Eleventh Army Corps under the command of General Oliver O. Howard. In this letter to his wife, Hubbard makes some disparaging remarks about the intelligence of white Southerners.

Camp near Brookes Station, Virginia
April 4, 1863

My own dear Nellie

I have just finished my monthly Reports for the Brigade and they will be sent off to-morrow. We have until the 5th of the following month to get them to General Head. Qrs. Mine this time have been delayed by waiting for one of the regimental Surgeons to complete his who has just returned from leave of absence. This afternoon I have visited three patients among the citizens here one a little girl 5 yrs old with acute Bronchitis and the mother with a bad cold who expects to be confined soon and wishes me to attend her. Their name is Jones. I also visited another family by the name of Stone the wife of the man suffering from sore throat. They are all in good times well-to-do farmers but now much straitened by the desolation of war. They are generally ignorant speaking a miserable dialect with the words "right smart" prefixed to everything. Example— You ask one of them where Mr. Smith lives & the reply is "A right smart piece down *yere*" or you remark it is a very stormy day & the inevitable answer is "yes right smart storm". Jones told me that he was 40 years old and never went 40 miles from the place where he was born in his life—was never in Alexandria, Washington or Richmond. They live in wretched log houses with the coarsest kind of furniture & live on "hog & hominy" the year round. Everything indicates the most primitive kind of civilization. Spinning wheels are found in almost every house, their farming utensils & implements are of the [*illegible*] and impractical kind and their minds as uncultivated as their soil. You miss the taste and neatness of New England homes—see no grounds tastefully laid out as a general rule, no shade trees planted & when Nature has not supplied the difficiency the houses are in all their native ugliness.

your aff. Husband, Robt. Hubbard

Yale University Library, New Haven, Manuscripts and Archives, Civil War Manuscripts Collection, Letters of Robert Hubbard.

William A. Sabin served with Company C, Third Rhode Island Artillery. Sabin offers his opinion on the performance of African-American soldiers in this letter to his friend Benjamin C. Gladding.

Beaufort, South Carolina
May 5, 1863

Friend Benjamin

Your letter of Mch 26st was recieved. And should have been answered before but I have been on Picket most of the time and had no conveniences to write. . . .

I have been on picket at a plase called Brick Yard point about 9 miles from Camp opposite the plase where the Gun Boat Geo Washington was sunk by a Rebbel Battery. the 1st South Carolina (nigger) is on outside Picket, one Company was stationed at the point where I was. There is great diference of opinion in regard to their efficiency. I find they behave well in Camp but they need a great deal of drill and instruction, and are not fit for responsible positions. One night a Corperal and two men saw an empty boat floating down the river and imagined it full of Rebels. they got frightend and came running into Camp a distance of two miles leaving an important post without a sentinal. they lack judgment and discression. And resemble the Indians. Good for gurilla fighting but drop a shell among them, and they scatter like sheep. I have been much amused by attending some of their *shouts* or religious dances—in which they form a ring singing and dancing for hours together. We added to the interest on one occasion by sprinkling pepper on the floor. I also witnessed a negro wedding. it took place in the open air, by moonlight. the bride was dressed in white with a wreath of white roses on her head. After the cerimony they had a big shout. all the wenches from the neighbouring Plantations were present. it beat all my Ideas of life in dixie. . . .

I do not think there will be any move made in this department, orders have been given to grant enlisted men furloughs. I like Beaufort better than the Head. Our Regt is at Hilton Head—except Co A and our Battery. I am well, and enjoying myself   Remember me to all who may inquire. and I hope to hear from you again soon.

I remain
Yours Truly
W.A. Sabin

Rhode Island Historical Society Library, Providence, Manuscripts Collection, Letters of William A. Sabin, Charles Ray Brayton Papers, MSS 304.

Charles A. Boyle enlisted in Company E, Fifteenth Connecticut Infantry. He was promoted to sergeant on February 1, 1864. He died October 10, 1864, of yellow fever in New Bern, North Carolina. Boyle comments on the treatment African Americans received from Union soldiers in this letter to his sisters Grace and Annie.

Suffolk, Virginia
May 15, 1863

Dear Home

I write this on my picket post on the Norfolk RR. I am lying on my back under a shelter constructed of logs & rails. . . . There must be as many as 2000 negroes within our lines here, and they seem to enjoy ther freedom. Ask them if they are not afraid that the rebs will drive us away and catch them, and they say "when you leave dis we leabe too, mas'r![") . . .

the Yankee soldiers do not treat the negroes very well, and are always ready to insult a female. The black women are not often molested by them boys, however, as they are not afraid of the white *heathen,* and are able to defend themselves against an "ordinary" Yankee. . . .

Connecticut Historical Society, Hartford, Letters of Charles A. Boyle, Civil War Box I.

Charles Ray Brayton served as a lieutenant in Battery C, Third Rhode Island Artillery. In this letter Brayton explains his decision to accept the lieutenant colonelcy of a colored regiment and offers insight into the prevailing views of African-American soldiers.

Morris Island, South Carolina
September 13, 1863

My Dear Father,

Yours of the 5th and 7th inst. came duly to hand by the "Fulton" on Monday morning. I have given the "Governor's offer" much consideration. Operations here at about ended. There is no chance for my promotion in the 3d at present as there is no vacancy in the Field. If I accept it makes me a "Field Officer" and will not injure my prespects for a higher position in some other Regiment in the eye of the Governor I think. It relieves me from all Company responsibility, which is no small consideration I assure you. The prejudice against Negro troops is fast wearing away and will vanish entirely in a few months, as I judge any troops will be acceptable if we fight France.[9]

There is a chance too of my being highest in Command in the Regiment as it is no sure thing that men enough will be raised to "Muster-in" a Colonel although enough might be recruited for a Lieut. Colonel's command, and Lieut Colonel must be "mustered-in" before a Colonel can be. Capt. Comstock, a senior to me in the 3d, has accepted the position of Major. My friends here all urge me to accept the position offered me. I have made application for a "leave of absence" but it has been refused, in order that I might consult with you, the Gov, and Col. Metcalf personally. Questions like these are unsettled in my mind. Will the Gov

---

9. From the beginning of the war, the Confederacy attempted to gain recognition from European powers. The Confederate government especially hoped that recognition, and perhaps even intervention, would be forthcoming from Great Britain and France.

think me less worthy of promotion if I accept the Lieut Colonelcey of a Colored Regiment? Can I be mustered in as soon as I arrive North? That is, will there be a sufficient number of men raised to entitle the Battalion to a Lieut Col?

You can ascertain these facts better than I, being at home. If sufficient men are raised to have a Lieut Colonel, or will be by the end of the month I shall accept the position offered. At any rate have my Commission sent on without delay by the "Arago" if possible so that I can get North and be mustered out here as a Captain. From the tone of both your letters I felt that you did not think it wise in me to accept, but I cannot see any better chance now and wait no one knows how long for another opportunity. Remember Lieut Col Greene at "Red Bank" with his Battalion of regulars. I saw the 57th Mass. charge "Wagner" as bravely as any white troops I ever saw.[10] Southern negroes are not worth equipping. They are entirely different from the Northern negro. Give me supreme command of a Regiment of Northern negroes and I will make as good a fighting Regiment as has left R.I. I know I shall be joked some at first, but time will tell and I believe that the Negro troops will equal the white in this war, that is those from the North.

I am well and in good spirits. Please see the Commission is forwarded as soon as possible. Hoping to see you soon I remain

Your aff. son,
Charlie.

Rhode Island Historical Society Library, Providence, Manuscripts Collection, Letters of Charles Ray Brayton, Charles Ray Brayton Papers, MSS 304.

In this letter to his sisters, Charles Boyle of Company E, Fifteenth Connecticut Infantry, describes an incident in which Union soldiers were instrumental in reuniting an African-American family.

Portsmouth, Virginia
Dec 25, 1863

Dear Home:

Christmas day finds me on duty as corporal of the guard. . . . Two black women came out from Portsmouth with a pass to go 5 miles beyond our lines to get three children,—sisters of the youngest woman, who had been at P. ever since our troops first occupied the place. She was at that time in town for the purpose of trading for her master; and was not allowed to go again outside the lines. But she had not forgotten her little slave sisters; and now that Gen Butler is here she easily procured a pass, and an order for a guard to accompany her. Two of the pickets volunteered to go, and guaranteed that they would bring in the children, while the order was for a guard of six men. They were gone from 10 am, until

---

10. It was the Fifty-fourth Massachusetts Regiment that charged Fort Wagner.

nearly dark; when the party appeared, bringing the emancipated little blacks with them. The motherly sister was so grateful to the guard that she could not cease in asking the "Good Lord to bless dem." The "proprietor" of these little chattels was mightily wroth when the purpose of the visit was made known to him; and his old vixen of a wife opined upon the Yanks and the negress with a tirade of abuse which was more forcible and vehement than womanly and dilicate. Of the sister who had come to the rescue, she said: "If I had a gun I would shoot the b—h through her nasty head!" But in the midst of this storm the boys entered the house and passed the little nigs "bodily" from the possession of this chivalrous family to the sister; and then searched the house for garments to protect their then almost naked limbs from the cold piercing wind. The great burly man did not make so much demonstration as did the wife, but the negro women were more afraid of him. "O, lor dem boys are de braves' fellers dere ever was." "If dey'd ben any cowards, dey'd nebber got dese yer chilin." "De ole man was big 'nuf an strong 'nuf to eat dem up; but dey warn't no mo' fraid on him—Lor!" "Dey went right in an fetch de chilin straight out!" Not only these women, but those whom they passed on the road, and who knew the parties raised their black hands and cried, "bress de Lor!" "You'se got de chilin at las'!" I asked the oldest of the girls, (about 10 years) if she could carry a pail full of water on her head;—she replied—"yes sir." (No doubt she could, for I saw, to day, a little black girl, not, apparrently larger than our Leslie, come to the spring, fill a water pail *full,* put it on her woolly little head and carry it steadily away without using her hand to balance it, and with apparent ease!)

The sister of these children said "I can work—dat I can! Bless de Lor for dat!" "I have tuk car mysef dese two year; an' I can take car dese young 'uns!" She told her guards that she was going to have a big party with music and dancing "jus all for dem," and she is going to send for them when she gets "ebryting ready."

I presume that none of the stout hearted soldier men who saw the group standing before the fire place, and heard the grateful girl try to thank God and the guards sufficiently for their aid in rescuing their little sisters, would not aver that they felt a choking sensation in their throats, and that they had a suspicion of tears in their manly eyes, but I am persuaded to believe that such was the case, even though they might deny it. . . .

Connecticut Historical Society, Hartford, Letters of Charles A. Boyle, Civil War Box I.

William Augustus ("Gus") Walker, captain of Company C, Twenty-seventh Massachusetts Volunteer Regiment, describes a Southern Christmas in this letter to his sister Frances French.

Portsmouth, Virginia
Dec. 26, 1863

Yesterday was Christmas & upon my word it beat all the Christmasses it has ever been my lot to witness, it is additional proof to my mind that the people down South are fearfully behind the times & sadly need christianizing. You know our ideas of Christmas have something of the Sabbath odor about them, we consider it a christian holiday & so early in the morning the chimes peel forth their song of praise, the churches are opened & from their altars ascend music & thanksgiving, families assemble together & bid each other a "Merry Christmas" while their hearts grow warm with the memory & renewal of their loves. It is a holy season & every christian heart rejoices at the anniversary of that day when the morning stars sang together & the angel hosts poured forth the refrain "Unto us a child is born, to us a Son is given."

With such feelings as these in regard to Christmas you need not wonder that I opened my eyes in astonishment when the realities of a Southern Christmas dawned upon my vision. I was awakened before daylight by the blowing of tin horns, the firing of crackers & small arms, as the day advanced these interesting exhibitions increased till the din was quite as great as any 4th of July up North. In the forenoon a procession paraded the streets like our "Antigius & horribles" "rag ships" &c. I noticed that citizens began very early to get elevated & throughout the day the amount of drunkenness was excessive. The tendency of every feature of the day was towards noise burlesque, & general looseness. And this was the Southern way of celebrating Christmas. I was disgusted at such a low state of morals, at such a heathenish way of expressing their religious sentiments.

Well the more I see of this sunny South, the more I am convinced it is no place for me. there is such an amount of *shiftlessness* pervading every department of society, that the fine sense of us yankees is constantly shocked. There is also an immense deal of discomfort even among people of wealth & refinement a total lack of those little things that are the results of taste & cultivation & add so much to the delights of home. One of the interesting social traits is *laziness* it affects everybody & is constitutional, it is fairly reduced to a science.

The daughters of the family where we board are only examples, they lie in bed half the forenoon & when up sit shivering round the fire wrapped in shawls. the poor Mother does the best she can & yet we have to wait from fifteen minutes to an hour for every meal & all this might be prevented but for the intense laziness of these girls. I have remonstrated & found fault & expressed my opinion in *very* plain terms, but for all the effect it has I might as well whistle they are impervious to sarcasm, hints or even shame. This laziness & tardiness seems to be carried into every thing, at church the congregation will hardly ever assemble until after the sermon is begun. One sees enough here to keep him growling continually & to ruin the best-natured disposition that ever was, unless he can become perfectly oblivious to the customs about him & be insensible to their annoyance. . . .

Write me a long letter soon my darling sister. My love to Lila & kisses for Frankie.

Your own loving bro
Gus

Historic Northampton, Northampton, Mass., Letters of William A. Walker, W. A. Walker Papers.

William Augustus Willoughby of New Haven, Connecticut, served in Company A, Tenth Connecticut Volunteers. In this letter to his wife Nancy, Willoughby offers his assessment of the war's impact on Southern society.

Deep Bottom, Virginia
August 1, 1864

Dear Wife

I am now in my tent *Fine Evening* having just returned from 24 hours Picket duty about ½ hour before the time for releif the "Jonnies" came down on our lines, with the intention of driving us in or finding where our lines run and how strong our force was. For about 40 or 50 minutes which next followed we had quite a sharp little skirmish fight in which we had 3 men slightly wounded and one *Edgar Beecher* of *Woodbridge Conn* seriously. The "Rebs" lost one man killed and 2 wounded. So we learn by deserter this Evening *We held our line. . . .*

As for *Richmond, Petersburg* and *Atlanta* I think their fall is a for gone conclusion and the delay will only make it the more disastrous for the "Reb" when it comes. *as come it will* Let no one dream those *Cities* are comfortably secure and safe. If I thought proper I might write you what I believe to be, and which I think will be developed at a proper time. and perhaps before many days or weeks at the most *Be Patient* I do not believe if "Father Abraham" should withdraw the *Federal Forces* to morrow from their territory that the "Rebels" could establish a Goverment, that would not break down from its own weight in five years. Their country is desolated from the Potomac to the Gulf of Mexico and from the Ocean to the Mississippi River. Citties Riddled with Shot and Shell. Rail Roads and bridges destroyed in one way or another Farm houses Barns and fences burned to the ground. their crops trampled down. and their whole Stock of cattle consumed for food for the Army long ago. All these, I say are not very pleasant phases to look upon for a bankrupt, and not a very enterprising people *and less skillfull* to start a machine and run themselves. with *slavery* as its motive power I believe it would either blow up or collapse in less than three years. Just immagine the Hudson River from New York to Albany without a single Village on either bank, and yet I believe this to be the case on the James River from Old Point Comfort to Richmond not a Village nor hardly a *Villa* While I think nature in very many things favors the James River. In one thing in particular the James River has the advantage that is in its approach and broad waters at its mouth Which I think far superior to the Hudson

Past 2 o clock PM I have just been releived from 2 hours guard duty from 12 to 2 o clock and all quiet in camp and on the Pickit line. I have five weeks from to day to serve yet the Government Officers do not seem disposed to discharge the members of Co A untill the Regiment is discharged in October some time So I may not get home until the middle of October I know it will not take a great while for 9 weeks to pass away yet 7 weeks will go quicker by 2 weeks which is of some account just now. I wish you would have a Custard or an apple pie when I come, or both. I have not tasted of any butter but once in most a year. I have not had a piece of pie that was fit to eat since I left Annapolis Maryland I must bring this to close So remember me to father W. and A. and Brothers Sisters and all relatives and friends both Sides

William Augustus Willoughby

American Antiquarian Society, Worcester, Mass., Letters of William A. Willoughby, W. A. Willoughby Papers.

Samuel Duncan, of Meriden, New Hampshire, colonel with the Fourth Regiment, U.S. Colored Troops, comments on the slaves' reactions to Union troops in this letter to his brother.

North East River Station, North Carolina
Feb. 25, 1865

My Dear Bro:

From this you will learn that I have at last rejoined my command, and I can assure you that it a source of great satisfaction to be back once more among my old army friends from whom I have experienced a hearty welcome. . . .

I have talked with many of the colored people of NC & the contrabands daily coming into our camp, and am perfectly satisfied that the rebels can derive but little if any advantage from the arming of their slaves. The slaves comprehend the great question at issue, and invariably assert that they would not fight for their masters, but are ready to fight on our side. They knew full well what our army signified to them as we passed into the city. they had hid away from the fleeing rebels, but all turned out to welcome us, and many a little woolyheaded darkie came jumping & dancing along the street & shouting "I'se broke my chain; I'se broke my chain," while the women were bowing & scraping and tossing their arms in the air and crying, "Bress de Lord; Bress de Lord. De year of jubilie hab come."

Dartmouth College Library, Hanover, N.H., Letters of Samuel Duncan, Duncan Papers.

CHAPTER FOUR

Politics on the Home Front

THE LETTERS IN this section discuss the political effects of the war at home. Soldiers and their correspondents discuss local elections and the draft, as well as some of the acts of violence committed on the home front (draft riots, Lincoln's assassination, the Confederate raid on St. Albans, Vermont). Many writers express contempt for those who undermined the progress of the war effort. Women correspondents reveal considerable interest in homefront politics, despite the fact that politics was generally considered to be outside the purview of nineteenth-century American women.

A. C. Hinckley, wife of the prosperous Massachusetts silk manufacturer Samuel L. Hinckley, wrote this letter to her son Henry, who was a student in Germany when the war broke out. Mrs. Hinckley describes the effects of the outbreak of hostilities on the "once quiet" city of Boston.

Boston, Massachusetts
May 1, 1861

My dear Henry,

I hope you get the newspapers for I could not pretend to describe the excitement our city & country has been in for the past fortnight & if I did you would not believe it but think it was woman's exaggeration, therefore I think it more dignified to be as silent as possible & content myself by saying you have never seen the like before, & I hope never will. it is some thing very sickening to hear the drum & the fife marching off daily regiments of noble spirited youth from our streets & all the underbrush of creation seems to have turned up into the common & among the streets of our once quiet city. Houses are being robbed by day & by night & where ever you go you are liable to find yourself in a mob in a moment. Nobody thinks of what they were doing last year on Mt Carmel or on Mt. Holyoke[1] & therefore you had better not, but rather rejoice that you are not shouldering the musket in a wicked war. I am loyal to the Stars & Stripes but pray most sincerely that they may not fight & your father has taken the only calm day that he has had for a fortnight to write you & I think he is taking a cooler view of

---

1. Mount Carmel and Mount Holyoke were two common vacation spots in Massachusetts.

matters now, but it is death to business as you may suppose. I send two scraps from the newspaper wh[ic]h were forgotten the last time. Did I tell you that my dear kind old Aunt Grant died on the 6th of April. Also Chief Justice Shaw. Peace to their ashes & all who are saved from seeing this countries disgrace.

Goodbye, says your ever affet Mother.

Historic Northampton, Northampton, Mass., Letters of Samuel L. and A. C. Hinckley, Henry Rose Hinckley Papers.

Sarah E. Fales wrote this letter to her son Edmund Fales, who enlisted in the First Regiment, Rhode Island Volunteers, on April 17, 1861. His first term of service was only for three months, and Fales was mustered out in August. He reenlisted as an orderly sergeant in Company L, Ninth Rhode Island Volunteer Regiment, in May 1862 and was promoted to first lieutenant in Company K, Twelfth Rhode Island Volunteer Regiment, in March 1863 and then to captain in the First Regiment, Rhode Island Volunteers, in September 1863. In this letter Sarah Fales describes the concern, prevalent among many Rhode Island men, about the possibility of a draft.

Middletown, Rhode Island
May 13, 1862

Edmund

Dear Son we received today your letter written May 10 and was very glad to hear you was geting a long so well and comfortable your time will soon be up now if nothing happens and then we shall see you home again. . . .

you ask how the Middletown boys feel about the draft I do not know much about the boys but some of the men have ben terribly frightend they met at the townhouse again last week not to raise recruits but to raise money to hire men to go for thim they voted $5.00 bounty some proposed raising enough to make a bargain with the railroad contractor to furnish Irishmen enough to fill out their quota[2] Father says there will be no drafting as long as there is a dollar left in the town, what do you think of that for patriotism and love of country in such times of danger as these we have reason to be thankfull it is not so everywhere

Father says he understands that those in the Service when the draft is made up are not subject to it in less than six months or a year the draft for the last three hundred thousand men has been postpond untill the first of september these are to be nine months militia men. . . .

---

2. In the spring of 1862, the federal government was beginning to consider implementing a draft. By the summer of 1862, Congress had passed an initial militia law which empowered the president to press state militia units into federal service. If state militia quotas were not met, a draft could be, and occasionally was, necessary. In addition, states and towns frequently offered cash bounties to induce men to enlist. In March 1863 Congress passed a national conscription law which nationalized the draft process.

I will close now as there is nothing that will interest you at present   we are all as well as usual. . . . write when you receive this so that we may know when you will start for home

so good by for the present
this from your mother
Sarah E Fales

Rhode Island Historical Society Library, Providence, Manuscripts Collection, Letters of Sarah E. Fales, Edmund W. Fales Family Papers, MSS 9001-F.

Edward F. Hall, of Company B, Third Regiment, New Hampshire Volunteers, expresses his opinion of those on the home front whose support for the war was wavering in this letter to his wife.

Hilton Head, South Carolina
Sept. 16, 1862

Dear Susan

A mail came in yesterday by the Steamer Arago, and I got a letter from you, with one from Eddie enclosed—yours was dated Sept 6th and Eddies the 7th. . . .

You say some complain of high taxes—probably they are the ones who thought a war with the South would be a nice thing—a mere play. an army of 100[,]000 could go through them like a dose of Salts. they are like the man who won the Elephant at a raffle. "dont know what to do with him." thought they could have a little *sport* with the Southerners free their Niggars, and get all through with it in a few months. having got more than they bargained for they now object to paying the costs—except in the way of Bounties to men who will step in and save their precious selves from the chances of a draft. . . .

I was glad to hear that you were both well and geting along so well. . . .

My love to everybody   Edward F Hall

New Hampshire Historical Society, Concord, Letters of Edward F. Hall, 1977–89.

In this letter to her son Mit who was serving in the Union army, Vesta H. Ingalls discusses her family's economic concerns, as well as some prevalent political issues.

Stoneham, Massachusetts
October 12, 1862

Dear Mit

I thought perhaps a few lines if they wasent quite so good might be better than none so I will do the best I can to interest you. when we got your letter last night and Charlie seen your Postscript No 2 about the Vermin you had accumulated he was in estacies   he said he was going to write to Mit to day   he thought he had

got a subject that he could spread himself on. you know why. Your Father &
Charlie is making locks as usual   we come pretty near changen our Location a
few weeks ago   Your Father made a bargain with Baker for his place & we went
to see the owners of House to Medford to see if he could have a lease of the
House for a sufficient length of time . . . but he found it was for sale and liable to
be sold any day and he thought it was a most too Risky. . . . I was sorry for they
had about thirty Boarders and I think we could make money   your Father saw a
Fellow from Woburn the other day that belonged to your Regiment   he was
Bugler has been wounded and been at home was going back the next day   he
gave him yours and Oliver address and he said he would try to see you when he
got back   he said he didnt care about going back again if he could help it as well
as not   he said they hadnt been fighting for the union at all this long time   they
were fighting for the Politicians   what is your opinion of it. what is the general
feeling among the Soldiers in regard to the Presidents Emancipation Bill which do
you think it will do the most good or hurt. let me see I believe you was the young
gentleman that was going to be so prompt about writing when you got to the
Army going to write once a week and here it has been two or three weeks since
we heard a word from either of you[3] till last Night   I want you both to be more
prompt in future unless you are so situated that you cant without too much trouble. in that Case I will excuse you write in Particular both of you   when you write
again how you get along and how your health is   I should have written before but
was waiting to hear from you   Your Father is going to write to you both soon
my wrist aches so I will close by subscribing myself

Your Affectionate Mother
Vesta H. Ingalls

PS   we shall put in some stamps but when you write to us we can Pay the letter
here and you can put them on the letters that you send elsewhere if you please

Historic Northampton, Northampton, Mass., Letters of Vesta H. Ingalls, A.CW.18.78.

---

*Caleb Blanchard of Foster, Connecticut, served with the Eighteenth Regiment, Connecticut
Volunteers. These three letters written by Blanchard and his wife Mattie demonstrate that
despite their lack of direct political influence, women frequently took an active interest in
politics.*

Foster, Connecticut
Nov. 9, 1862

Dear husband
    I now seat myself to answer your letter which I received yesterday, I was very
glad to hear from you and to hear that you was well   your letter was very encour-

---

3. Mit Ingalls's brother was also serving in the Union army.

ageing it would be more so if I could hear that peace was declared and you was a
comeing home but I must wait patiently but oh how hard it is to be seperated
from so good and kind a husband and stand and wait patiently for the plotting
and planing of a few political leaders   the old democrats are haveing everything
their own way in the election I supose they think they will have a glorious time
yet the more I see and hear the less confidence I have in our ever haveing peace
restored to us again   I think these United States will be a divided land when the
fighting ceases if that ever is and I think it will soon for I think they have got most
tired of it   at the first of January the President has declared the slaves of rebel
owners free   what do you think that will amount to   please write and tell me   I
am thinking there will be a great change in what way I am not able to say but I
hope for the better but I guess I will stop writing about such things or you will
think I am crazy but I must say one more word and that is I think that most all of
our head Generals rejoice to think that Seymore is elected[4]   I wrote to you last
week and did not get a chance to send it untill last night   I was all confused when
I wrote and my eye was sore and it plagued me to see   my eye is better now but is
not quiet well I think it is a humor   I am well other ways and our little girl is
quiet well I think it is a humor   I am well other ways and our little girl is
quiet well she lays here on the bed sound asleep but I am expecting she will
awake very soon   she goes to sleep every day between nine and ten oclock and
has a nap of an hour and a half and two hours and then she has two more short
ones in the afternoon one about three oclock and another between five and six
and then she is awake untill eight and then I undress her and get her to sleep and
put her to bed and I dont have any more trouble with her for she sleeps as sound
as a nut all night wakes up as good natured as need be in the morning   she hardly
ever cryes unless she feels bad or gets mad and then she lets you know it   I think
she has got spunk enough   they all think a great deal of her   I expect Hannah
thinks it is a long time since she see her   I have not heard anything from them up
there since I come down here   I asked Nancy to write she did not say whether
she would or not   Ruth and Andrew is down here so you see we are all to home
but you mother was calculating to get a turkey and invite us all home but she says
that she shall not now you are not here

Andrew has come down to paint fathers new wagon   he has not got it from
Walkers yet the boys have all gone down there to day to see if it is done   I am
glad to hear you say that you like better than you did to McHenry[5] I guess you
have made a good change I should think they were all sesesh there   I hope the
25th boys was enough for them   did you get any of those nice things   I should
think the provost marshal was sesesh   I hope you will not have to go away to
guard bridges but stay there if you like the place   I supose you feel as though you
had gained liberty since you got out of the fort   I dont want you to have to go
into the feild but I supose you would have to go if you was ordered but I cant

---

4. Horatio Seymour was a Democrat who opposed many of the Lincoln administration's policies,
especially the Emancipation Proclamation. Seymour was elected governor of New York in 1862.

5. Fort McHenry in Baltimore, Md.

think you will have to go   it would take all my hope away if I should hear that you had got to take the feild but I must close now   so good by until next time

from your loveing wife
Mattie Blanchard

Back River, near New Orleans, Louisiana
March 22, 1863

Dearest Wife

it is with pleasure that I seat myself to write to you agan   it is a very beautiful sabath morn and I should like very much to spend it with you   I think it would pass very pleasently but as we are seprated from each other I find that I pass a great many pleasent moments in conversing with you with my pen   we talk of moving our camp over the other side of the Brige as soon as it gets warm enough we shall go into tents   it will be a more healthy location   March has been the coldest Month we have had this winter but to day it seems as though we were goin to have fine wether   we have got a good place here and I hope we shall stay here the rest of our time   the news have been very favorable the last week   it seems as though the war was drawing to a close   the elections in the free states will almost decide it   I wish a portion of one army could be at hom and shoot the traitors there the coperheaded peace party are doing all they can to encourage the rebels and to thwart the designs of the Adminstration[6]   why do the union men allow them to go on with their work   they are puting the swords [in our backs] while the rebels are shooting us in front   could they hear the bitter curses and threats they would flee before their rath   if they still persist and go on with trea-son it will not be safe for them to show their faces when the union patriots get back it is an insult to us our familes and our country that will never be forgoten there are a great meny democrats in the army but they almost disspise the name now they have come out here to fight for their libertes and the union with all its free instutions   and those mean unprincibeld villians are trying to murder us by electing rank rebels to fill places of trust and honnor   I hope ther is men enough left to defeat them   if they would onely go into the rebel ranks we should know where to find them   there is a reconing day coming wo be unto them   I went up to Haver de Grace I saw a good meny that I was aquainted with   J Adams is well and ruged and thinks he shall go home in about 3 months   he says his family is well   I had a very good visit there but should rather be stationed here than up there   I could not get eny picture taken   I shall have to wait until after they pay off then I can go to the city as they are goin to let them all go then and I shall look out for a chance

6. Those Democrats who wanted to end the war by coming to terms with the Confederacy were called copperheads.

Foster, Connecticut
March 26, 1863

Dearest and best of husbands it is with great pleasure that I take my pen again to write to you and let you know we are both well as usual and hope this will find you the same   there is not much news to write about   I suppose you get as much war news as I do   I feel very much interested in the spring elections the democrats in this state have not decided upon who they will run for Govenor yet and the town meeting is next Wednesday   I am affraid Gove Buckingham will loose his place[7]   I think they had ought to let the soldiers wives vote while they are gone dont you   old Sol Bennet is as big a traitor as any south and there is a great many more of the same stamp around here   they take the Hartford times and they get over to the store and have a glorious time over the news if it is in favor of the south   they had ought to be shot I hope their will be a time when they will have to be punished for treason   they had ought to be now when we have sent our best men off and have nothing but a set of blacklegs left   they had ought to be made to know their place   I dont think much of Gen Banks movements at New Orlens do you   he is most to choice of the negro and favors the slaveholder to much to suite me[8]   I dont know as I understand what I read   I do often wish when I am reading that you could explain it out to me just as you used to   I am heartily tired of this war and would be glad to hear that it was near the end but think we shall have to waite a spell for the joyful sound   I dont know what you thought of my letters that I wrote when I was up to Daysville and I hardly know myself what I wrote   I had just heard that you played cards and you cannot tell nor immagine how I felt about it   it come upon me so sudden I was not thinking of such a thing did not know as you used cards at all and was thinking of the same man that went away and hopeing he would return the same and I still hope so and dont think I shall be disapointed   cards can do you no good and pray dont use them any more for the sake of yourself and for your friends   there has been many a young man ruined by beginning to play for amusement   they are very enticeing   I know that and when a man is alone he gets lonesome and does that which he ought not to do   you have taken lessons from a father and a brother what a thing it is for a parent to set such an example for his children   you are a father now and dont bring disgrace upon your childs head   I dont want you should feel hard towards me for what I have wrote for I mean well and want you should express your feelings about it   I and Addie are all alone this evening   the rest of the family have gone down to Geo Woods to meeting   Geo and his wife have experienced religion and are going to be baptised   melvin Foster is going to work for Geo this year and is going to move up there   Fosters says he used to know you when you

7. The incumbent Republican governor, William Alfred Buckingham.
8. In December 1862 President Lincoln replaced Gen. Benjamin Butler with Gen. Nathaniel P. Banks as commander of the Union forces occupying New Orleans. Whereas Butler had ruled with an iron fist, Banks was more conciliatory in his handling of the Southern inhabitants of the city.

lived to the Artic   he told Charles about you and he and [*illegible*] & Charls Leathrup going to providence once and driveing by some fellows   I suppose you know all about it   I canot write much more to night as it is nine oclock I dont think I shall write only once a week because I cannot get them to the office Charles is going out to work and father will have all his work to do alone so I shall have to depend upon the Hartford times   they get them regular every saturday good night with a kiss from Mattie

Connecticut Historical Society, Hartford, Letters of Mattie and Caleb Blanchard, Caleb Blanch-ard Letters.

Dr. Robert Hubbard, surgeon with the Seventeenth Connecticut Volunteer Regiment, communicates his fear that people on the Northern home front might elect officials who oppose the war in this letter to his wife. Hubbard expresses the opinion that women on the home front must use their influence to dissuade men from voting for such candidates.

Brooks Station, Virginia
February 25, 1863

My darling Wife

I improve the opportunity of writing a word by Lieut. Gray who leaves to-morrow morning for home. I only wish I could avail myself of the Irishman's privilege & bring the "lether meself" for I do so wish to see you all very much. I think Dr. Mc is becoming more contented and am of opinion that if he could see his folks at home and talk with them he could persuade them to let him remain unmolested. He would with the experience he has had with the duties of his office prove more useful to me than a new assistant provided he was contented. If I am convinced that he will make a sincere effort to stay I shall be inclined to defer my vacation and recommend him for a leave of 10 days to go home. This I think will be sufficiently magnanimous on my part as it will meantime throw a great deal of labor on my shoulders as Gregory is still at Dumfries & I should have the entire care of the Regt. and the Brigade business beside. However I do not mind that as I am very well indeed and ten days passes very quickly I find.

I am disappointed to-night in not getting a letter from home for I am confident that there was one in the mail. It was brought into camp this evening but the Chaplain & Col were both absent and not finding anyone readily to receipt for it he took it back to Brigade Head Qrs. Now was not that provoking? However we shall receive it in the morning. We shall move into our new *house* to-morrow I think and it will make us a very comfortable domicile indeed.

I hope the people of Connecticut have not so far degenerated as to allow that arch traitor Thos. Seymour to be elected Governor of the State.[9] It would be a

9. Thomas Seymour was a Democrat running for governor on a peace ticket.

disgrace that would go far to reconcile me and in fact nearly all her sons who are now fighting her battles to a voluntary exile from her borders. We cannot yet believe that she has fallen so low as to commit the care of 20,000 loyal sons now in the field to the tender mercies of a man who avows himself openly, & sincerely I doubt not, in favor of any and every means of crippling them in their honest & patriotic endeavors. Should such be the result of the coming election it would be a just retribution for the Union Armies now in the field to fall back into the free states, removing thereto the theatre of war & let them see & realize the infernal spirit that animates the fiends now in arms against the most just & liberal constitution ever bequeathed to an undeserving people—undeserving if such should prove to be the guardianship of their heritage. The rebels will doubtless use the willing tools thus placed in their hands as did England the traitor Arnold[10] & then spurn them in similar manner from their presence. God forbid that I should ever witness as humiliating a spectacle. No father could have exercised toward his children more tenderness and self-denying spirit than has Governor Buckingham towards our soldiers in the field & I pity the cowardly hearts of those who now behind their backs and in their hour of secret trial deliberately betray him & them should they meet face to face.

You have & can have no idea of the feeling that the bare possibility of the election of such a man has upon the soldiers here. It is not that a professed democrat is likely to be elected; for policies we care nothing for we hail every man as a friend who extends to us a helping han[d] whatever his political antecedents or associations and consider not more our enemies those who are in armed rebellion in front than those who are plotting treason & trying to execute it behind our backs. In accordance with military principles the enemies in the rear require our first attention. But I did not intend to say a word about political matters and only a few about anything to-night but you see I have almost unconciously been drawn into this strain. I know ladies are not usually interested in such matters but the time has come when they as well as the sterner sex must put a shoulder to the wheel. They must frown upon such tendencies as are now being exhibited & if that is not sufficient spit upon those who manifest them if indeed they are worthy to be spit upon by their respectable female acquaintances.

Yale University Library, New Haven, Manuscripts and Archives, Civil War Manuscripts Collection, Letters of Robert Hubbard.

Robert Hale Kellogg of Company A, Sixteenth Regiment, Connecticut Volunteers, wrote this letter to his father and described how the Lincoln administration was attempting to ensure the election of a Republican governor in the state of Connecticut.

10. Revolutionary War traitor Benedict Arnold.

Plymouth, North Carolina
Mar. 18, 1863

Dear Father,

March 18th while we were in New Berne, I recieved a very beautiful and good letter from Mrs Hawes of Hartford wife of Rev. Joel Hawes. I send it to you for safe keeping as I prize it very highly. I answered her letter at once and expect an answer soon. I think such a correspondent worth having.

I hear nothing from my West Point reccommendation, and almost fear it will amount to nothing but even if it does not, I am more than repaid by knowing that my Col. could give so good an opinion of me. and I *know* that there is further promotion in store for me, and that before long for *your* sake & *mother's* sake I am glad of this but for my own part I don't care a great deal for it. I sometimes think though that it would be rather gratifying to meet a certain young lady I was formerly acquainted with on a standing nearer equality, than when we parted, but still I am not sure but this is an unworthy and wrong desire.

Friday Evening

I didn't finish and mail this letter yesterday, and I am now glad of it, for last night witnessed a most remarkable occurrence, about which I must write a little. About 9 o'clk last evening a large list of names sent from the *War Department* came to the Regiment, and orders were given for these individuals to get ready *immediately* to go on board the transport which was in readiness at the dock, and in a very short time the Lieut. Colonel, Major, Adjutant, three Captains, & several Leiutenants with 94 enlisted men, left Plymouth on the steamer "Col. Rucker" for where?—*Connecticut,* and *to vote for Gov. Buckingham*—Now Father is this *right?* I admire & respect Gov. B. but I believe I would almost rather see him defeated than to see him elected in a foul way. but I have forgotten to mention the very important fact that these men with hardly an exception, were *Republicans* & men who will vote for Gov. B.[11] I think, to say the least, this is a very bad precedent, for our party may not be *always* in power, and if the opposition *should* be successful we cannot consistently blame them for following our example. Another noticeable fact is, that our men, went *fully armed and equipped.* I fear that our Nation is rapidly drifting toward a *military despotism.* This abuse of arbitrary power in a free land & people will work incalculable mischief. When I view the corruption and wickedness in the country I tremble for our future. it is not the South alone that has sinned, but the whole Nation, and all ought to thank God that he has not destroyed us, but instead blessed us with victory after victory. When will the end come? But I know it is wrong to be impatient or to distrust God's power at all,

---

11. In Connecticut's gubernatorial election Thomas Seymour, a Democrat who advocated coming to terms with the Confederacy to end the war, challenged the incumbent governor, W. A. Buckingham, a Republican and staunch supporter of the war effort. The race was very close, and the tactics of the Lincoln administration that Kellogg describes played an important part in securing a victory for Buckingham.

and I do try to look forward to "the good time coming." It is with joy that I see revivals of religion springing up all over the land, and I begin to believe that this will exert a greater power in bringing the war to a close than anything else, for the people need to be aroused from their slumbers and made to turn from their sins, as individuals & as a nation, and the Heavenly Spirit is falling not only in the north, but in the South particularly in the Southern *Army.* We have strong reasons for hope, I think. I wish I could *talk* with you Father, and I would like to see you & mother very much, as I hope I shall if I am alive next Thanksgiving. . . . Write very soon after the reception of this, and oblige

Your aff. son

Rob Kellogg

P.S. I rec'd a "Berkshire Courier" the other evening from Mother, & thank her very much for it. I like to recieve papers very much. Address as formerly Plymouth N.C. via Fortress Monroe.

Connecticut Historical Society, Hartford, Letters of Robert Hale Kellogg, MS 68013.

In this letter to her brother Henry P. Fowler, Adelaide Fowler describes reactions to the draft among Massachusetts residents.

Davnersport, Massachusetts

July 1863

Dear Brother,

It will soon be dark but I am going to write a little this evening and tomorrow will finish the letter. We have had remarkable stormy weather of late, but to night the sky is clear and the prospect is good for a short season of pleasant weather. I dont think there is any news to write unless it is that Clarence has got home; he graduated week before last, is well, and has two places in view where he can preach as a candidate one is Charlton the other I do not know. It is not impossible but that he may be drafted, he was enrolled in Canton; you have no doubt heard of the riot in New York. Isnt it dreadful! It is now quelled or soon will, as there is a strong military force in that city. Last week Tuesday there was considerable disturbances in Boston quite a mob gathered in the streets and some depridations were committed and a few lives were lost.[12] But the people of Boston anticipated some resistance to the draft and were in a measure prepared for it. I went to Boston last Wednesday with Clara Dr Boris and Ellen, and although the city was

---

12. Congress passed a conscription act in March 1863 which allowed draftees to avoid service by hiring a substitute or paying $300. Draft officers began drawing names on July 11, 1863, in New York City. On July 13 many residents of the city who opposed the law on the grounds that it favored the rich began to riot. The riot lasted until July 17, ending only when federal troops arrived to enforce the peace. Boston also experienced a riot in response to the draft, but as Fowler explains, authorities in Boston were well prepared for any disturbances.

as quiet as usual yet you could see that great preperations were being made to punish the rioters the ensuing evening should there be any disturbance. The second Cavalry Regiment now recruiting were arming and equiping themselves for duty and in one of the streets I saw about thirty horses or more all saddled and bridelled and quite often you would see Artilerymen in squads of two or three patrolling the streets they were ordered from the Forts. Also two or three of the returned Regiments were ordered out. But the mob finding themselves to weak for the military soon dispersed. I enjoyed myself very much although I did not have a chance to go around much because Ellen could not walk. Clara went to have their Photographs taken and did not want to go alone so she wanted me to go with her. It is growing so dark that I cannot see to write more. *good night.*

Monday Afternoon

We were quite disappointed at the nonarrival of your letter this morning, because we have been accustomed to receive them so regularly. I dont remember whether I wrote you that Frank and Fairfield Gray were drafted, they are but their names were not in the Mercury[13] it was a mistake I suppose there are several in the list—Joseph Fowles is written Towles I believe. I dont know who of the drafted men are going from this way it is about time for them to report themselves. My oppinion is that there will be a precious few who will go. I have heard that Benjamin Porter was going but I dont know how true the report is. The draft comes pretty hard for the poor folks that cant pay the three hundred dollars and dont want to go but i think that if the Government had drafted when it was first talked about and not fooled the people so many times there would be less trouble I am glad that the draft has taken place only it had ought to before now for one man ought to go as well as another. Now it is high time for people to show their patriotism if they have any; of course there are some cases when there has been two or three drafted from one family that are hard but the majority are wise dispensations of Providence. Every man ought to feel willing to do something for this war and I wish it was so. A great many persons think that spending their breath in useless word is all that *they* ought to do and leave the work for others to do you ask them who and they say negroes. The draft has brought a few of such persons out, they must send thier sons or sacrifice three hundred dollars (not half enough) and this is the reason why I think the draft is doing good. . . .

I will close now   best wishes for your welfare

from Addie

Peabody Essex Museum, Salem, Mass., Letters of Adelaide, Sally, and Henry P. Fowler, Fowler Family Manuscripts.

13. The *Mercury* was a local newspaper the Fowler family was sending to Henry.

In this letter Lieutenant Colonel Lyman, formerly of the Twenty-seventh Massachusetts Volunteer Regiment, writes to a friend still with the regiment. Lieutenant Lyman describes the reactions of the citizens of Northampton, Massachusetts, to the news of the draft riot in New York City.

Northampton, Massachusetts
July 23, 1863
Lieut. Wright,

Dear sir,

I have been waiting in anxious expectation of receiving a letter from you ever since my arrival home. I will wait no longer, but see if I cannot tempt you to write by writing you first. I have written to most of the Captains but only Knight, Moore & Walker have replied. I shall write to the Lieuts. as I get time, those who choose can have a correspondence with me, judging from what I hear from their of late I have not got so many friends among the officer as I had reason to suppose. I am very sorry it is so. I have the satisfaction of feeling that I done the best I knew how for the Regt. while connected with it. Every power of my mind & body was devoted to its interests. I never allowed personal feelings or interests to come between me & what I considered the best good of the Regt. my conscience is clear in the matter & if the officers do not appreciate my labors for them & are willing to hear & believe the false stories circulated by my known enemies calculated to injure me I cannot help it. I am out of the way & cannot defend myself & must submit. I will do so as gracefully as I can.

News of all kinds has been very exciting for two weeks past you will get the most of it through the papers, but the little items which only concern the locality in which they arise you will not know in that way. I wish I could picture to you faithfully the ups & downs or the excitement in this usually quiet town, you would be pleased to witness it I know. the excitement in relation to war news is about the same every where. the most exciting war rumors we get just at night either thru the Hartford Evening papers or the Telegraph. some have been perfectly fearful both for & against us. but *the* excitement of the week has been the draft. The riot at New York frightened every body & all said we should have one here on the night of the draft. the old grannies run up & down the street saying there was surely going to be trouble doing just the thing to creat a disturbance. On Monday morning it was at its hight. news came that Cheapside bridge had been burnt, several buildings in Greenfield burnt or destroyed & the most extravagant rumors you can imagine all (the grannies) were anxious to know if the Lyman Guard[14] was ready for assisting in quelling this horrible riot which was to

14. The town of Northampton had organized a home guard to handle wartime emergencies. It is unclear whether this home guard was actually called the Lyman Guard, or if Lyman was using this term humorously, in reference to Northampton inhabitants' request for his advice.

be. you may believe I enjoyed it. I of course *"having seen service!"* was consulted &
was just wicked enough to rather help it on that is, say something which would
be likely to increase their fears. Imagine me sitting on the Court House steps
which you know over looks the whole of "Shop Row" & watching the movements of the different squads. Here is Sam Mills Sam Lyman Dr. Fisk & one or
two men of that style in one. Here Dick, Joe Kellog & some of the younger
grannies in another, Starkweather of the "honorable guard" was going from one
to the other assuring them every thing was "all right" & not to be frightend, yes
say they "but so & so's Irish girl says that something terrible was going to happen
& we must be prepared" a paper was started pledging the signers to meet at a
given signal the ringing of the Court House Bell (don't tell any body what the
signal was!) & fall in with the remains of the Lyman Guard & fight to the death.
the brave fellows, I would like to have seen said list, but would have been better
pleased to have had just a little trouble, just enough to have warranted the striking of that Bell, how I should have laughed I know to see the imortal braves in
line. by the way it was arranged that I was to lead them, how I did ache to have
something turn up & see their knees tremble. Some I recon would not have heard
the signal. I tell you it was fun & I enjoyed it. They breathed freer when it was
known that the Lyman Guards muskets had been hid away out of the reach of
the mob & 600 cartridges ready made. the muskets were carried away by three of
us one dark night & hid in a room not a thousand yards from this building. the
cartridges men made in my office *on Sunday,* think of that & you will not longer
doubt that we were a frightend people. Capt. Childs Henry, Joe Williams Charly
Lavake & myself were the wicked ones on that occasion. well the muskets & cartridges remain where they were put & nary a Poor Paddy has felt the effects of
them, all now is as quiet as ever. the R.R. Co. watch their bridges yet every night.
my *pistols* go, so I think they (the bridges or pistol, as you please) are safe   a secret
police patrol the town every night & I feel perfectly safe. I occasionally hear a
picket fire, but that don't disturb me in my quiet home.

   News about town is very dull, no resistance will be made by the conscripts to
reporting when ordered in this section comparativly but few will go to war, either
be exempted for disability or pay their mony. it comes rather yes *very* hard on
some. young married men with a small family perhaps just starting in business
cannot raise $300 only by borrowing taking all they can earn perhaps for a year.
think of Lee & Porter Tinnes as a sample *both* drafted. the two Clapp boys in
South St. Ed & Martin, & lots men of such cases. but they must go, this wicked
rebellion must be put down & I believe it will be. the blows are falling upon it
thick & fast. we are all sorry Gen. Mead did not attack Lee on the North side of
the Potomac the 2 time, but its of no use to cry for spilt milk, up & at them
again.[15]

---

15. After defeating Lee at Gettysburg, Union general George Meade was unable to attack Lee
again before the Confederate troops crossed the Potomac River into Virginia.

You have had some change in your Dept. since I left all for the better I hope, but some part of it I am afraid will not work so well. I have just learned that you are on another expedition it is so strange to me that the 27th could not be treated like other Rgt. in the Dept, what other Regt. ever, while doing Guard duty, in the city, was called upon to go on expeditions? you must grin & bear it I suppose. I am glad I am out of it & wish any others who want to be was. I have no desire to return to the service. I have had many flattering offers & could get most any position I might ask for within reason. I should never expect to be so pleasantly situated in any other Regt. as I thought I was in the 27. how nice it is they did not find out what a bad man I was while with them, I should have felt very uncomfortable. I never wish to be treated better by any body of men than I was by the officers of the 27 so kind & considerate of my feelings, so ready to obey, even anticipate, my wishes, as they were. I never shall forget. I cannot believe the men, officers & non coms[16] of the Regt. are so ready to turn upon me. perhaps I am not correctly informed of the real feeling which exists among the officers. I hope I am not.

Your friends in town so far as I know are as usual. Georges wife I see riding out occasionaly   she is looking bad.   Ansels wife looks as tough as ever. the young ladies of your acquantance are anxiously & patiently waiting for your return hoping that their present prospect of being old maids will soon after cease. the best of them remain stedfast occasionally one of them flies off marrying some "Home Guard" fellow or, one who can not even join a Home Guard. there are many very pretty girls here now, lots that I don't know, working in some of the Factories I presume. then the younger set have grown to be young ladies   it is supprising how fast they are becoming women   think of it. I have one as big as any body larger than her mother. she will be smitting some body very soon. Bill Turner is really engaged to Martha Clary, several other reputed engagements, hurry up the war & come home & make your selection—well another sheet of nonsense & I won't bother you any more, but will stop short, make my regards to all who enquire for me. I shall be very much pleased to hear from you, write fully in regard to the Regt. & oblige Fred, your friend

L Lyman

Historic Northampton, Northampton, Mass., Letters of L. Lyman, W. A. Walker Papers, A. L. 18.298.

Mary Parmelee of New Haven, Connecticut, wrote this letter to her brother Henry Spencer Parmelee, who served with the First Regiment, Connecticut Cavalry. She describes the effects that the New York City draft riot had on New Haven.

16. Noncommissioned officers.

New Haven, Connecticut
July 26, 1863

My Dear Brother

Yours of the 20th reached me yesterday. Whether it has lain in the office I don't know—I have been away. . . .

It was a season of trouble all around, the New York riot coming in with its terrors & forebodings. . . . We felt apprehensions of such trouble here. The Draft on Monday passed off very well—almost every available young man in this region being drafted. . . . That day the riot commenced in New York & as the draft here was to be continued on Saturday we watched the state of affairs in the great city with intense anxiety. Had the riot there continued until the renewal of the draft here we should have had trouble, for there was no lack of disposition. There was an exchange of thieves & vagabonds some going to New York to assist in the ready-made tumult, others coming here to stir up ones. The governor & city made quiet preparations for trouble, the New York mob was quelled & on Saturday the draft was concluded without turbulent excitement. . . . we had a moonlight ride to Killingworth. . . . We stopped at the hotel where father & I were quartered when we visited Killingworth two years ago. . . . The old town is a hard place;—ignorance & rum show themselves in half cultivated or entirely neglected lands, in old, weather-beaten houses & in the uncouth dress & appearance of the people. They are all rebels, calling "old Lincoln" a tyrant, opposed to the draft, some openly asserting their preference for Jeff. Davis' sway. I only wish they were subject to it—every soul of them! Of all who there talked with father upon the state of the country but one heartily sympathized with him. Such as they support & are politically educated by the Register.[17] . . .

With love yours,
Mary

Yale University Library, New Haven, Manuscripts and Archives, Civil War Manuscripts Collection, Letters of Mary Parmelee.

Mary B. Burnham wrote this letter to her son Lewis who was serving in the Union army. The Burnhams (including Lewis) were confused as to when his term of service was up, and Mrs. Burnham expresses frustration with the government for not giving the soldiers this information.

Essex, Massachusetts
Aug 2, 1863

My Dear Son,

We received a letter from you last evening, dated July 17th. We were very sorry to learn, that you were still unwell at Baton Rouge but hope it is nothing serious.

17. The *Register* was a Connecticut newspaper that opposed the Lincoln administration and the war.

I think, could you but learn that you were to start for home, in a day or two, it would revive your spirits at once. It would be better than medicine.

Still I advise you to keep up your courage, if you possibly can, for your own good, for fear it will injure your health, dwelling on it so much. Although I get discouraged myself, sometimes, I feel as if I could not bear it, this continual suspense, thinking that the next letter, will tell us, when you are to start for home. but the next letter comes, & still you do not know, any more about it than you did before, but I still have hopes that the next letter will tell us. If they keep you there till the 15th of Aug. it will be but two weeks more but I hope ere this letter reaches you, that you will be on your way home. But I thought it best, to continue to write you, once a week, as we had done, to keep your courage up, for fear you might be kept longer. We thought as you did, that after Port Hudson fell, you would be released. I think now, that Government does wrong, to keep the men, after their time has expired, for which, they were enlisted. They wont get near so many men to reenlist, as they would if they let them go, when their time is out. That is, they cannot get them, of their own free will, unless they are compelled to go, as is the case, with drafted men, if they cannot pay 300 dollars or get a substitute. So that it comes hard, on a poor man. And I would ask, what is a man good for, who is compelled to do any thing, compared to one, that does it of his own free will?

I am very glad you was not in the fight near Fort Donaldson,[18] for, as you say, you might have been taken prisoner and in that case, it might have been a long time, before you could have got home. And then, we should all have been so disappointed for we are all looking forward to a happy reunion. We have got some strawberries, & blackberries preserved for you, when you get home which I sincerely hope will be soon. Isabelle Florence & myself went to the Falls, after blueberries, last Thursday afternoon. We filled our baskets, about 9 qts. I suppose in all. I wish you could be here to have some.

Father is still here & I think will be here when you arrive, he is as well as common. We have had a great deal of wet & foggy weather, the past month, so have not got through english haying yet. Lucy is well.

Your affectionate Mother
Mary B. Burnham

Sunday   it is very hot here to day. Next wednesday the 5th will be your Birthday, 19 years old. As you was sworn in to the United States service the 19th of September, you should have been released the 19th of June & not kept till 15th of August.[19] There is nothing right, nor just, about it. For if a man enlisted for a certain time, he would never know when that time was out but Government could keep him forever.

Peabody Essex Museum, Salem, Mass., Letters of Mary Burnham, MS 0.308.

18. This is perhaps a reference to fighting near Donaldsonville, La., in July 1863.
19. Lewis Burnham had enlisted for a nine-month period of service.

On October 10, 1864, approximately twenty-two Confederate soldiers who claimed to be civilians interested in hunting began arriving in St. Albans, Vermont, in small groups. On October 19 these soldiers robbed three St. Albans banks. While some of the soldiers took money from the banks, others patrolled the streets of the town, preventing the citizens in the immediate vicinity from alerting any others. After completing the robberies, the raiders stole horses and headed for Canada. A posse of St. Albans citizens chased the raiders into Canada, managed to arrest thirteen of them, and turned them over to the Canadian authorities. After a lengthy trial the Canadian court allowed the raiders to go free, claiming it had no jurisdiction over the matter. The raiders brought approximately $175,000 in U.S. currency to Richmond. However, the primary purpose of the raid was not financial but to force the U.S. government to withdraw troops from the war theater and place them at points Northerners believed might be vulnerable to other raids. Anne Eliza Brainerd Smith, wife of Vermont governor John Henry Smith and resident of St. Albans, describes her personal experience during the Confederate invasion in this letter to her husband, who was away from home.

St. Albans, Vermont
October 20, 1864

My dearest—

We have had (to use Cousin Joe's forcible expression) a "Raid from hell!" For about half an hour yesterday afternoon I thought that we should be burnt up, and robbed. William[20] gone to B[urlington] and Ed, Mr. Inglis and Joe & Eddie up to Warner's with the apples[21]—but I hope you don't imagine I was one moment frightened, though the noise of guns, the agitated looks of the rushing men, and our powerless condition were startling enough. I ordered the house shut and locked, hunting myself for weapons, but nothing could be found but your carved pistol *empty*. However, with that in my hand I stood in the door feeling *enraged* but *defiant*. I[n] a few minutes Stewart[22]—pale enough, galloped up, and asked for arms, I gave the pistol, and he told me they[23] had turned north, but were expected back on the Sheldon road.

A number of pickets ran on to Aldis hill, where they could see, and blazed away every few minutes to let the raiders know they were in readiness. After Stewart left, we found the rifle, and I started down street to give it to somebody, but in a moment I met a man who said he was after it. We then found another pistol, and in a few moments some men rushed in to the back yard for horses. I

---

20. The Smith family's coachman.
21. Eddie was the Smiths' son Edward C. Smith. Ed, Mr. Inglis, and Joe were probably neighbors. Warner's was a cider mill.
22. Stewart Stranahan, Mrs. Smith's brother-in-law.
23. The Confederate raiders.

gave Mr. Beeman [from the] bar factory, Major. Ed who had just got in from the cider mill (I feared the horses and all were captured) took Kitty, and two others took Nellie and Diamond.[24]. . .

I worried very much about you, thought you would suffer great anxiety on our account, but my dear, never after this, think that I shall be frightened or that I cannot do all that my best judgement dictates. That may be worthless, but it will probably be an active exercise. . . .

How foolish and frantic our people have been not to heed your warning.[25] I hope this affair will settle matters at once. Good bye. God give you grace to act wisely in these trying times.

William, when he heard the rumor in B[urlington] groaned, "Oh my God! The horses are gone!!" Our little Ed's spirit was superb. While Julie[26] and some of the rest were crying terribly, he was awfully mad. "What did you let that rifle go for?" says he to me, "It is the only thing in the house that I can use!!"

St. Albans Historical Museum, St. Albans, Vt., Letter of Anne E. B. Smith.

In this letter Sarah A. Gay writes about her sorrow at President Lincoln's assassination to her husband, John O. Gay, who had enlisted in June 1864.

North Hingham, Massachusetts
April 17, 1865

Dear Husband

I guess I will try to write hopeing that I shall be able to finish my letter before I send it   we recived your kind letter yesterday morning and I felt to rejoyise with you over our resent victorys but a few minutes later and how changed all though turned to sadness   it hardly seemed true that our presdent is no more & that he should meet his fatal blow in the theatre how sad   I wish now more than ever to have your year out   it seemes to me as though there would not be much safty around there but as I write this I hear that small voice whisper, I am the protecter, yes, how thankful that there is an over ruling power one that does all things well

I have been to church apart of the day   the flag is up at half mas and the church is draped in black crape every thing looks mournfull and still how much we have to be thankfull for   a little more than three months more and we shall meet if it is his will   I look forward to that day as the happest day of my life but one that one was when I felt that my saviour had [accepted] of me & next when

24. Major, Kitty, Nellie, and Diamond were horses.
25. Governor Smith had been calling for greater vigilance against possible Confederate raids along the Canadian border. Until the raid at St. Albans, Vermonters did not take his concern seriously.
26. Julie was the Smiths' daughter.

you & I were one, may the lord still bless us   we feel as though we had got home
and should injoy ourselfes if you were here or when you got home   the neibours
seem to be very much pleased to see us   I have wrote longer letter than I expecd
to be able to but I must say good day   with my love & babies write soon.

From Sarah A. Gay

Yale University Library, New Haven, Manuscripts and Archives, Civil War Manuscripts Collection,
Letters of Sarah A. Gay.

CHAPTER FIVE

The Personal Sacrifices of War

THIS SELECTION OF letters contains discussions of the personal and family disruptions brought on by the war. Soldiers and their correspondents devote considerable attention to financial matters and economic hardships and note, in particular, the new burdens being assumed by New England women. The writers here also reflect on something more intangible: in their letters of love and devotion, New Englanders express their heartfelt grief and concern for absent loved ones.

John H. Norton of Hartford, Connecticut, wrote this letter to his sister Lissie, in which he details some of the positive effects the war was having on home-front businesses.

Hartford, Connecticut
May 1, 1861

My Dear Sister Lissie,

Your nice long letter was received Sat. noon and sent it to Ellen Monday. I have been intending to write for some time, but I have so much other writing to do, that I do not get time. There has been an Election parade here to day the smallest one I ever saw, rained most of the time Pa & Mrs Norton have been down to Day, all well at home. Pa said that the windows were done for the house he said he should not have got them now, but he ordered them long time ago. I was up home a week ago   Mrs Norton is having a fine parlor. I saw the Furniture, it is *perfect folly* his getting any more, the house is so full now you cant move   There is nothing going on here but "war"   I enlisted in a company and was going but Ellen heard of it and came down on an *Extra Train*   Pa sent a letter to Dear Fay by her not to let me go and I did not know but you would be on by Telegraph. the company was more than full so I stayed at home but I did want to go, it was the *first* company in the state. Geo L. Burham was Cap. but he is now promoted to Leut. Col. and J R. Hawley is now Captain. G. Buckley is in that Co. all of them ware nice fellows. they are in N. Haven, the first & second Reg are ordered to New Haven the third & fourth here. forty Company in all. It look quite warlike here Co.s drilling all the while, there are ten Cos here now, and ten more coming next week. There has not been much Sunday here for the last three weeks   We are getting up the Uniforms at our store. We have got an order from the *state* for *one Thousand* overcoats and are running the Tailors shop night & Day & Sundays

besides. We have sold a great deal of Flannel & Army Cloth. They have got up a
Company in Suffield   Roland Burbank is Cap   willis Pomeroy is first Leut. all
Cigar Makers   Major Hatheway can not go, he is Quarter Master General of Conn.
and is very busy fitting out troops—the Suffield Co. is in the fourth Reg. We sold
them about 400 yds Flannel Monday. One Sunday the News offices isued three
editions of Extras, and boys were selling them all day. They cheer the Ministers in
the pulpit here—Eugene was up last Saturday said he had been to Charleston and
had just come from there, he has enlisted in the ninth Reg. New York. Horace has
failed and assigned over. It is very hard times out west, the exchange is so high
that our Customers wont pay. I saw them Troops from Boston that were attacked
in Baltimore[1] shook hands with a great many of them, they parted through here
about 2 oclock one morning there were two thousand down to the depot to see
them—but I must close, give my love to *all* excuse this, & write again

Your Afec Brother
John H. Norton

Connecticut Historical Society, Hartford, Letters of John H. Norton, MS 6504D.

---

*In this letter to her son Henry, A. C. Hinckley describes how some women reacted to the
enlistment of their male relatives.*

Boston, Massachusetts
May 21, 1861

My dear Henry
    Your letter dated April 21st reached me only a few days ago at the same time
came one to your father datd 30th, we were beginning to get a little impatient to
hear from you, for in these *uncommon* times one cannot help being anxious about
every thing & every body. I cannot say that I know much, for the people, whom
God pleases to take to himself, for our future seems very black & dubious. The
blissful days of peace & prosperity have passed & the only cry now is how can I
draw in my expenses & in fact how can we live if this state of affairs continues?
. . . War times in Northampton[2] are very gloomy & I think your father rejoices
that he has not got to encounter the gloomy faces there. They have sent off a regiment & have formed a *home guard,* as there is no police to protect the town &
rowdies are very numerous. You will laugh when I tell you, that Mr. Sam Welles
Dr Barrett & such like are *drilling* like young boys. I think it is almost worth a

---

    1. A great deal of prosecession sentiment existed in Baltimore, the capital of Maryland, a slave
state which remained in the Union. On April 19, 1861, a mob attacked the Sixth Massachusetts
Regiment as it passed through Baltimore on its way to Washington, D.C., in response to President
Lincoln's call for troops.
    2. Hinckley's husband, Samuel, owned two silk mills, one in Boston and the other in North-
ampton. The family owned a second home in Northampton, where they usually spent the summer.

journey to see them. We have distress & suffering on every side here. Mothers & sisters haunting the neighboring towns & the State & common for their sons & brothers who have enlisted, by stealth & gone away or are preparing; I am so glad that you are not here for I am afraid you would catch the fever. Oh my dear Henry how I do long to see you, the year is almost round again when we said Goodbye & I feel as if I could not wait for another one. . . .

My blessing goes with this.

A.C. H[inckley]

Historic Northampton, Northampton, Mass., Letters of Samuel L. and A. C. Hinckley, Henry Rose Hinckley Papers.

Henry W. Baker enlisted in the Seventh Regiment, New Hampshire Volunteers, in October 1861. In this letter to his sister, who lived in Worcester, Baker explains the arrangements he was making to provide for his mother and his chairmaking business while he was away.

Boscawen, New Hampshire
Oct 12, 1861

Dear Sister

It has been a long time since either of us have written but I do not believe that we have been forgetful of each other. *My* friends are not so numerous as to allow of *one* being droped from this list, least of all a Sister from whom I have received so many proofs of regard.

I had a letter a short time since, from Annie, but she said nothing of you or Mary. I conclude that you have been as well as usual or she would have spoken of it. How are Mary and family? Does the Drs business increase?

You may have heard before this letter that I expect to go into the army soon. I had a promise of a place in the 4th Regiment but lost it by no fault of my own. I am now confident of a Lieutenancy in Gen Abbotts regiment in a company to be commanded by J.S. Durgin of Fisherville. We shall probably go into camp some time next week. The only uncertainty is in this, that I may fail to raise my share of men. I have now but half my number but expect to have the others this week.[3]

This is no hasty move of mine. I have thought of it all summer and weighed as well as I was able, the arguments for and against. My chief objection was in leaving mother. This I would not do unless she can be as well cared for as if I were here. I have now got this provided for. Ted & Leana will move here and take charge of things generally, which will be satisfactory to all parties. Mr. Blodgett will make what chairs they can sell, he working by the piece. I have a large lot of turned stock on hand, so that but little more will be needed while I shall be gone. I shall make Ted my cashier and send home, from time to time my pay. Whenever

3. Commissioned officers were expected to enlist a certain number of recruits before they could officially assume their positions.

you want your interest, notify him and I will give him directions about it. I shall leave my affairs in such condition as to be settled by others satisfactorily in case I fail to come back again. Of course I understand the liabilities of war, but I *expect* to come home to tell of adventures "by flood & field," but if I do not escape so fortunately I shall leave enough to provide for all who have claims on me and there are less to mourn for me than most men leave behind   I go because I feel it to be a *duty*. If I should stay safely at home, I *know* that in after years, I shall feel asshamed to confess that I left others to do *my* duty for me. I hope to hear from you soon and let me know what you think of this matter. I will write again before going.

Yours Truly,
H.W. Baker

American Antiquarian Society, Worcester, Mass., Letters of Henry W. Baker, Civil War Papers Collection.

This letter is from Maria H. Berry of Lynn, Massachusetts, to her son Abram Hun Berry, who enlisted as first sergeant in Company I, Eighth Regiment, Massachusetts Volunteer Infantry, in August 1862. Berry was commissioned second lieutenant in the beginning of May 1863 and had risen to first lieutenant by the end of the month. He was commissioned adjutant for the Eighth Regiment in August 1864.

Lynn, Massachusetts
January 12, 1862

My Dear Son Hun

How very strange it seems to me that you are in the Reble country not as a Reble but a Volenteer   how it can be possible that you can love military life so dearly and still stranger that now wish to be in battle   I hope the Lord may prevent it is my Daily Prayer. I happened to read a lecture the other day by Henry Ward Beecher and in it he says A Mother that has Brought up six sons is able to Legislate   now I am one of those that had done that same thing and if goverment will only accept me I will turn the affairs of state the right way that is what *I* would call *right.* . . . it does seem that neither General Burnside nor government know how to act or what to do   this Rebellion ought to have been put down long before this time   why God permits it to continue so long I cannot tell   there is something yet behind the scenes that we do not see   that awful Battle of Fredricksburgh seems an inhuman Butchery just so at Vicksburgh but enough of that   only if you are called to go do your duty my Darling son and may he that never sleepeth nor slumbereth guard and protect you and your friends cover your head on the day of battle and shield you in his Everlasting Arms and Bring you in safty to us again. your last letter to me was just after Christmas do write often. . . . Now Hunnie you have promised me never to smoke or touch or taste ardent spirits of any kind and if you forget me you forget your God there are so many Temptations of every kind that you are exposed to. . . . Anna is at New York enjoying herself so she says but oh how lonely at home but I will not say any thing about it. . . . our little Baby grow finely she is one of the lovelys of the earth if you could see her her quiet cuning little ways you would almost eat her up. give my respects to all that ask about me. now my Darling with a kiss I will say Farewell

from Mother

Lynn Historical Society, Lynn, Mass., Letter of Maria H. Berry, Berry Family MS/P100.4.

John Gilbert of Cornish, New Hampshire, served with the Third Regiment, New Hampshire Volunteers. This letter to a family friend reveals the economic difficulties many soldiers' wives faced during their husbands' absence.

Port Royal, Hilton Head, South Carolina
Feb. 4, 1862

Dear Sir

I thought I would write a few lines knowing that you are the only friend to me and my family. I take this privilege In addressing myself to you although I have no right to do so. My family are suffering by all accounts I can hear through the neglect of the select men of the town of Cornish they take the advantage of my wife because I suppose she is a woman they deny her the pay which the State of New Hampshire is bound by law to pay her[4] every town in the State of N.H. pays the Soldiers families their lowest dues whatever in fact the law allows them It appears to me there must be a many ignorant men in the town of Cornish or else they want to cheat my wife out of her rights and what is justly due to her Perhaps they may have the Idea that the money comes out of their own town but it comes out of the State as well as the town. My wife tells me in her last letter that they deal with her as if she was a pauper and on the town which is absolutely wrong, by giving her a little flour once in while and a little wood nows and thens perhaps they think they will get out of it by dealing with her in this kind of manner but I tell you Sir they will have to pay her the 12 Dollars per month which the law specifies she shall have as a soldiers Wife this will be seen to if I get home once again for the town of Cornish shall be answerable for that amount of money. I wish my dear friend if it would lay in your power to help her to get her money that you will do all you can towards it out of kindness to me and compassion to my family.

---

4. The state of New Hampshire had passed a law requiring towns to pay $12 each month to the families of enlisted men during their terms of service.

Dear Sir

Those verses I sent you I hope you have received them but I have not had an answer from you I hope you will write and let me know how they suited you I have sent you some other verses and music which I suppose you have not received yet which when you do get them I hope will suit your sentiments. I am going to send Ellen a letter also to day with my kind respects and best wishes towards you I remain your sincere Friend

J. Gilbert

New Hampshire Historical Society, Concord, Letters of John Gilbert, 1990-001 (m).

In this letter to her son Henry P. Fowler, serving in Company D, Fourteenth Massachusetts Regiment, Sally Fowler voices concern about how army life was affecting his moral character.

Danversport, Massachusetts
Feb. 23 1862

Dear Son

We recieved your letter last evening of which you give an account of the arrest of a great many Soldiers and Officers I was aware that some of the Officers were intemperate as well as the soldiers but did not suppose it were possible they could make such beasts of themselves, I think these two Regiments must be exceptions to all others especially the 14 Regiment, I dare say thier are many Companies that are temperate, or nearly so, what good can arise from drinking Liquor I cannot concieve, I have read considerable in the newspapers about them th[r]owing away Liquor I wish they would throw it all away except for medicines I should think the sight of those persons would disgust any decent person in a company of soldiers I hope all your associates are sober men they all speak of the 14 as being the best Those ring are very pretty Sarah gave one to Cousin Marion they are the right size if you have time to make any more make them largier they are as handsome as coral, Gov ration are very good if you alway fare so well you have nothing to complain of in regard to food which you never have Thier has been great rejoicing here over the late victories,[5] Father wrote a note to send to you in aunt Mariens letter but by some mistake it was forgotten till after it was sealed, Tomorrow you will be 23 year old Last year as well this year thus far have been eventful to every one especially to the troops, if you have time in your next we should like hear about your adventures on the other side of the river Father will write this evening so I will close all send love It is a treat for Sarah to write she enjoy it much she will write   Mother

Peabody Essex Museum, Salem, Mass., Letters of Adelaide, Sally, and Henry P. Fowler, Fowler Family Manuscripts.

---

5. Gen. Ulysses S. Grant had captured Fort Henry and Fort Donelson in Tennessee.

*This letter from Sarah Fales describes how the absence of her son Edmund Fales, serving in
Company L, Ninth Rhode Island Volunteer Regiment, affected work on the family farm.*

Middletown, Rhode Island
May 4, 1862

Edmund

Dear Son I have received your letters three in number and was very glad to
hear from you each time   I have been very anxious to hear of your safe arrival at
Washington   we are all as well as usual, here we have no extra help. Father has
done your part of the work so far the grain land is finished and the corn ground is
allmost ploughed   the troup of lambs are doing nicely except one witch I think
will not live, there have been a great many boys here to hire out since you left but
we do not think they would fill your place very well. Father says he and Tony can
do the boys work, we miss you very much indeed. . . . we received your clothes
from George Shinmorns but the over coat cannot be found, Ward says you asked
him to take it and that was the last he heard of it, Father got your money and has
put 2.25 Dollars in with your other money at the Savings bank Fall River he was
there yesterday   George told him he had recieved a letter from you, but I did not
get mine untill today, I hope you will be comfortabbly settled in the City and get
enough to eat, take good care of your health as you possibly can   sickness is to be
dreaded more than anything els among so many, write my Son as often as you can
you never can know how anxious I am to have letters from you   we cannot tell
anything by the papers you know   they are so contradictory   do not wait for
answers   I will write allways when I can   you know there is not so much to write
about here as there is there, if you should be sick be sure and let us know it and if
we can send you anything that you need   may God bless you and return you safe
and in health to your loving parents again once more, do what you know to be
right at all times and leave the rest

this from your Mother
Sarah E Fale

PS the City have voted to pay $10 a month during service.[6] I suppose Father
will get yours when it is due, excuse all mistakes you know I write so seldom we
all send our love to you Tony included   they have raised a Flag on the swamp
meeting House and had quit[e] a celebration at the time   every boddy seems to
be awake and doing what they can, but I hope there will be less fighting than they
anticipate so good night from Sarah E. Fales

---

6. The city voted to pay $10 each month to the families of enlisted men during their terms of
service.

Dont for get to write often and let us know how you fare   have you got stockings enough and what have you got for shirts

from Mother

---

*Diana Phillips writes about hometown and family news, as well as her anxieties for her hus-
band's safety, in this letter to her husband Marshall, who was serving with the Fifth Maine
Volunteer Regiment.*

North Auburn, Maine
June 10, 1862

Dear husband,

I received a letter from you to night   was very glad to hear from you, I feel
sory your health is so poor, I want you to come home before you get so sick you
cant come   the news comes to night of another battle at Richmond[7]   I have not
seen the paper to night so I dont know the particulars. shall hear tomorow   you
spoke about numbering the letters we send to each other in this month, I think it
will be a good plan, I think I have written three letters to you in this month before
this one. one dated June 1st and one June 3d and one the 8th so I will number this
one the fourth   if you have received those other letters you can number them. I
saw Mr Austin French to night and told him about John French and about the
money, we are all well and want to see you, very much   Abbie is to Mr Lyons yet.
she received a letter from Alfred Brown tonight   he says that one of his brothers
at home is very sick, and is not expected to live so he has got to go home, I have
not seen any of your fathers folks this week, I presume they are well, Sarah is
here yet she and her family are well, Capt Burbank has resigned in Cavilry   Zeb
has been promoted to Capt. to-day has been the first warm day we have had this
month   I have got squashes cucumbers beets beans peas onions corns turnips and
cabbage all up planted on that small peice of ground below the stable   Clara
Walker has promised me some tomatoe plants   I shall send for them as soon as it
is warm enough, I suppose you have it very warm there where you are, the report
is that George French is wounded but how nor when I cant find out, Marshall if
you was at home safe and well it would be all I could ask, I hope to see you soon,
I cant help thinking about your being sick, I am afraid you dont let me know how
sick your are be sure and come home before you are so sick you cant, for I dont
know what I should do if you did not, I hope you was not in the last battle at
Richmond   I shall feel very anxious till I hear from you after the battle   it is

---

7. This is possibly a reference to the battle of Fair Oaks, Va., on May 31, 1862.

twelve o clock in the evening   so good night from your anxious wife anxious for your safe arrival home

Diana Phillips

Maine Historical Society, Portland, Letters of Marshall and Diana Phillips, S-166mb 6/3-6/8.

Edward Klein of Clinton, Massachusetts, served with the Twenty-fifth Regiment, Massachusetts Volunteers. Klein's letter reveals the attitude of some of the early volunteers toward those men who enlisted to receive a bounty. He also expresses some concerns about the family's finances.

Newbern, North Carolina
July 24, 1862

Dear Brother

I take my pen to write you a few lines to let you know how George[8] and I am at this time   we are better than when I wrote that letter to Father. we have been on guard duty since that time and are feeling quite well. . . . do you send the Courant[9] every week if you do I do not get them   I have not got any since the last one in June   you spoke in one of your letters about sending them to me so I thought I would ask you about them as I did not get them   now I should like to have you send them if it is convenient for it is quite a treat to get them and see the news   I want you to let me know who there is in Clinton that it takes 75 dollars to get their patriotism up so that they can enlist but I think that they had better enlist and let the town keep the 75 dols to give to some unfortunate soldier who gets his leg or arm shot off or wounded in some other part of his body but money makes the *mare go* so I suppose I will make money also *to war* but I hope the men will not wait long before they enlist for government wants the men as soon as they can be got   now Parkman I want you to let me know if Father and Mother use the money George and I send home or do they save it for us   if they are saving it and Father is in debt I shall not like it if he does not use it for if they think because we are out her[e] away from the comforts of home and are not having home comforts while here and that they will save our money until we return so that we can have something to buy some luxuries with but I do not want them to do any such thing but I want them to get out of debt if they are in debt and then they can enjoy some comforts which they do not feel like buying now. . . .

I wish you would write if Father gets my check and send your letters to Newbern until you hear from me and I will let you know if we change our camp

8. George Klein, Edward's brother.
9. The *Courant* was probably the local newspaper of Clinton, Mass.

to any other place   But I must close for my paper is about written over
Good Bye

From Edward

Boston Public Library, Rare Books and Manuscripts, Letters of Edward Klein, July 24, 1862, Ms.Am.2150 (1–2).

Levi Perry served as a corporal with the Fourth Maine Volunteer Regiment. In this letter to his mother, Sarah Hall Perry, Perry worries that she will be unable to look after the farm after her only other child enlisted.

In Camp
July 26, 1862

Dear Mother

I will write you a few lines this evening   I received a letter from Chandler[10] this morning   was glad to hear that you was well but I was surprised to learn that he had enlisted   I think he has done wrong for he promised me when I left home that he would stay and take care of things at home   now there is no one to look to things but you   I shal not be contented again untill there is different arrangements made   I suppose he has left home ere this. I think you had better dispose of the young cattle as soon as they require any tending   I suppose while the warm weather lasts they can take care of them selves if not I should advise you to get rid of them at once for you will have hard work   make it as easy as you can   I wish Chan was here now I would give him a small piece of my mind   I was down to the landing a day or two ago and could have shiped on board of a Baltimore schooner and left U.S. in the lurch and I wish I had for I dont think the disgrace would be as bad as it is to have every thing as Chan has done at home at any rate I could stand it better. it may be all for the best but I cant see it in that light   if he has not gone before this reaches you tell him and the rest of them to join an old Regiment if they can do so and I think they can if they have gone to Augusta

All the old Regiments are situated in healthy places and there will be a good chance for them to get used to camp life before they are put into the harder parts of a soldiers life and beside they will learn their places and duty quickere and therefore stand a better chance in battle than they would in a Regiment only partialy drilled   this I know from my experience which is not much I know but I will stop this now.

I am in first rate health but there is considerable sickness in camp   over half of our company is off duty   there is but few of them verry sick and part is playing up to keep clear of work.

---

10. Perry's brother.

Adam Gray died this morning I suppose you remember him he used to lived near us in Rockland   I have nothing more to write at present so I will close   give my love to all the family and friends and accept this from your affectionate son.

Levi

Maine Historical Society, Portland, Letters of Levi Perry, S-1954mb 93/15 ms178.

Henry P. Fowler of Danversport, Massachusetts, served in Company D, Fourteenth Massachusetts Volunteer Regiment. In this letter Fowler's father explains the war's effect on several local businesses, including his own.

Danversport, Massachusetts
Sept. 29, 1862

I have nothing in particular to write. We had the heaviest battle of the War in Maryland I should think and I think on the whole the Rebels had the worst of it.[11] But it was not so decisive on our part as I expected. I do not think the Rebel Army will stay a great while where they are they will be afraid of having there supplies cut off as they must now come through Virginia. They will either make another raid into Maryland or retreat and that very soon. The Presidents emancipation proclimation will have the effect to close the rebellion if all the loyal states hang together, and I think they will for the President I think would not have issued it if he had not know the border states would have agreed to it. They will adhere to the Union stronger than ever as by so doing they can sell all their slaves to the Government.[12] I have no doubt that this Winter will close the war but it will be a good while before the Army will be discharged on a great part of them. Tanning buisness is quite good now. Roper has bought 210 Western hides for me to tan   he has done very well on what hides I have worked in for him yet. He bought the last in Buffaloe. Labour is very scarce   I have to do all my work alone which makes a slow job of it. I think buisness may continue to be good through the Winter. Shoe makers are getting better pay than they have had before for years. When you wrote last you spoke about having a horse. Unless you can send him home I should think you had better sell him if you can   you cannot keep him unless you keep him under cover as the cold rains this fall will kill him if he is exposed to

---

11. The battle of Antietam, Sept. 17, 1862.

12. Lincoln's proclamation did not affect slavery in the border states; an earlier Lincoln proposal had raised the possibility of compensating slaveowners in the border states if they freed their slaves, but border state representatives rejected this plan. Only in the District of Columbia did Congress, in 1862, enact a plan of compensated emancipation.

them. You may be oblidged to move and lose him, but you know best what you can do with him.

Father

Peabody Essex Museum, Salem, Mass., Letters of Adelaide, Sally, and Henry P. Fowler, Fowler Family Manuscripts.

Justus F. Gale of Company A, Eighth Regiment, Vermont Volunteers, writes this letter to his father in an attempt to settle a property dispute that had its roots in his parents' separation.

Algiers, Louisiana
Nov. 7, 1862

Dear Father

It is with much pleasure that I seat myself to answer the kind letter that I received the 4th dated Oct. 12. It came to hand while our regt. was up the rail road at Lafourche, our regt have been out on excursion two weeks to morrow. the force that went with us and we have drove the rebels back 100 miles from this place; our regt havent done any fighting for the rebels that we was sent to whip picked up their heels and skedaddled before we got to them; they burnt the place whare they was quartered and set fire to the rail road bridge and left leaving much of their camp equipage some cannon &c.

I was verry glad to hear from you & the rest of the family and to hear that your health is so good—for I think it must be hard for all of you being sick so much this summer and fall. You will have to excuse me this time from writing much about affairs around here for I have got to go back up whare the Co. is at Bayou Buff about 70 miles from here I came down here yesterday with Wesley and Corporal Brown to guard a load of stuff that was confiscated up the road.

I suppose I must write something to answer the questions you asked me concerning our property affairs; it is a hard thing for me to answer these questions for three reasons, if I comply with your wishes and please you it will displease Mother, and if I do as Mother wishes me to do that will not bee satisfactory to you, and if I give up the farm it will bee against my own will for if I live to get out of this war I think I shant care about roving any more. as concerning the bond I gave you I calculate that I fulfilled it up to the time I enlisted and then left things in as good shape as I could for the comfort of you all. but if the laws of our State are such that a man can take the advantage of another because he has volunteered to go to fight the enemys of our free land—then I suppose I shall have to submit to it.[13] If I could see that it would bee for the benefit of all that I agreed to

---

13. Gale's father had deeded the family farm to Gale in exchange for a bond in which Gale promised to provide for both his parents. His father had attempted to convince Gale to deed the farm back to him, which would enable him to make a property settlement with his wife, whom he was divorcing. It appears that Gale's father was considering taking legal action to regain the property by claiming that Gale's absence prevented him from fulfilling his bond to provide for his parents.

take care of I would do a most any thing that would add to your comfort but I cant see as any such thing as deeding the farm back will benefit you all & as to the troubles and fusses you have among yourselves, I dont consider that I am accountable in the least for any such affairs, and another thing you spoke of that was another companion; I calculate to take care of what my bond binds me to take care of and no more, I never shall consent to have you bring another woman theire to add to the fuss and troubles that are already in the family. I dont know as I ever shall live to get home so it may not make any diferance with me—but time only can tell. I hope you wont feel that I am trying to hurt you or that I am against you—for I am sorry that you have so much trouble in your old age—but I must try and show respect for one parent as well as the other.

Vermont Historical Society, Montpelier, Letters of Justus F. Gale, Gale-Morse Papers, MSA 50.

Henri Eugene Bacon of Pawtucket, Rhode Island, served as second lieutenant with Company F, Eleventh Regiment, Rhode Island Volunteers. In this letter to his wife, Bacon mentions some of the financial difficulties she faced as a result of his absence.

December 11, 1862

Dear Wife

Your favor came to hand to night and I hasten to answer it. Would not advise you to make a long stop in Oxford under the circumstances for I do not think I would like to trust Dr Paine to tend him in such a case. I did not care to have you send me a statement of what you had spent but what you had on hand for I told you I did not know how much I left. Was that [*illegible*] of 9.75 paid for Boots Paid to Gates. If so he charged more than he agreed to—the price was 9.00. I am very well aware how much it takes to live and knew when you came to the Business yourself you would not wonder that I could not pay in advance. Am pleased to know that you have furnished yourself with good clothes and wish I could see you when you come out. Others can look on and admire but poor me—must draw my own pictures. . . . You may imagine the most powerful self sacrificing love that ever existed between a man and woman and that would be no more than mine for you—I hope you do pray for me if you are conscientious about it. As for the parting for that better world I wish that we could go together—I could not bear the thought of being separated for Eternity—and hell would be a heaven to me if you were with me—I hope that we may so live that when we die we shall both participate in the realities of heaven together. You are the last one in my thoughts when I lay me down to rest at night, and the first when I get up and so it will always be. There is no woman on this earth that can draw my love from you. I know my heart and will and so do you—and whenever you feel as though you

were forsaken and neglected—remember these words—I will always love you—
and you alone.

With many kisses
I remain
Yours   H E Bacon

Providence Public Library, Providence, R.I., C. Fiske Harris Collection on the Civil War and
Slavery, Letters of Reuben F. Thornton and Henri Eugene Bacon.

---

*Harrison Clarke writes here about the war's impact on the textile industry in this letter to
one of his former coworkers, Allen F. Cameron, who served as a sergeant with the Fifth
Regiment, Rhode Island Colored Artillery (Heavy), and as a first lieutenant with the
Eleventh Regiment, Rhode Island U.S. Colored Artillery (Heavy). Cameron had been
employed as a weave room overseer in a cotton mill in Rockland, Rhode Island.*

Rockland, Rhode Island
March 6, 1863
A.F. Cameron

Dear Sir,
    You need not feel surprised because of my writing you at this time   I have
frequently made the attempt and as often failed. I have already quite a correspondence with members in nearly all parts of the army but yours and indeed I am
fond of such, because I presume on a greater degree of accuracy with reference
to their doings and movements when having it directly from them, than when
through the varying columns of the many Newspapers I see. They are *so very
conflicting* Written, some for political schemes, some for financial effect, and for
sensation generally. All of which is very unsatisfactory to one who wishes to
know the facts as they are, be they pleasing or not so pleasing. I presume you have
been kept posted as to things generally and events transpiring around here, so
that I can add nothing new of interest. Ponaganset Mill is running full time, aver-
aging about 545 cuts per week, 40 yds each   Cotton worth, 94 c pr. lb. Print cloth
18 c pr yd. Cannot tell as will run longer than April, think however shall though
cotton is outrageously high and cloth does not bring corresponding prices. We
begin to get cotton from foreign countries. Considerable from South America and
some from Central America. In fact nearly all the cotton in use whether domestic
or not has passed through the speculators hands to Europe and then reshipped
back hence its high price, which need not necessarily have been—so it is, But we
shall yet see brighter days.
    I am not discouraged yet: I did not expect at such times as these things could
well move on without being disarranged   War is the greatest curse of man, but
when waged for the right, his greatest privalege and holiest cause. But we are not
all patriots enough at these times to engage in the maintenance of rights if we
were we should all be with you now battling and fighting the enemies of our

country. You have I suppose heard of, or seen the conscription bill as passed by the last congress. I think it a very good thing. The same should have been done eighteen months ago and ere this, the rebellion would have reached its height and waned to nothingness. This new bill provides for calling out of all or as much as the Executive sees fit of the militia fit for duty between the ages of twenty and thirty five years, with all the unmarried to forty five This is the class to be drafted first, Second all between 20 and 40 years—married or single. It is supposed 600,000 men will be called for in a few days which will indicate somebody is in earnest. I will send you a paper containing the new bill in a few days so I will explain no more at present

Hoping soon to hear from you I remain respectfully,

Harrison Clarke

Providence College, Providence, R.I., Phillips Memorial Library College Archives and Special Collections, Letter of Harrison Clarke, March 6, 1863, R.I. U.S. Colored Art. 11th Rgt. Collection.

In this letter to her son Lewis, a soldier in the Union army, Mary B. Burnham relates some town gossip concerning a liaison between a local acquaintance and another soldier's wife.

Essex, Massachusetts
March 29, 1863

My Dear Son,

We received a letter from you, last wednesday the 25th We were very glad to hear from you, You thought then, by the preparations going on around you, that you might have to go into Battle soon. But your Father concludes by the papers, that you did not have to, I hope that it is so. But should it be otherwise, I hope you will be spared. That God will watch over you & that you may yet live to come home safe & sound, in body, & limb and that we may all live to see the happy reunion. I hope that this war may be settled satisfactorily before long, but not under *Southern* rule. I hope they will see the folly of their ways, & surrender.

Last monday, school closed. I thought the scholars did well, but I suppose Isabelle & Florence will tell you about that. . . . We hear bad stories, about George Warren Andrews who it is said visits a Mrs. Craft often & stays for days sometimes, who has one daughter eleven years old, & whose husband is in the army. We understand the other day that she left her daughter at Mrs. Fields, the coloured woman, and that Mrs. Crafts & George went to Salem & had their likenesses taken. They are the Town talk, at present. . . .

Try & write us once a week if possible. Sunday evening all gone to bed but me

From your affectionate Mother
Mary B. Burnham

Peabody Essex Museum, Salem, Mass., Letters of Mary Burnham, MS 0.308.

Josiah B. Corban enlisted in the Second Connecticut Volunteer Artillery and was promoted to first sergeant early in 1863. This letter to his wife Lydia expresses Corban's admiration for the sacrifices his wife had to make and for her capable administration of the family's affairs.

Fort Ellsworth, Virginia
June 24, 1863

Dear Wife and Children

I felt very much relieved to receive yours of the 20th to day. I felt rather disappointed not to get one yesterday but for some unknown reason there was not a single letter came into the fort. we have always had some for some of us every day before. I have not felt remarkable keen lately. one reason is the hot weather and another is so much excitement as we have had lately the rapid movements of both armies and some reverses in our own has caused a kind of bad worried feeling in my stomach. my work has not been hardly enough for exorcise some of the time lately. I eat considerable although I dont have a very good apetite. my food dont relish so well as it has generly but I guess I shall feel better shortly especialy if our union army should have as good sucess as I wish it might. it is the general opinion of Officers and Soldiers here that the war will be closed in the course of the summer. I understood that Col Wessels said yesterday he thought the Rebels were making their last and most desperate struggle if they should get defeated down at Vicksburg and old Lee should get a pretty thorough whipping in Va I dont believe they will be likely to continue to fight a great while longer.[14] but if they happen to defeat Hooker[15] there is no making any calculation how long they will fight. we must keep up as good courage as possible and trust the all wise ruler of the universe to bring about peace when he shall see it is best with all his future designs and plans. if we all live to see that time and are permitted once more to unite in the enjoyment of each others society how very thankful we wil be. O may that time speedily come and the ravages of this wicked war and bloodshed cease.

last saturday and sunday when we could hear the firing so plain they were fighting at Aldi about 40 miles from here the battle was between the Cavalry and Artillery on both sides. the Rebs got badly beaten and driven some 15 miles to Ashbys Gap where or near where Lee's main forces are. our Cavalry [captured] quite a large number of the Rebels prisoners with their equipments. I am glad you have sold that waggon out of the way. I guess you have got about a fair price for it. I guess you manage affairs as well as any one could in your situation. who would have thought once that I should have left you and come to the war. I never would if you had not been the most Patriotic of women and willing to make any sacrifice in your power to save our Government from ruin. you deserve a great

14. Corban refers to General Grant's siege of Vicksburg, Miss., which resulted in the surrender of that city on July 3, 1863.
15. General Hooker, commander of the Army of the Potomac.

deal of Credit and praise for your courage in trying to get along with so much hard labor and extra care as you have upon you since I left. but I hope and pray that your life and health may be spared and that we may all be spared to enjoy each others society many years after our Government has been restored to us. 25th I got that butter the 12th and it lasted till yesterday. it tasted good till it was gone   I could dispose of all you could make and not half try. the boys all thought it was first rate butter and want some more if they could get it. Capt Gold told me had a letter from you and that you want me to have a furlough. he did not tell what was in it besides. he said I must write to you and tell you that he had no power to give a furlough and that he musnt to. it is not to be expected that any one can get one until the present excitement is over. if they do then, I dont much think we shall ever see any fighting here and I dont believe the 19th will ever be sent off into field service but be kept to Garrison Forts somewhere because they are so nice and clean. I remain the same as ever your own Husband lover

J B Corban

I dreamed of being at home how I wish it might come to pass. I wish George and Julia would write often[16] they cant think how much I want to see them they seem very dear to me all the time   when shall I. I want George to tell me about the Ponies and all the rest of our stock and crops grass and so forth. much love to all enquiring friends.

Connecticut Historical Society, Hartford, Letters of Josiah B. Corban, MS 69465.

Lewis R. Caswell, a resident of Marblehead, Massachusetts, wrote this letter to his brother Henry, who was serving as a sailor. Caswell details the high prices at home that were a result of wartime inflation.

Marblehead, Massachusetts
Oct. 19, 1863

Dear Brother

I now take this opportunity to write a few lines to inform you that I am well and all the rest of the familly and hoping that you are the same. mother she is about the same as she was when you went away. she has recived two letters from you the last one was dated sept 15 and she was glad to hear from you after so long a passage. tom he has gone in the twenty third regiment   everybody is geting married and going to the war   the town pays one hundred dollars to every one that goes. the tenth battery goes to day for the seat of war   there is about forty marblehead men in that battery   they have been in camp two mont[h]s   their is now two marblehead companys at camp stanton (Boxford)   i will give you the names in print it is now 11 O clock   i have jest come home from the shop we have

16. George and Julia were the Corbans' children.

had quite a party to night   Bob Knight Jim Brown and the rest of them seting round and drinking same as usual. i have bought our winters fuel, coal is $8 dollars a ton and wood is $8 dollars a cord. i have got to work up now and to buy a stove fruit and vegetables plenty of it. good picked fulwins apples is selling at seventy five cents a Barrel   your tax this year is two dollars. we have to pay god dam dear now for tobacco 90 cts lb rum 90 cts a gal all the change we have now is postage stamps   i have not seen twenty five cents in silver for six weeks

   they have been drafting men up to Boston to day for the war there wont be no drafting in marblehead she has got one hundred men to spare. . . .[17]

I Remain Yours   Affectionate Brother
Lewis R. Caswell

Peabody Essex Museum, Salem, Mass., Letters of Lewis R. Caswell, MS o.255.

Stephen S. White of Royalston, Massachusetts, served in the Thirty-sixth Regiment, Massachusetts Volunteer Infantry. In this letter his wife describes her efforts to keep the family financially stable during White's absence.

Royalston, Massachusetts
Feb. 16, 1864

Dear Husband

   We are all well and get along first rate. I received a letter from you dated 14th of Jan. No 14 last Saturday it was 30 days old it takes longer and longer for the letters to come. I went to Mr Bullard to day and paid that Note, so I am getting quite a lot of your Notes into my hands.[18] he sent his respects to you and said he had been looking for a letter from you but had not got one. he said he was agoing to attend a wedding to night   Haman Brown is married to Nancy Wood tonight There was a man came here to day with Mrs Jefferson Richardson to see if I would rent a part of the house but I thought I could not very well, if I had Chambers I would. I think now I shall get it fixed up and so rent a room to some School girls if I have a chance, for then I should not have to move out my things and I should be getting enough to pay the fixing. in paying Mr Bullard I took bubs 10 cent Note that you sent him so if you happen to have another new one you may send it to him. I sent you several when I sent the 1,50 to Crab Orchard. I hope you have got it before now. Irving asks a great many questions, how things are made, so the other day he asked me how they made him. Emma is so large now she helps considerable.[19] you need not think I am short for money for I shall get some for my webs in 2 or 3 weeks, and I can do very well now. It is so cold I am a

---

17.   The conscription act required each congressional district to fulfill a quota which, if it could not be met with volunteers, was to be filled with draftees.

18.   White is referring to notes of credit debited to her husband.

19.   Irving and Emma were the Whites' children.

going to leave off writing and go to bed it is about 9 oclock. I thought I would not send my letter this week till I could write you I had got that Note. I am glad you are well and hope you will take care of yourself so that you will keep so. My Wood is all saved up and it only needs splitting now and I have got it paid except the 2 cords of hard Wood and I guess I can pay that next month. so you see I am getting along pretty well. Feb 17th It has blowed so and been so cold that I have not sent to the Office to day; I hope it is not so cold where you are. The Children say they shall not let you enlist again.

Henry How is here again I guess he has reenlisted. I am surprised at so many of the soldiers reenlisting but I am glad of it. I wish I could here from you oftener. I think a good many times I could do more work if I could. you must favor yourself all you can and take care of your health. you do not write me the names of any of the men that are with you. I wish you would. there ought to be some good men with you. Write as often as you can, Mrs Giles said her husband is a going to try and get a furlough to come home this Spring, and you write what you want I should send you by him if he comes you will se him before he starts I wonder where Burnside is a going to take his army now[20]

I shall be glad when this War is over and you get safely back to us, but I hope you will not think of working for Newton again.

L. W. White

I paid Mr Bullard 48½ dollars and I am glad it is paid, for he came in last Nov or december and after sitting a few minits he said, well what about that money. I thought then I would pay the first money I got, for I do not know but he thought we should cheat him out of it. but he is very kind.

Massachusetts Historical Society, Boston, Letters of L. W. White, Royalston Papers.

Henry Snow enlisted into Company H, Twenty-first Connecticut Volunteer Regiment, in August 1862. He was mustered out on June 16, 1865. This letter from his mother, Eunice Snow, expresses concern for her son's religious salvation.

Greenwich, Connecticut
Feb 21, 1864

Dear Henry

I received your War Records Feb 18 last Sat date Feb 6 and last night I received your letter date Feb 12. was verry glad to hear from you and to hear of the Meetings you have I am glad to hear that you are not affraid of Man that you are determined to serve the Lord let others do as they may I have felt quite anxious about you I was affraid you did not feel as you should in your situation now I

---

20. In February 1864 General Burnside made numerous public appearances, including some in Massachusetts, in an effort to recruit new regiments.

hope you feel to give yourself up to the Saivour trusting in him   no doubt you have a great many temptations to encounter but we have the promise that he will keep us from temptations if we trust him   have our minds fixed on him   we need not fear he will be with us and comfort us   Oh what a blessed Saviour   we have to go to   he has promised to be with us in times of trial what precious promises I think many times what should I do if I had no Heavenly Father to go to

their has been some verry interesting Meetings in this Town   their has been a great a number of convertions   I attended one eve   their were a number spoke and told what the Lord had done for them. I have often hoped you would be as good a Man as your Father. I think he was a Christian. I had a letter from Mrs Niles the other day she informed me of the Deaths in E. Hampton   she says Newton is rather failing he is verry feeble I did not think he would live till this time when I left   I suppose he is not much alarmed about the future perhaps if you should write to him and entreat him to turn to God and live   perhaps he would hear if you could be the means of saving one soul what a blessed thing your Aunt Huldah has been sick a great while her health is better but she is verry Nervious   they are afraid she will be deranged   I hope not. We read in the paper that Grants Army had a battle on the extreme left[21] is it verry muddy, now it is not quite as cold now as it has been it is good sleighing and has been for ten weeks rite along   I never saw so long a time of sleighing before. I hope you have got your box before now. How far were you from the bloing up of that Fort   it must have been an awful time.[22] is any of the boys in your Co that are anxious is your tent mates any of them   I will send you some Money you need not send me any if I want any I will let you know   you may send your letters without postage stamps they will let soldiers send them without it will save a little of your Money when you are short   do they talk of paying you off have you bought you a watch yet   I do not think of any more to write we are all as well as usual except colds

this from your Mother
Eunice Snow

Your aunt sends her love to you   I will send you a dollar and fifty

Connecticut Historical Society, Hartford, Letters of Henry Snow, MS 66721.

Daniel Webster Brown, of the Seventeenth Regiment, Maine Volunteers, wrote this letter to his mother. The letter reveals the difficulties Brown's mother faced in trying to run the family farm in his absence.

21. The reference here is unclear as Grant at this time was headquartered in Nashville, waiting for word on his appointment as lieutenant general.
22. Again, this reference is unclear.

Camp near Brandy Station, Virginia
April 8, 1864

Dear Mother,

I take my pen in hand to drop a few lines to you. I saw Maj. Mattocks this afternoon he said he had got your letter and I believe he said he had written to you, he said he had spoken to the Col. about my furlough but says if you want me to come home you had better write to the Col. I had given up all idea of coming home but the Maj says he thinks I can get one if you will write and tell the Col. just how it is. he said I had better have you try for he thinks I had ought to have a furlough. he told me to write to you and have you write to the Col soon, and let him know as soon as the Col gets your letter and he would do all he could The way they have to do to get a furlough is to have their folks write that It is actually kneed of his coming home and I think there is kneed of my being their for a few days to the thins and as you are slim I think you have a good excuse to write to the Col. Say that your oldest son has died lately and you have but two small boys to take charge of a large farm and that you health has been very slim for some month and that you want to see you son this spring and have him fix things for you I don't care so much on my acct but would like to see you very much, and may never have the chance if I don't get it this spring, for we have got to see some dangerous works I expect but have always been very lucky, but may be the first one that is picked of[f] this Spring, for no one can tell what is to take place. If you don't feel like writing to the Col you could get Uncle Cyrus to fix it, you want to fix it in good shape for I will have to go to Corps headquarters when the furlough goes in to show that it is actually necessary for me to bee their. Let no one know that I am trying for a furlough but Uncle Cyrus and then it will be no harm if I don't make it go. . . .

from your son
D Brown

Maine Historical Society, Portland, Letters of Daniel W. Brown, S-1962mb 94/12 ms228.

John Peirce of Beverly, Massachusetts, served in the Twelfth Unattached Company, Heavy Artillery. Peirce's frustration over his wife Clarissa's precarious financial situation is obvious in this letter.

Washington D.C.
June 23, 1864

My Dear Wife

I got your letter and was glad to hear that you was all well at home i feel mad to think that they do not pay you the state wages if they do not send it to you you hade better take the order and get some one to go with you to Boston[23] i

23. Peirce had sent an order home authorizing his wife to receive his pay.

think you wold be sure to get it it is to bad not to pay a Soldier as the state agreed
to the State Treasuer told me in Salem that the wages wold be sent to you with
out any troubel it is a shame to decieve a man in that way   i never wold enlisted
but i was pro[m]ised 32 from the state aid and Wages the wages every two months
  when i know my famely is not provided for i shell be of littel use to the
goverment   i have felt first rate becaus i thought you hade enough to get along
with at home if you do not get the order again that you gave to the town
Treasuer i will send you a nother   i sent you a letter the 22d with 10 dollars i send
you some in this. i am well and enjoy as good health as ever i did in my life   about
the state pay makes me mad if writing will get it it will come   some of the mens
Wifes have been to Boston and got it it is to bad to go to have that troubel when it
ought to be paid to you without going after it.
    Ad gets the letters that is sent to him and he sends one once in a wile he is well
enough to do his duty
    I should like to hear the littel rougue talk i am glad she is well and fat   i sup-
pose Tim is in his kindom com by this time dont you Clara   i owed the sutler
4 dollars and 1,50 for the Military regester. the pay master said he thought we
should be paid again in July   i am sorry John got disoponted about his jacket   i
think the money will come soon from the state   six of the boys started for the
navy this morning, one is discharge a day or two ago   his name is Carr he was
sick   the Co will have to be recruited soon   after we got paid off three of them
went off and got drunk   they are chained to geather walking in front of the guard
house now   it takes all sorts of fallows to make an armey   i have no troubel with
officers or men   i will send my Pictuer about a week i should like to have yours
when you get the state pay   my Love to you all good Luck

Yours Ever
John Peirce

Peabody Essex Museum, Salem, Mass., Letters of John Peirce, John Peirce Papers.

---

*Edwin Horton, a resident of Chittenden, Vermont, was a soldier in Company C, Fourth
Vermont Regiment. In this exchange of letters, Edwin and Ellen Horton discuss the personal toll that Edwin's absence has taken on their marital relationship. Edwin likewise comments on the growing tension between his wife and his mother and expresses his anxieties
over the rumors of Ellen's alleged infidelities.*

Chittenden, Vermont
May 6, 1864

Distant Husban
    it is with the greatest pleasure I now seat my self to answer youres of the 26th
whitch I received to day   I have received the box that you sent me   I should have
answerd it before but hav bin wateing to hav my picture taken to send and to day

I hav been down and had it taken   I will send it in this letter   now Ed when you
get this picture I guess you wont say enney more about my getting annother chap
for you will see by this that I hav grone so homly that a fellow must be a fool to
hav enney thing to say to me when there are so menney better loocking ones
around   I suppose if I laid out evrey sent of my mans wages on my back and
flirted my self around the streetes as some do that I know of I should stand a
better rite but that isent my stile and if there is enney that dont like my stile here
they can take less of it   I hav paid Fay and it done me good to fore I think he
needs it as bad as enney one could   he hadent a decent shirt to his back I tell you
Ed they are pretty shiflas   I doant know what they will do when they come to hav
an addition to there familey and they will ere the corse of seven month if nothing
happenes   Tomas Hendry and wife are goin to Washington to liv they will start
one weeke from next monday they are a goin to sell there things of[f] at [auction]
   oure folkes hav got there chaimbers done of this spring   they are plowin oure
gardin to day and I hav bin to work in the yard   I worked till I blisterd my hands
and then I had to stop   you had a letter the other knight from a young lady   I
thought I had got a lov letter but it wass from miss Browns nease   she rote to the
post master to know if there wass a familey here by the name of Brown   I shode
the letter to Dick and he has answerd it   I got a stamp by the meanes and if it had
bin enney one but hir I hav let hir had it but I thought I wood not let hir hav it
you see that I am getting as mean as the best of them and I mean to play my part
with them   I guiess you thought I was prety rough to go see Smith about yore
bounty but I did not go alone   youre father went with me and I dont think that
uncle Jo ment to go and so I had him go with me to see about it   I shall hav to
close for the want of paper   please excuse this bad righting and right soon   oure
folkes send there best wishes to you

youres ever with mutch Love
Ellen Horton

Chesnut Hill Hospital, Philadelphia, Pennsylvania
July 7, 1864

Dearest Ellen
   it is almost to weeks since we parted and the time has seemed real long to me[24]
   I never have had time seem so long as it has since I came back   I havent heard
from you yet but I am in hopes to hear from you tonight   if I dont I shall think
you have given up the notion of writing to me any more   this is the third letter I
have written to you and I cannot think of writing any more until I get one from
you   my finger is getting along first rate   I presume they will send me to the regiment next week and I dont care if they do   it is so lonesome here. I wouldent be
lonesome here or any where else if you was only with me but I suppose it will be

---

24. In June 1864 Edwin was wounded in the hand. He was allowed a brief furlough while recover-
ing. He did not return to active duty until August.

too long years before we shall be allowed to meet again   I hope Nell this will find
you enjoying yourself first rate   My God Nell I never felt half so bad about anything as I did to leave you that morning   dident you notice I dident bid you good
bye it was because I couldent speak   I dont never want to come home again until
I come home for good   the war news is so bad now I guess their is no doubt but
what I shall have to serve my time out but I am going to apply to go to the regiment right away   if I have to serve my time I am going to serve it in the field
time dont seem as long there as it does here   well Nell I must close. . . . please
write soon   give my respects to the old folks   this from your true and loving
Husband

                                                                Edwin Horton

        dont show this foolish letter to any one

                                        Camp Near Petersburg, Virginia
                                                        Jan. 14, 1865
Dearest Ellen
        it is with pleasure I now seat myself to answer your welcom letter of the 11th
I am well and hope this will find you the same   I have not received the box yet
that you sent   I guess it must be lost if you have got the receipt of the express
company you must present it to them before it runs out   I believe you have to
present your claim within thirty days or you cannot get any dammage   Now Nell
I am sorry that you have got into trouble with mother because it will cause a
good deal of talk and if she is wrong their will be a good many that will side with
her in order to keep the row along, and it will only give you a bad name in the
end   Now Nell Since their is so much said about Soldiers wives I was in hopes
you would carry yourself strait enough to avoid all stories but Nell I dont care
what she says about you or me but as long as I am away a good many will believe
her for that reason I was in hopes you would keep on the right side of her   you
know that when she gets a little miff against any one she will go to all lengths   if
it was only her to talk about us and their was no one else to here it and spread the
news and to enlarge every story she told I shouldent care but you know their is
always a thousand that likes to have their nose in all such buisness for these reasons alone I should have liked it much better if you had kept on good terms with
mother and maintained a good name and lady like caricter   now nell their isent
any news of any account here we are laying here in camp within rifle shot of the
Joneys and all we have to do is picket duty and guard duty but we dont know how
soon we may have to fight[25]   we are liable to kick up a row any day   their is a
good many Joneys deserting and coming over to us lately almost every night

---

25. The Fourth Vermont Regiment was participating in the siege of Petersburg, Va. Soldiers
encamped in trenches to avoid sharpshooters and artillery fire. Throughout the winter of 1864–65,
Union troops slowly pushed the Confederates back, cutting off the city's last remaining supply lines.
The Union army captured Petersburg on April 3, 1865.

some comes through our lines   now Nell I will close and I hope I shall have a
more interesting subject to write uppon the next time I write   I am real Sorry
I rote such a lot of stuff in that letter since it has cause so much trouble but a
better way is Nell not to show any of my letters   I dont never show any of yours
I always burn them up as soon as I read them   I dont burn them because I am
ashamed to keep or to read them to others but I burn them becaus I dont think it
is a good plan to keep a lot of old letters for others to read and chuckle about as
soon as a mans back is turned   now Nell *please* excuse me for this time and write
soon   I presume you will be verry glad to excuse me this time and never want me
to write again on this subject   I make such awkward work of it   you must excuse
me under the consideration that I am not posted on the subject   now Nell please
write soon and write all the news yours with much Love

Corporal Edwin Horton

Camp Near Petersburg, Virginia
Jan. 29, 1865

Dearest Ellen
    it is with the greatest pleasure I now seat myself to answer your welcom letter
that I received last night   I am well and hope this will find you the same   I am
verry sorry that you are so down hearted you must not care what they say just
keep cool and they will get sick of blowing after a while   I think that we will be
about as gay as they will [a]verage if I live to come home they will not dare to
spout on us then   we will get them foul for some of their tricks   now my dear
Ellen their is no news of any importance   we are laying here in camp doing pick-
ett & guard duty and we do some fatigue such as building breast works and forts
we are so near the Joneys that they can shoot us in camp any time they choose
the Joneys are deserting bad now   their is a good many comes into our lines
every night   John Noyes is back here now he is feeling well and is doing duty
now Dearest Nell I rote to you for a pair of boots please send them as soon as you
can   you can get father to buy them   he is a good hand to pick out boots   now
Dear Ellen be a good girl and try and enjoy yourself as well as you can   dont get
down hearted but put on a good che[e]ck and not mind anything about what they
say it never will make any differents to me what they say but dear Nelly their was
a fellow here in my tent the other day and he said that he had heard that you was
sasaing around all sorts with any one you could get a chance to   I told him to dry
up or I would smash his mug for him he was from Rutland and I dont know what
his name is   he first commenced to talk about your folks and then he spoke about
you and I commenced to talk with him and told him that you was pretty near con-
nection of mine and he Apologized and said he was sorry and said he wasent
aware that you was anything to me and begged to be pardoned if he had hurt my
feelings   now Dear Nelly dont mind anything about this   I thought first that I
wouldent say anything about it to you but finaly I have and I dont want you
should feel bad about it   I dont believe any such stuff   I dont think you would

misuse me in that way   Now Nelly please write soon and excuse all mistakes and be a good girl and I never shall go back on you if all the rest does you are all the one I care anything about that lives in that place and if I thought you was going back on me I should be one of the miserablest creatures that ever lived   I think when you fail all is gon   give my respects to all enquiring friends

yours with much love
Corp Edwin Horton

Vermont Historical Society, Montpelier, Letters of Edwin and Ellen Horton, MSS 21, no. 16.

CHAPTER SIX

The Morse Family Correspondence

THIS SECTION CONTAINS an extended exchange of letters within the Morse family of Woodbury, Vermont. These letters reflect the correspondence to and from Benjamin F. Morse and his nephew Franklin ("Frank") B. Morse, both of whom enlisted in Company E, Eighth Vermont Volunteer Regiment. Not only did these men share many wartime experiences, their ties on the homefront also were intertwined. Until her death, Benjamin's wife, Rosina, occasionally boarded with Franklin's parents, Ira and Huldah Morse (Benjamin's brother and sister-in-law), during Benjamin's absence. Despite some tensions on this issue, Rosina and Benjamin's son, Willie, also boarded with Ira and Huldah. Both Benjamin and Franklin Morse survived the war; Franklin married Samantha Gale in 1866, and Benjamin married three more times after the war. He also served as selectman, lister, overseer, justice of the peace, and notary public in Woodbury. He died in 1924.

The letters in this series demonstrate the many ways in which those at home worried about loved ones at war and coped with the financial and family pressures caused by the absence of family providers. They also provide a glimpse of how the men at the front attempted to cope with tragedy at home.

Collection of Carole A. Fontana, Letters of Benjamin F. Morse.

Woodbury, Vermont
Apr. 24, 1862

well frank how are you getting along and what are you adoing about these days   hope you are well and enjoying your self as well as you can and take good care of your self. look out for your things as well as you can, i want you should read your testament all you can, i feel better about you where you be than i should if you were here and acted as will cameron does, for i think you are engaged in a good cause. since we wrote the other letter the snow has almost left us there is not mutch in the fields the going is bad you can think something how it used to be about this time of year   harrisson has got to be father   they have got a little girl and the last we heard they thought Debbie could not live   it looks a little like winter to day   it frose last night and to day it snows some and blows. i shall send you acount of a sleigh ride fast day April 10th.[1] leroy and willie[2] have

---

1. Towns and even entire states commonly proclaimed fast days, when citizens were expected to fast and pray, usually for specified problems or dangers.
2. Leroy Morse was Franklin's brother. Willie Morse was Benjamin's son and Franklin's cousin.

been a sliding some to day. is there anything you want that we can send you if
there is write and tell what and you shall have it we often think of you and hope it
is all for the best that you went. put your trust in him who does all things well
                                                          from your Mother
      i want you should write whether you get our letters

                                                    New Orleans, Louisiana
                                                            May 29, 1862
Dear Rosina
      I have received 3 letters from you since you last wrote and if I was ever pleased
it was to [hear] from you and *willie* and if I can continue to get as good news from
Vt I shall be quite contented   I got one today dated the 7th of May & *Andrew*
got 5 from Eu *frank* got one   we are all quite well so that we are on duty   we the
8 Vt have been citty police for about 10 days had to be up part of the night it was
considerable hard for us as did not understand the business but got along very
well   made a good many arrests & now we are back to our quarters & we have
orders to go somewhere & we shall probaly go to night or in the morning   the
rebels are very quiet here in New Orleans dare not eaven insult us if they do take
them right to camp[3]   as to coming we hope to by fall but I cant say as I do much
before but shall be glad to come you may bet high on that   if we were in a cool
climate it would be better but still the regiment is quite healthy here & I think we
shall move away from here soon   as to sending sugar if you have not you hadnot
better send any to me for we cant tell on[e] day where we shall be next   as to
your going to plainfield to make a visit I shall be glad to have you go & take all
the comfort you can but I am afraid that *Willie* will get that dipthera & you know
goes hard & with your poor health it would be about sure with you both there
are so many cases there you could not hardly escape runing in to it before you
knew it   but you must do as you think best   I shall not finish this letter till I find
out about your geting the government pay   we have not got it yet but expect to
soon & then I will see what can be done about it   by the way I believe you wrote
that you paid *Kidder* 10.30 if so he has cheated you the raskall for I know that that
should be 7 dollars and interest 3 years up the first of last Apr which would
amou[n]t to 118.25 so that he took at least 2.00 but let it go I will look it up if I
come home   if this gets there before you go to P[lainfield] write a line & let me
know about how long you will stay and write at any rate whether you go or not
we get mails quite often from the north and if one friends write often they will
get letters   often they are old   we dont mind it   good night and angels attend
you and keep you safe is the wish of your Husband

                                                               May 30
      good morning   in regard to the government pay you cant get it till they pay us
here & then the pay role will have to be sent to Washington & to the states trea-

---

      3. The Eighth Vermont Regiment was part of the Union forces occupying the city of New
Orleans.

surer & as the money is alloted to you you can draw it without an order. We have
signed the payrole & think it will be put adoing soon but it will be some time
before you can get it. my hand trembles so that I cant write much more this time.
if you write direct to New Orleans untill you hear again this from your Husband
with much love kiss *willie* & tell him to be a good boy I think you made a very
pretty selection for your dress & *Willie* waist tell him that papa was real glad to
get his letter & that he must write again next time little heap how I want to see
you both & shall some time if we shall all live & I think we shall but must leave
that to a higher now power to decide we have got to get ready to move

yours with much love
B F Morse

LaFourche, Louisiana
June 7, 1862

Dear Rosina

How do you & *Willie* do this morning. I hope that you are quite well & enjoying yourselves we are about 50 miles north of new Orleans in a very good p[l]ace
plenty of good air & eggs & chickens & some of the boys make quite free with
them but I wont take them without paying for them there is aplenty of Rebiles
here there is not but two companys here & we are not full as we left the sick at
new Orleans I dont think that we have many that are dangerous sick we *Morses*
have been remarkably favord about our health we have been able to do duty the
most of the time I am better than when I wrote last & so that I feel quite well I
think *Frank* is on the gain. . . . it seems strange to me we should [be] so favord but
think that it must be the prayers of our friends at home what a good sound there
is to the word *home* I think that we shall all know how to value it if we ever get
there if our best wishes could make it so I am sure that you all would all be well
& happy up there the next time that you have a chance drink some west woodbury water for us & you needent be pertickler where you get it either but then
the water that we get it not the worst water that ever was the most of it comes
out of the Miss river there are aplenty of black Berries here but we cant buy anything of the whites here but can of the blaks & some of the boys pass 5 cts tick-
etts for 25 cts if we had the whole Regt here I think that it would be the best
place we have seen since we left Vt. as to how long we shall stay here I dont know
anything about it we are guarding the Rail Road at presant the Rebels bur[n]t
the Briges when they left new Orleans they have been Repaired up to here we
came through some wet mean country but the land is dry here the plantations
look well but the negro is a lasy creature at the best if ever I come home I shall
not be an abolition[ist] not that I think slavery is right but it is a bad instution to
medle with let them that have got it bear the curse of it. you will see them of all
collers white gray & black the most of them dirty & rag[g]ed some of their masters have been away & their left to look out for themselves etc. how do you do
master *Willie* are you well & do you go to school my gratest wish is to see the
day that I can come home & see you & *Willie* & I will trust that that day will
come that is my prayer & there I must leave it to the rulers of the universe.

Write oftener cant you   I know that it take a long time for a letter to come but if you write often we shall get them often after they get started   as the Port of new Orleans is open there is steamers coming in from Boston or new York quite often direct to new Orleans till you hear again   I will close by sending my best wishes & love to you & *Willie*

from your Husb
B F Morse

as to taxes I think you wont have to pay any only on the land and not that unless you get the government pay

LaFourche, Louisiana
June 14, 1862

My Dearest Rosina

I received your letter mailed May the 21 & was so glad to hear from you that I hasten to write again but felt bad to think your throat plauged you   but you must do all you can for yourself if you can get the money take good care of your self & if there is any medicine that will help you get it. we have not got any pay from the United States yet but there will be 52 dollars due you the first day of July if I live & it will surly come some time & if *Ira* will waite till you get that so that you can get your medicine I shall feel under renewed obligation to him for it[4] for if I loose you & *Willie* it seems as though all was lost   I dont know as I can get home till the war is over in any case   So take good care of your self as you can   if your work is to hard for you you had better pay for your board again[5]   I am afraid that you are not as well as you represent but if I knew that you was I should feel agrate deal better than I now do   if I get any pay I shall send you some out of what I get here as I dont need it & I think you will get it sooner than you will the other way. . . . there [is] a union assosiation formed in new Orleans & they had agrate time raising the United States flag over the city Hall the other day   it was the citsens that raised it & they fired a national Salute & the band played Hail Columbia in grate [style] they have a good band in new Orleans   Since that there has been flag raising this side of the river by the people. . . . When we first went to new Orleans the people all looked dag[g]ers at us and dasent go out alone for fear of assa[ssi]nation   befor we left we met smiling faces and we could go where we pleasd in perfect safty   there was one p[l]ace that they would set a cupt of coffe[e] & some buscuit in the window for me when I was on police in the city & I could eat & drink and not leave my beat & they would not take a cent   I will close by sending love to you & Willie   how I want to see you you know

from your own Benja F. Morse

---

4. Benjamin is referring to his brother Ira Morse (Franklin's father). Rosina and Willie owed money to Ira, and Benjamin expresses his hope that Ira will wait to be paid so that Rosina can buy medicine.

5. Rosina and Willie had been boarding with Ira Morse but had moved out on their own again.

Woodbury, Vermont
June 22, 1862

well frank we recived your letter last night and was glad to hear from you
maild June 9 we think it come quick father has been this morning down to
a[u]nt Abbagails to get grandmother B glad to hear that you are well and fare
better than you did i think of you every time we eat and wish you some of our
bread and butter be a good boy read your testament

leroy[6] is well he goes with his father almost everywhere he goes he and willie
get along first rate

write often as you can

i cant write much more for orlando and kattie[7] are agoing to ride out this
afternoon

tell Benjamin that rosina is afailing she is verry weak we do all we can

this from your Mother

Bayou Allmanse, Louisiana
July 30, 1862

Dear Rosina

I take my pen to write you a few lines how do you do this morning I am
afraid but poorly no tounge can tell how I want to come & see you to you my
thought[s] are first in the morning & the last at night I often think that if I could
only come home for a short time but I cant there is to be no more furlows some
times I see you in imagination & for awhile talk in my mind as though we were
together these moments are the happiest moments of my life here & I will still
hope that we shall be blest with the privelige of seeing eatch other yet. we are all
well yet we are about 30 miles west of New Orleans the land is low & swampy
here the weather is very warm there are not many crops growing here we are
quarterd in an old tavern *Frank* & your humble servant ocupy the corner bed
room our furniture consist of one bed stid one settee one table 2 old chairs so
you see we are pretty well off etc. the inhabitants most all left here when we
came there is one family of Vermonters about 3 miles below here that seem to
be quite neighborly. . . .

August 6

I have been wating for your letter & to day the long looked for & precious
letter came & with it your & *Willie* degauretype no words can tell you my feeling to see how you have failed. I want that you should be as careful of your self as
you can and if we are permited to meet again on earth it seems as though my

6. Leroy was Frank's brother.
7. Orlando was Frank's brother. Kattie's relation to the Morse family is unclear.

happiness would be complete   how I have wished & prayed that it might be so for the last few weeks my mind has been on you continualy   I should come home if I could money or no money but I cant as I know of but I shall try   I cant write much more this time for the train leaves in a few minutes.   keep up good courag as you can & if we are not to meet again on earth let us try to meet where there will be no more parting without spot blameless. for evry harsh word and action I want you to forgive me   write often

yours with love for ever
B.F. Morse

Woodbury, Vermont
Sept. 7, 1862

Absent Brother [Franklin]

i now take my pen in hand to let you know that i am well and haint lost any fingers neither   i should not think there would be mutch fun for you to lose the one you did   if i was a going to shoot off one i should shoot the forward finger on my right hand so i might get a discharge but i suppose that you did not think when it was shot off whitch finger you should shoot   We received a letter from you last night dated aug 23d telling about you losing your finger   Ester got a letter from a soldier in the 2ond vt regt saying that Charles was dead   he has been sick about 2 Months   he died with the dysentary   he died the 27 of august   We have got through haying so has Mr mcnight and Mr Cameron   Mr bailey will finish in one day   Jony Morse has got a little drum and he can play better than orlando and leroy wants one but father thinks he aint able to buy him one but when i get some money i shall buy him one   harrison and Mira and harison little baby has been over here   benjamin is to work at kial morses   harison is to work for david nevens   i should like to know what kind of stuff that ring was made of that you sent home in a letter   i guess it was made out of some of the rebbels back bone   i guess it would jest fit that finger that you had shot off   you had otto have keept it but i suppose that when you sent that ring home you did not [k]now that you should have your finger shot off but you must be care full and not shoot off any more   i am up stairs in the bed room a riting and celia is out in the other room riting a letter to you for orlando   orlando has got to be so nervers that he cant rite but i cant think of mutch more only i hope that you will come out victorious but it looks rather doubtfull now for every where they have a battle the rebbels lick us bad   i cant think of any more now so good night

this is from your brother
George Morse

Woodbury Sep the 7th 1862

Absent nephew

i take this opertunity to enclose a few lines to let you [k]now that i am well and wishing that these few lines would find you the same   did a mesketoe step on your finger and breake it or did he bite it off   in the last letter that granpa

Ainsworth[8] received you sent me your love in one corner so in answer to that i will rite a few lines i cant rite any more now

celia Ainsworth[9]

frank be of good chear i will write next time take good care of your self be a good boy   Mother

Algeris, Louisiana
October 22, 1862

Dear wife

how do you do this morning   how I do hope that you are geting *better* you must try to get well if possible for you & willie are all that I have to encourage me   my leg continues to gain but it seem to me rather slow. my health is good. the weather is very warm & pleasant here now & dry   the river is 15 feet lower than when we came here   but you can hardly think how much I want to come to Vt but dont know yet how it will be but we must be patient & take things as they come. I wanted to go to Camp to day but the Surgon wouldent let me   it is lonsome for me to stay in the Hospital but think that I shall get out soon   I have been most 7 weeks now   *Andrew* has been out along time but cant do any duty *Frank* has been put on to duty again. I received a letter from you last Sunday morning the 19 & was writen the 6th of Oct   was very glad to get it for I hadent one before for a long time   the last one before that was writen the 7 of Sept so I think that there must have been some lost   you wrote that if you had a dollar that you would send it   you mustent do that for if they wont pay me I cant send you any & to think that you cant have a dollar for your own use it is to bad   when this month is out they will owe us government pay 130. dollars   if you haint got that first 2 months alloted pay & it is a shame for them to keep us out of our pay in this way   now I want that you should have things to make you comfortable   you dont write whether you have any medicene or not   if you can possiably get it have all that you need for I think that the pay will come some time   perhaps that *Ira* will wait for part of his pay so as to enable you to have some money to help your self a little   I aint home sick but for only one thing & that is home   that is where I want to *be*   if *Ira* has a chance to sell a part of the hay for a fair price you had better have it sold   I wish that I knew how you get along. the general health of the Regt is good   Government made good promises they said that we should be paid evry two months that they money would be ready in the bank for our familis & that if we got killed that our families would be entitled to all back pay 100. bounty & a pention & it is probily truc. . . . but I should rather that they would make less promises & perform more but we must do the best that we can to   did you get a letter from me with some nuts in it I sent one & as you haint said anything about it I dident know   there is some talk that we are going to be

---

8. Grandpa Ainsworth was Huldah Morse's father.
9. Celia Ainsworth was Huldah Morse's sister and Franklin's aunt.

paid this week but they have said that so much that I shall believe it when I see the
pay   there is not any war news here by the time that we get it it is 2 weeks old
there some think that the war will end by the first of Jan & I hope that it may for
it seems as though there had been blood enough shed   to think the way that they
kill each other up there in Virginia   I hope that Capt Hall will come back soon for
we need him   Liutenant Day dont seem to care much for any body but himself
there is talk that he is to come back soon. now *willie* how do you do   mama told
me that you picked up potatoes   did you pick up as many as you can eat   do you
carry in wood for mama   if you are well you must & if papa ever comes home he
will fech his little willie & mama something   O how I do long for the day that we
can meet again   I believe that the day will come & my prayer is that it may come
speedily   let us try & keep up good courage   from you own Benja as ever   if you
get any money dont send it here for I get along very well   I received two postage
stamps   was very glad because they come from you but you mustent send any
more for you need them more than I do   kiss *willie* little heap   how I want to see
him & his mama

Benja to Rosina & Willie

Woodbury, Vermont
August 2, 1863

Dear Brother [Franklin]
    I will now write you a few lines to let you know that we are all well   we
received 3 Letters from you last thursday dated July 5th 10 & 12–16 and was glad to
hear from you   as to our pictures we shal get taken as soon as we can and send
them to you   I have been over to Granpas after him to help to do our haying   we
dont have any hay weather more than 2 days in a week and them 2 days are rainy
days so you see that we get along rather slow & our school fineshed yesterday and
we had a good school to   it was keep by Miss Ena Darling to Montpelier   They
have been Drafting up this way lately   I sent you some dailys that had a list of the
drafted in   those that was drafted in Woodbury payd 300   All but one or two and
that cleard them   you know the dra[f]ting law is the meanest law that ever was
made   if they wanted men why did not they draft men and not money   money
wont put down this Rebeldom but they dont want to stop this war   the officers
are geting to big pay   But I should not think that rebs could hold out much longer
but *dam* them they will fight as long as they can have a place as big as a [mos-
quito] would want to shit on   but I must draw to a close for this time

from you brother
George A. Morse

Woodbury, Vermont
November 22, 1863

Absent frank
    As the rest have gone up to build Enice a shed, i will write you a few lines to let
you know that we are all well and hope that these few lines will find you well as
can be expected. it snows a little to day the first snow that we have had   the

ground isnt frose mutch and i guess we shant have sleighing yet   i suppose the boys will write all about the party that they went to last thursday night out to Mr Jacksons   it was thanksgiveing day. i thought of you a great deal that day and wonderd what you had to eat   how i wished i could send you some thing but keep up good courage as you can the time will soon pass a ways that you will come home. how thankfull you ought to be to think that you are spared so long while so many are taken a way that went with you. If there is anything that we can send you write what it is and we will send it to you   we dont care what it costs if it will do you any good   leroy wants i should write to frank that he remembers that drum that frank is agoing to buy for him   he and willie get a long first rate   they can not bare to be separated   they are together all the time. . . . we are going to have our degauratipes taken and send to you   we have had so mutch to do that we could not leave verry well   your father health is not verry good but he works   you wrote last winter about letting Benjamin have two dollars   did he ever pay it back to you   we would like to have you write to us about it so we may know. when you have money, take the good of it dont be afraid to buy what you need   we will send you more when you want it. just write and let us know. be a good boy and put your trust in him who doeth all things well

this is the wish of your Mother

The next letter accompanied a care package the Morse family sent to Benjamin and Franklin. Although serving in the same regiment, the two men had been separated. The package and letter reached Benjamin first. He then sent it on to Franklin, with a note attached.

Woodbury, Vermont
December 14, 1863

Benjamin and franklin

we send you this box of things   it is all for you except there is a small peice of cheese that Eunice send to Andrew   she would have been glad to have sent him as mutch we did to you but he wrote to her not to send him anything. there is two bags of sasaug meat. . . . dont know wheather it will come out there good or not   the rest of the things we sent for you two   divide to suit your selves   I believe we got all that you sent for but the ink stands and them we could not find if we can get them at Montpelier we will send them some other time   I dont know as the gloves will suit you but they were the best that we could do.

Ira sends two pounds of tobaco   if you dont want it you can sell it. i take a great deal of comfort in fixing a box to send to you hopeing it will do you some good   franklin you will find a ball of yarn in the box   Maria Cameron sent it to you to mend your stockings with and her best wishes for your well fare

we are all well and hope that you are as well as can be expected   willie is well and goes to school   it is hard going here not any snow   it rains hard now has raind most of the time for two days. they are about all enlisting in Woodbury David Powers has enlisted and orlando has been so crazy to go that we concluded

to let him go. . . . the town pays three hundred and twenty five dollars the government three hundred and bounty make six hundred twenty seven dollars   we
think that he will go into the 11th regiment but cant tell yet   there is where the
most of them are agoing

    please write as soon as you get this for we shall want to hear

H[uldah] F. Morse

Bashear, Louisiana
February 4, 1864

    Well Frank how do you do   well I hope   I am feeling pretty well to day but I
haint been as well since I came here   I received this Box yesterday & felt anxious
to get it to you   the sasuage meat was spoilt so that I threw it in to the Bay   the
gloves are damaged by laying next to it as you will see   the nut cakes are spoilt
but I send them so that you can see how nut cakes look   I took out a little gum &
cinnamon & tea   there w[a]snt but one fine comb & thought that you needed it
more than I did   the boots are mouldy but I dont think that they are damaged
there is a silk handkerchief in the glove   my boots are just a fit   I send you &
Andrew a loaf of Bread   I hope it will get to you before it is spoilt   write as soon
as you get it so that I may know that you get it safe   I want to see you & Andrew
very much   write both of you

[Benjamin F. Morse]

Woodbury, Vermont
Jan. 3, 1864

    well franklin how do you get along this evening and how do you stand it   we
would like to see you verey mutch   we are as well as usal   orlando has enlisted
and has gone to brattlebourgh   i couldent do no other way with him   i dident
want him to go but go he must   i want you should take care of your self as well
as you can   i shall be glad when you can come home and Benjamin so he can see
to his [affairs] for our folks are mad all the time because they cant do jest what
they are a mind to but i shall take care of his stuf untill he come home or orders it
otherswise. write as often as as you can so we may know how you get along and
Benja write all the news   write whether you got that box all wright or not and
how thos boots fited   it was the best that i could do and gloves evrey thing is
high here   i have got 19 head of cattle this winter and have hay enough to winter
them on

this from your father
Ira Morse

*Huldah Morse's letter to her brother-in-law Benjamin gives an indication of the family ten-
sions caused by Benjamin's absence. Benjamin's wife Rosina had died; however, Ira and
Huldah Morse continued to care for Benjamin's son Willie, a situation that led to a dis-
agreement over how much Benjamin should pay for Willie's board.*

Woodbury, Vermont
Feb. 15, 1864

Absent Brother

    we received your letter and was verry glad to hear that you was better, and
also that you wont let frank reenlist again if you can help it we dont want him to
enlist again out there, they may try to make him think that if he enlists again he
wont have to stay eny longer than he will now but one year aint so long as three
years and they will keep them as long as they can tell him to wait till he comes
home and then there will be time enough to enlist again you know that it is so
far out there that we cannot send you anything and have it get there enytime. Ira
carried the last box that we sent to Montpelier the (15) day of last December and
they said that it ought to get there in two weeks

    Willie is well has been to school everry day this winter, the school finished last
saturday we had a good school willie has learnt well and has been a good boy
when it was cold or bad going George[10] took the team and carried them to school
you wrote that one dollar a week was high for keeping of him, it *was* Rosina's last
request that he should stay here for it was like home to him, and if that is your
mind that he should stay we shall keep him if we dont have enything for it for it
would be almost like takeing one of our own boys for he has been with us so long
it aint the money that we want it is to see that the boy is well taken care off i
hope it will be the will of the lord that you should return and take care of your
boy your self and know things as they are for i think that if you knew the parti-
cilars of things as they be you would feel different about somethings than you
now do everything shall be done as near right as can be done guess i have wrote
about as mutch as you can read

this from with respect
Huldah Morse

Woodbury, Vermont
March 2, 1864

Absent but not
    forgoten frank

    we received your letter to day (marked No 5) and was glad to hear from
you, about your [re]enlisting i think we have wrote enogh that you might know
what our minds was the bounty is of no consequence if you ever get home you
shall have a liveing without the bounty if Benjamin dont enlist we had rather
that you would not for i cannot think of your going back there again, but i suppose you wil make up your mind to do one or the other before this reaches you,
your Father has had some notion of buying the young place back again but thinks
it is a little to mutch for him and George to cary on but if you was here to help
them guess they would get along with it, Mr youngs folks are at barnet yet James
enlisted in a new Hampshire regiment went out and was gone a spell and was

---

10. George Morse was Huldah's son.

sick and come home on a furlow and then he got his discharge, Mr Hatch folks
are at Masschusetts to work   Mr wheatey he stays on his place as yet   David
Powers enlisted when orlando did

March 3rd

leroy wanted i should write to you that little calf that he took care of that
winter that you went away had got to be a cow and he was a raising the calf to
make a ox for him to work when he got home   willie has got a little calf for him
now and he thinks he shall have a cow some time   your father has been down to
Esthers to day   the commisioners sat to day on luthers estate   Nick and the old
man have got every thing in thair hands so the rest cant get anything

George has gone to a party to night down to schyler wells, he thinks he is
about as large as enybody he wears your frock this winter that you left   John
Batchelder one of your cousens that went out with your uncle Truman has died
and is agoing to be brought back this week   the funerel is next sunday at the
south school house   he will be burried beside his Mother   we are all well and the
boys have a good time a slideing for there is a good crust now days   one of your
aunt lucindas girls is here now   how long i shall keep her i dont know she is most
(8) years old, it is verry plesent here now and not but a little snow

i want you should write what money is good out there so we may know what
to send when we send you eny i will send you three ten cent postage scrip in this
i suppose that is good out there   i guess i have wrot enough without it is better
be a good boy   take as good care of your self as you can   i suppose you haint
many clothes to see to

i want you should write how all the things come in the box so we may [k]now
and what to send next time

this from your
Mother

INDEX

Abolitionism, 7, 13–14, 59, 62, 70; *see also* Antiabolitionism
Adams, Enoch George, 27
African Americans
letters written by, 15–17, 21, 47–48, 92–94, 142–43
New Englanders' views of, 13–17, 84, 89, 93–94, 98
and racial prejudice, 61, 74, 85, 87, 95–96, 157
as soldiers, 86, 91–92, 97, 102–4
treatment by Union soldiers, 100, 103–5, 108
Alcott, Louisa May, 1
Antiabolitionism, 63–64, 74–77, 90, 96; *see also* Abolitionism *and* African Americans
Antietam, battle of, 139
Appomattox, surrender at, 52–54

Bacon, Henri Eugene, 141–42
Baker, Henry W., 131–32
Baltimore, 1861 riot in, 56, 58–59; *see also* Sixth Massachusetts Regiment
Banks, Gen. Nathaniel P., 34, 115
Beecher, Henry Ward, 132
Berry, Maria H., 132–33
Blanchard, Caleb, 114
Blanchard, Mattie, 22, 112–16
Boyle, Charles A., 102–5
Bradley, George, 29–30
Brayton, Charles Ray, 103–4
Brooks, Isaac Austin, 60
Brown, Daniel Webster, 148–49
Buckingham, Gov. William Alfred, 115, 117, 118
Bull Run, first battle of, 25, 27, 29
Bull Run, second battle of, 71
Burbank, Calvin M., 45–46, 83–84
Burnham, Mary B., 124–25, 143
Burnside, Gen. Ambrose E., 29, 67, 74, 81, 97, 98n, 132, 147
Butler, Gen. Benjamin F., 32, 104, 115n

Caswell, Lewis R., 145–46
Chancellorsville, battle of, 78
Clarke, Harrison, 142–43
Connecticut, letter writers from, 13, 29–30, 35–37, 39–40, 64–70, 73–76, 79–80, 96–98, 101–5, 107–8, 112–19, 123–24, 129–30, 144–45, 147–48
Conscription
militia draft of 1862, 72, 110
national draft of 1863, 23, 77n, 110n, 119n, 146
negative views of, 162
positive views of, 77, 143
Contraband, 84–85, 90–92, 97, 103, 108
Corban, Josiah B., 22, 144–45
Cudworth, W. H., 78–79

Davis, Jefferson, 30, 31, 58, 65, 77, 124
Draft riots
in Boston, 119–20
in New York City, 23, 79, 119, 121, 124
reaction to, in New Haven, 124; in Northampton, Mass., 121–22
Duncan, Samuel Augustus, 51, 79–80, 108

Early, Gen. Jubal, 49
Economy, New England, 4–5
effects of war on, 17–19, 39–40, 59, 111–12, 129–30, 133, 135, 137–43, 145–46, 149–50
Emancipation Proclamation (1863), 13, 74n, 97n, 112, 113, 139n
criticism of, 74, 77
support of, 97–98, 139

Fales, Sarah E., 110–11, 135–36
Forten, Charlotte, 16, 17, 21, 92–94
Fort Jackson, 32
Fort St. Phillip, 30, 32

Fort Sumter, 8, 36, 58, 86
Fort Wagner, assault on, 14, 86, 104
Fowler, Adelaide, 119–20
Fowler, Henry P., 139–40
Fowler, Sally, 134
Fox, Daniel Burt, 26
Fredericksburg, battle of, 44, 132
Freeman, Thomas D., 15–17, 47–48
Frémont, Gen. John C., 65, 67

Gale, Justus, 9, 11, 92, 99, 140–41
Gay, Sarah A., 127–28
Gettysburg, battle of, 45–46, 80n
Gilbert, John, 21, 133–34
Gill, Henry B., 39–40
Glines, Henry C., 35–37
Grant, Gen. Ulysses S., 49, 134n, 144n, 148

Hall, Edward F., 76–78, 87–88, 90–92, 111
Halleck, Gen. Henry, 70
Hinckley, A. C., 109–10, 130–31
Hinckley, Samuel Lyman, 58–60
Holmes, James Edward ("Ned"), 44–45
Hooker, Gen. Joseph, 27, 29, 74n, 98, 144
Horton, Edwin, 46–47, 50, 151–54
Horton, Ellen, 21, 150–51
Hubbard, Robert, 10, 22, 101, 116–17

Ingalls, Vesta H., 111–12

Jackson, Gen. Thomas ("Stonewall"), 34n, 65n, 92
Jenks, John Henry, 88–90, 99–100
Jewett, Charles E., 37–38

Kellogg, Robert Hale, 13, 69–70, 117–19
Kent, John H. B., 41–42
Klein, Edward, 137–38

Larry, Meschack Purington, 15, 81–82, 98
Lee, Gen. Robert E., 49, 52, 80n, 122, 144
    surrender at Appomattox, 52–54
Lincoln, Abraham, 13, 65n, 67, 107, 124, 130n
    assassination of, 51–52, 127
    and emancipation, 65n, 70, 139
    see also Emancipation Proclamation
Little Women (Alcott), 1
Livermore, Mary, 2, 19

Lovell, Gen. Mansfield, 32
Lyman, L., 19, 121–23

McClellan, Gen. George, 37, 65n, 67, 70
McDowell, Gen. Irvin, 34
Maine, letter writers from, 38–39, 44–45, 81–82, 98, 136–39, 148–49
Massachusetts, letter writers from, 26, 40–42, 47–48, 51–54, 58–62, 70–73, 80–81, 105–6, 109–12, 119–25, 130–34, 137–40, 143, 145–47, 149–50
Meade, Gen. George, 80n, 122
Millard, Dr. Henry J., 52–54
Morse, family correspondence, 155–66

New England
    culture, 5–6
    education, 3
    residents' criticism of the South, 10–14, 41, 55–56, 83–85, 87–88, 94, 105–6
    intemperance, 99
    literacy, 101
    women, 41, 106
New Hampshire, letter writers from, 25–27, 37–38, 45–46, 48–51, 62–64, 76–80, 83–84, 87–92, 99–100, 108, 111, 131–34
New Orleans
    Union capture of, 30–32
    Union occupation of, 156–58
Nickerson, Thomas, 9, 28–29
Norton, John, 5, 17, 129–30
Norton, S. H., 13, 74–76

Olmsted, Frederick Law, 33

Parmalee, Mary, 123–24
Peirce, John, 51–52, 80–81, 149–50
Perry, Levi, 138–39
Petersburg, Va., siege of, 48, 152–53
Phillips, Diana, 136–37
Phillips, Marshall, 38–39

Religion, New England, 6–7, 11–13
    and New Englanders' views of the war, 56, 69–70, 78–79, 118–19
Riggs, John Harpin, 14, 73–74, 96
Rhode Island, letter writers from, 28–35, 43, 55–58, 60, 84–87, 94–96, 102–4, 110–11, 135–36, 141–43

Robert, W. H., 30–32

Sabin, William A., 102
St. Albans, Vt., Confederate raid on, 20, 126–27
Sargent, George H., 25–26
Saxton, Gen. Rufus, 93
Scott, Gen. Winfield, 58, 65, 67
Second Great Awakening, 7
Seven Days battles, 37–38, 71
Seymour, Thomas, 116, 118n
Shaw, Col. Robert Gould, 86
Shepard, Samuel B., 64–68
Sherman's march, 51
Sixth Massachussetts Regiment, mob attack of,
    130; see also Baltimore, riot in
Smith, Anne, 20, 126–27
Snow, Henry, 147–48
Spinney, George A., 40–41
Spooner, Fred, 55–58
Spooner, Henry, 10, 94–96
Storrow, Samuel, 70–73

Thornton, Reuben F., 43
Turner, George, 14–15, 84, 87

Uncle Tom's Cabin (Stowe), 100
Upton, George, 48–50, 62–64
U.S. Sanitary Commission, 1, 32, 33n, 50
USS *Merrimac*, 59–60

Vermont, letter writers from, 21, 46–47, 50, 92,
    99, 126–27, 140–41, 150–56
Vicksburg, battle of, 79, 132, 144

Walker, William Augustus, 12, 13, 61–62, 105–6
Washington, D.C., defense of, 71
White, L. W., 19, 146–47
Willoughby, William Augustus, 68–69, 97–98,
    107–8
Women
    effects of war on, 126–27, 132, 144
        economic, 62, 148–49
        political, 112–17
        social, 143, 150–54
    letters written by, 32–35, 92–94, 110–16,
        119–20, 123–28, 132–37, 143, 150–51, 155–56,
        159–66
Wormeley, Katharine Prescott, 21, 32–35

A NATION DIVIDED:
NEW STUDIES IN CIVIL WAR HISTORY

James I. Robertson,
GENERAL SERIES EDITOR

Neither Ballots nor Bullets:
Women Abolitionists and the Civil War
Wendy Hammond Venet

Black Confederates and Afro-Yankees in Civil War Virginia
Ervin L. Jordan, Jr.

Longstreet's Aide:
The Civil War Letters of Major Thomas J. Goree
Thomas W. Cutrer

Lee's Young Artillerist: William R. J. Pegram
Peter S. Carmichael

Yankee Correspondence: Civil War Letters
between New England Soldiers and the Home Front
Nina Silber and Mary Beth Sievens, editors